THE TATTIE LADS

The untold story of the Rescue Tug Service in both world wars and its battles to save ships, lives and cargoes

IAN DEAR

BLOOMSBURY

LONDON · OXFORD · NEW YORK · NEW DELHI · SYDNEY

Conway
An imprint of Bloomsbury Publishing Plc

50 Bedford Square
London
WC1B 3DP
UK

1385 Broadway
New York
NY 10018
USA

www.bloomsbury.com

CONWAY and the 'C' logo are trademarks of Bloomsbury Publishing Plc

First published 2016

© Ian Dear

British Library Cataloguing-in-Publication Data
A catalogue record for this book is available from the British Library.

Library of Congress Cataloguing-in-Publication data has been applied for.

ISBN: HB: 978-1-8448-6401-0
ePDF: 978-1-8448-6403-4
ePub: 978-1-8448-6402-7

2 4 6 8 10 9 7 5 3 1

Typeset in Janson Text by Deanta Global Publishing Services, Chennai, India
Printed and bound in Great Britain by CPI Group (UK) Ltd,
Croydon CR0 4YY

To find out more about our authors and books visit www.bloomsbury.com.
Here you will find extracts, author interviews, details of forthcoming
events and the option to sign up for our newsletters.

To all those members of the Rescue Tug Service
who lost their lives on active service, 1939–1945

CONTENTS

INTRODUCTION

I FIRST CAME across the term 'Rescue Tug' when I was writing the history of the *Royal Ocean Racing Club* in 1998. One of the Club's founding members, EG Martin, had been awarded the OBE in 1919 for his work in establishing the Admiralty's Rescue Tug Service during the First World War. It sounded intriguing, but I couldn't find out anything about it. In 2011 I met Captain Christopher Page RN, the then head of the Naval Historical Branch, and he kindly said he would make enquiries, but he fared no better.

Then in 2013 I was invited to the unveiling of a blue plaque for Martin at his childhood home in Brixham. The ceremony had been arranged by Martin's great niece, Clare McComb, and to my surprise – and pleasure – I was introduced to several veterans of the Rescue Tug Service. Then Clare rang me and asked if I was interested in writing a history of the Service; if I was, she would arrange for me to be lent the archive of the Deep Sea Rescue Tugs Association, which was being disbanded. Two of the veterans, Len Reed and Jim Radford, came to see me with Clare, and I was handed a huge amount of material, including photographs, newspaper cuttings, operational and administrative reports from The National Archives, and copies of the Association's newsletter, *Towrope*, full of members' first-hand accounts of their time in the Service.

It looked as if much of the research had already been done. I became even more interested when I was told that though part of the Royal Navy, and therefore entitled to fly the White Ensign, the contribution of the Rescue Tug Service in the Second World War had been excluded from Stephen Roskill's four-volume official history of the Royal Navy. Yet the Service had developed what a wartime American newspaper called 'a new type of naval vessel – the British fighting escort tug', and had saved millions of tons of shipping, both warships and merchant ships, not to mention the crews and the precious cargoes.

Could this be true? It seemed it was. It was also true that the official history of the Merchant Navy had not mentioned the Service either, nor had numerous other books on the war at sea. I could find only one that made any attempt to describe what the Service was about. The convoy historian Arnold Hague wrote a three-page chapter on it in his book *The Allied Convoy System 1939–1945: Its Organisation, Defence and Operation*, which was published in 2000. The chapter's penultimate paragraph reads: 'Such instances [of salvaging ships] were numerous and the majority owed their success to the Rescue Tug Service and crews, of whom little has been written and in consequence little remains known even to those who study the maritime war, 1939–45.'

I hope I have done something to correct this. It is a 'warts and all' account and it may give the reader some answers as to why the Admiralty's Rescue Tug Service has been written out of history, and why one rescue tug had *Filius Nullius* (belonging to no one; orphan) as her motto.

AUTHOR'S NOTE

I HAVE GIVEN convoy numbers in the text wherever possible as an interested reader can sometimes trace more information about a particular incident on the various websites dedicated to convoys. I have deliberately excluded giving details of the U-boats involved in the incidents described in this book as I preferred not to clutter the text with too much information. But, again, an interested reader can trace these through the convoy websites and from looking at the ships that have been torpedoed on www.uboat.net

The files listed in the chapter notes – ADM, MT and T – all come from The National Archives. I am aware that these documents, on which this book is mainly based, have their limitations, and aware, too, that there are gaps in the narrative the written records have been unable to fill. Also, there are many stories of bravery and resourcefulness, which, for one reason or another, I have not been able to include.

There are interviews with veterans in Robin Williams' film *Mayday Tugs of War* (see www.maydaytugsofwar.com); and the rescue tug *Restive* appears in Carol Reed's 1958 film, *The Key*, about those commanding her in wartime, available on DVD.

A donation from the advance on royalties for this book has been made to the Mission to Seafarers.

ACKNOWLEDGEMENTS

I WOULD LIKE to acknowledge the help of Len Reed in writing this book. Without him managing to gather so much information over so many years about the Rescue Tug Service, and the men who served in it, it would have been an impossible task to construct any coherent history of it. I also owe a debt of gratitude to the late Deane Wynne, the editor of the Deep Sea Rescue Tugs Association's newsletter, *Towrope*, and to his successors, particularly Cliff Hubbard, who gathered the reminiscences of the veterans quoted in this book and preserved them in print. Other veterans and their families have generously helped me, too, lending photographs and allowing me to use extracts from personal memoirs, published books and *Towrope* contributions. To them I say a big thank you.

Clare McComb was also unstinting in her help, and generously gave me details of her great uncle, EG Martin, which I might never otherwise have been able to track down.

When I have used quotes from *Towrope* or other sources, I have naturally asked the permission of whoever wrote them. Where that member is dead I have tried to contact his family to request permission. This also applies to any photographs I have used from the Association's albums. However, I have not always been successful in tracing everyone, and would like to hear from anyone who should have been credited.

GLOSSARY AND ABBREVIATIONS

A-A Anti-aircraft.

AFD Admiralty Fleet Dock, a floating dock that could be towed where required.

AFO Admiralty Fleet Order.

ASDIC Anti-submarine acoustic device developed secretly between the wars. The initials are purported to stand for Allied Submarine Detection Investigation Committee, but research has failed to find evidence of any such committee. It later became known as sonar (SOund Navigation And Ranging).

ASW Anti-submarine warfare.

Attack transport A classification in the US Navy for a troopship that carried its own landing craft to take its troops ashore during an amphibious landing.

Beam ends When a vessel is forced on to its side by wind and sea. The phrase derives from when the vessel's position is so extreme that its deck beams are vertical with the water.

Bollard Upright circular metal fixtures on a ship's deck or dockside, usually used for securing mooring ropes.

BEM British Empire Medal.

Bulkhead Vertical partitions in a ship.

Bunker In steam-driven vessels where coal or oil was stored.

Cable As a nautical measurement, it is one-tenth of a nautical mile, or 200 yards.

CAFO Confidential Admiralty Fleet Order.

CCRT Captain-in-charge Rescue Tugs.

C-in-C Commander- or commanders-in-chief.

Davits Small cranes that lower and lift a ship's boat by its bow and stern.

Dog-watch The watch between 16.00 and 20.00 on board a ship is always divided into two dog watches of two hours each. This avoided the same personnel being on duty at the same time every day.

Dreadnought Generic term for a large, fast, heavily armed and armoured battleship, deriving from the revolutionary HMS *Dreadnought* launched in 1906.

Fairlead Deck fixture for leading a rope in a required direction.

Fleeting in Improving the haul on a rope.

Fo'c'sle Abbreviation of forecastle, the forward part of a ship.

FOIC Flag Officer in Charge.

GI Term for US soldiers. It stood for 'galvanized iron' or 'general issue'.

Gnat torpedo British name for German Naval Acoustic Torpedo.

Gunwales A projection above the deck of a ship or boat to prevent water coming aboard.

HA/LA High angle/low angle. A dual purpose gun.

Hawsepipe Pipe in a ship's fo'c'sle that leads the anchor chain to the anchor.

Hawsers A heavy rope or steel wire used for mooring and other purposes.

HMRT His Majesty's Rescue Tug.

Hotchkiss machine gun Heavy automatic air-cooled weapon of French design, a standard weapon in the First World War but obsolescent by 1939.

Hove to Not moving.

Hydrophones Underwater microphones to detect submarines.

In ballast Without cargo.

Limpet mines Explosive device used by frogmen on both sides during Second World War. It was attached to an enemy vessel with magnets.

Log Instrument measuring a vessel's speed by means of a rotator towed astern.

Luff tackles Single and double block where the rope's standing part is secured to the single block, the other end being rove through the double block.

MBE Member of the British Empire.

Messenger rope Light rope, which could be thrown or fired across to a vessel. It was attached to a larger and heavier one like a hawser, which could then be brought aboard manually or by a capstan.

NOIC Naval Officer in charge.

North-Western Approaches Northerly part of the Western Approaches.

OBE Order of the British Empire.

Oerlikon 20mm Swiss autocannon derived from a German design. Used in and against aircraft, the licence to produce it in Britain was granted just before the fall of France in 1940.

PO Petty Officer.

Pom-pom Two-pounder automatic anti-aircraft weapon with multiple barrels. So-called because of the noise it made when firing.

Poop The raised deck at the after end of a ship.

Q-ships Merchant ships fitted with concealed guns to sink U-boats that surfaced to challenge or attack them.

RA Rear Admiral.

RFA Royal Fleet Auxiliary.

RNO Resident Naval Officer.

RNR Royal Naval Reserve.

RNVR Royal Naval Volunteer Reserve.

R/T Radio telephone which transmitted and received voice messages.

Scantlings Standard dimensions for materials used in a ship's structure.

Sheering See yawing.

SNO Senior Naval Officer.

Stone frigate Naval slang for naval shore establishments.

Taffrail The after rail at the stern of a ship.

Tannoy system Public address system used aboard a ship or in barracks.

TDC Tug Distribution Committee.

Three Sheets to the Wind Drunk.

Towing horse Curved rail at stern of a tug fixed athwartships so that it lifts the towing wire or rope clear of the deck or any obstruction.

Trot boat Boat used to take crews to where their tugs were moored.

'tween decks Abbreviation of between decks, the space contained between any two whole decks of a ship.

Western Approaches Rectangular area whose north and south boundaries were the two extremities of the British Isles and extended west to 30 degrees of latitude, which passes through Iceland.

Whaler Royal Navy's standard ship's boat, a 27 ft overall, ketch-rigged centreboard sailing boat which could also be rowed.

Whelps Ridges on the drum of a capstan to help the anchor chain or rope from slipping.

Whip A rope rove through a single block for hoisting.

Windlass A horizontal winch, a smaller form of capstan.

W/T Wireless telegraphy, which transmitted and received messages in Morse code.

Yawing In rescue tug terminology this was when a towed vessel veered from one side of the tow to the other. It was not unknown for a towed vessel, which could not be steered, to come up parallel with the rescue tug towing it.

1

THE LIFELINE
NEARLY CUT

WHEN THE FIRST World War erupted in August 1914, submarines were mere adjuncts of the dreadnought surface fleets Germany and Britain had amassed. The use of German U-boats as commerce raiders had been studied in Germany before the war, but it wasn't until a small and obsolescent U-boat sank three old British cruisers in September 1914 that the U-boat High Command was alerted to the potential to cause havoc with Britain's commercial lifeline. However, U-boat commanders later claimed the real impetus for this new type of warfare came from a short story written by Arthur Conan Doyle, the creator of Baker Street detective Sherlock Holmes. Published in July 1914, it described how a small European power, deploying just eight submarines, decimated Britain's merchant fleet, forcing her to sue for peace.[1]

Fictional it may have been, but Conan Doyle's tale was a good example of Oscar Wilde's dictum that life imitates art. Despite having just twenty-one U-boats operational – only nine of which were diesel-powered with the range to reach England's Atlantic coast – at the end of February 1915 the Germans launched an unrestricted U-boat campaign. All merchant ships, including neutral ones, would be attacked and the Laws of Naval Warfare would be ignored. However, fear of neutral countries, particularly the United States, entering the war diluted the campaign and on 18 September 1915 it was abandoned. It had shown what U-boats could do, but not nearly enough had been available to obtain the campaign's objective of bringing Britain to her knees. When asked after the war how his naval staff had so badly miscalculated the numbers necessary, one German admiral had ruefully replied that it 'had put too much faith in Sherlock Holmes'.[2]

In December 1916 – by which time more and longer-ranged U-boats had taken a serious stranglehold on Britain's commercial trade – the German government instigated a second unrestricted U-boat campaign by declaring a war zone around the British Isles, and that any vessel found there after 1 February 1917, whether Allied or neutral, would be attacked without notice. The Germans knew this would almost certainly bring the United States into the war, but with the armies in France still locked in stalemate, the betting was that Britain would be starved into submission before the Americans had time to intervene effectively. It was a gamble that nearly succeeded.

The British Admiralty had so far refused to introduce the convoy system, but the threat of this new campaign must have prompted it to do more to save those merchant ships that remained afloat after being mined or torpedoed. 'It was considered that there would be a very good chance of getting some of these vessels into port,' one document recorded, 'if arrangements could be made for tugs to be held available for assisting such vessels. The plan was, therefore, conceived of basing tugs – to be termed 'rescue tugs' – round the English and Irish coasts and in the Mediterranean for the express purpose of rendering prompt assistance to damaged ships. All tugs detailed for this work were to be armed and fitted with wireless.'[3]

To oversee this decision a Tug Distribution Committee (TDC) was created on 2 February 1917 within the Admiralty's Trade

Division. Then on 2 May 1917 a rescue tug section was formed to control all rescue tugs and their dispositions, which was attached to the Admiralty's War Staff as a section of the Trade Division. The TDC's chairman, Captain EPFG Grant CB RN (replaced later in 1917 by Captain CR Wason CMG RN), was appointed to head the section as Captain-in-Charge Rescue Tugs (CCRT), and was given a staff of two commanders, or one commander and one lieutenant-commander, and one assistant paymaster who would also act as the TDC's secretary. The TDC would continue in being as a standing committee to co-ordinate the work carried out by tugs under the control of the director of transport and shipping, and the director of the Trade Division.[4]

After preliminary investigations, the TDC informed the Admiralty of the acute shortage of ocean-going tugs and that a redistribution of those available was urgently required. Subsequently, all tugs were brought under the committee's authority and a search overseas for suitable tugs was instigated. The Admiralty requisitioned some, but others were hired and were still managed by their civilian owners.

Organising the country's tugs more efficiently was only a part of the answer. No one knew what kind of tug was best suited for ocean rescue work in wartime, or how it should be equipped, much less what techniques were needed. Towing was, and is, a highly technical branch of seamanship, and while efforts were always made to save the crew of a torpedoed ship, saving the ship itself – often in adverse weather a long way from land – was quite another matter.

In fact, a start had already been made to remedy the lack of ocean-going tugs, as the Admiralty had purchased two 457-ton Stoic-class tugs being built in Britain for the Argentinian government. *Stoic* was launched in March 1915 and *Cynic* in October 1915, and in January 1917 the Admiralty had ordered three more, *Dainty*, *Dandy* and *Spry*. The pulling power produced by their 1200 indicative horse power (ihp)[5] engines made them capable of towing most cargo ships, and their endurance and speed of eleven and a half knots able to reach any casualty.

A month later the Admiralty ordered six more tugs, later called the Resolve class, which were based on the design of a commercial tug, *Sir David Hunter*, built for South African Railways in 1915. At the same time the government's Department of Transport and Shipping ordered the first three of what became known as the Frisky class. These were based on *Racia*, an ocean tug built for the legendary Dutch tug company L Smit and Co., the world's foremost experts in ocean salvage.

Unfortunately, this knee-jerk reaction was overtaken by events as later that year the government introduced a crash shipbuilding programme for merchant ships. This kept the shipyards working to full capacity, and at the end of September 1917 none of the tugs ordered had even been laid down. In any case, by this time the Admiralty construction department had been persuaded 'that taking the plans of an existing commercial tug and collaborating with a builder to modify them for naval purposes was not the ideal way to design or build a rescue tug. In evaluating their requirements, the Admiralty felt that a smaller tug than the Frisky or Resolve types could handle the majority of mercantile casualty work more efficiently and economically. The Admiralty specification was discussed with several builders under the designation of 'Rescue Type' tugs, and the first drawings of the class appear to be the result of co-operation between Ferguson Bros of Port Glasgow and the Naval Constructor.'[6]

The result of this collaboration was the 440-ton Saint class.[7] They, too, were something of a compromise and had a number of design faults – though strongly built, their stability was not as good as it should have been, nor was their endurance – but they were the first to be designed from the keel up as a rescue tug. They were armed with a twelve-pounder gun and such ancillary equipment as smoke-generating apparatus and hydrophones, but the towing arrangements were primitive, and the lack of a motorboat showed the Admiralty had little appreciation of what the work of a rescue tug would entail. Sixty-four were ordered, of which forty-six were built. They were constructed between April and August 1918, seven of them in Hong Kong. It is doubtful if any of them were used operationally before the Armistice was signed on 11 November 1918, though a handful were deployed. However, some played their part during the next and far bigger conflict to come.

On 3 February 1917, two days after the start of the second unrestricted U-boat campaign, the United States President, Woodrow Wilson, severed diplomatic relations with Germany. He may have still hoped to avoid war, but the famous Zimmermann Telegram put paid to that. This revealed Germany wanted an alliance with Mexico if the United States entered the war, a move that would have directly threatened American territory. With the destruction of shipping continuing, involving a further loss of American life, President Wilson declared war on Germany on 6 April 1917.

THE CONVOY DEBATE

Their Lordships at the Admiralty had determined that in the age of steam, convoys, which had a long history, were no longer the best method of protecting merchant ships. Convoys made them, the sceptics argued, a larger target; there were too few warships to escort every convoy, where the presumption was that the escorts had to equal the numbers of ships it contained;[8] convoys created large areas of smoke that could attract the enemy; they took time to assemble; and the arrival of so many ships at a port at the same time would create congestion and incur further delays.

A later analysis of U boat warfare and convoys showed these arguments to be almost entirely fallacious,[9] but to ship owners time was money, so the last two points had also made them opposed to convoys. So much better, they agreed, for merchant ships to sail on their own along routes patrolled by the Royal Navy. Besides, merchant ships had no experience in 'keeping station' within a convoy and of following the diversionary manoeuvres necessary to minimise attack.

By voicing this last concern, convoy sceptics – of which the First Sea Lord, Admiral John Jellicoe, was one – gave the impression, at least to the British Prime Minister David Lloyd George, that they considered the Merchant Navy not to have the ability or seamanship to learn convoy discipline. This was, as Lloyd George later scathingly commented, 'simply the arrogance of superiority which induces the uniformed chauffeur of a Rolls-Royce to look down on the driver of what is contemptuously stigmatised as a "tin Lizzie",'[10] a comment that must have gone down well with their Lordships.

The Merchant Navy's official historian of the First World War, Archibald Hurd, wrote that the captains themselves had doubted their ability to maintain convoy discipline: 'When the merchant captains were approached upon the subject of introducing ocean convoy, they answered that the thing was impossible. They could not do it. They and their ships were ill-fitted for such a system.'[11]

This proved nonsense, though of course there were initial difficulties, and almost certainly similar encounters to the one recalled by a US Navy officer escorting a convoy from Gibraltar later in the war. On urging a straggler by megaphone to move back into position, the skipper, a 'very canny Scot', replied, 'I dinna ken, I dinna ken into position. This ship is no liner; she is an auld box.'[12]

The Admiralty had already introduced a number of other anti-submarine measures. Merchant ships were being armed, and the Auxiliary Patrol formed to protect Britain's coastal waters.

Further out, the shipping routes were covered by small warships, such as sloops and destroyers, and Q-ships had early successes in luring surfaced U-boats close enough to sink them with their concealed guns. Depth charges were first used in 1916, but equipping warships with them took time, and hydrophones to detect a U-boat were never very successful. Minefields caused the U-boats some problems, particularly when in 1917 the Admiralty, with great reluctance, replaced British duds with ones based on a German design.[13] As the war progressed aviation – particularly dirigibles – played an important reconnaissance role.

But these measures could not counter the ferocity of the new unrestricted campaign. The increased numbers of U-boats[14] was the main reason for its success, but there were other contributing factors: patrolling warships were spread too thinly to prevent attacks; U-boat commanders became adept at detecting Q-ships; and, as armed merchantmen became more common, their attackers rarely exposed themselves by surfacing before sinking them.

Inevitably, the Admiralty's objections to convoys came under ever-closer scrutiny, and when the cross-Channel coal convoys – or 'controlled sailings' as they were tactfully called to dampen the Admiralty's scepticism – proved successful after they started in February 1917, some thought the argument won. But still the Admiralty sought other alternatives, and in March 1917 it arranged for ships with cargoes deemed of national importance to have dedicated routes within three triangles. The bases of these triangles were certain longitudes and their apexes the ports of Falmouth, Queenstown on the south coast of Ireland (modern-day Cobh), and Buncrana on Lough Swilly in Northern Ireland, which Archibald Hurd later named as the main bases for the new rescue tugs.[15]

The scheme was initially supported by ship owners, but the areas soon proved too large for the number of warships available to patrol them. Of the eight hundred and ninety merchant ships assigned to them between March and May 1917, sixty-three were sunk – seven per cent of the total, a very high rate of attrition. In June it was even higher at eleven per cent,[16] and ship owners now started to call them 'death traps'.

Another measure the Admiralty introduced – a reminder that the transition from sail to steam had still not been completed – was to introduce compulsory towing for commercial sailing vessels through zones where U-boats were known to operate. By their very nature these vessels were slow, and their routes erratic, making them difficult to protect, but they often carried valuable cargo the country could ill afford to lose.

The TDC stipulated that the tugs undertaking this task were to be called 'relay' tugs, though they could act as 'rescue' tugs at the discretion of the senior naval officer (SNO) where they were based. 'Rescue' tugs, on the other hand, were to be employed solely for salvaging damaged merchant ships and could only be used for other work with the Admiralty's permission. Slowly, the concept of a rescue tug was beginning to take shape.

CONVOY TRIALS AND TRIBULATIONS

While the Admiralty dragged its heels over convoys, the government introduced measures to counter the very real threat of Britain being starved into submission: non-essential imports were reduced to a minimum, or stopped completely, and the use of existing tonnage was reorganised to concentrate more merchant ships on the shorter North Atlantic routes to increase the stockpile of imported wheat. It was less dramatic, short-term measures like these that probably saved Britain from immediate collapse, as one historian has plausibly argued.[17]

However, according to Lloyd George, it was political pressure to establish ocean convoys that eventually saved the day. In his memoirs, he wrote caustically that had 'we not found some means of dealing with the menace not then visible to the fear-dimmed eyes of our Mall Admirals, and had we not put into operation ideas which never emanated from their brains and some of which they resisted, others of which they delayed', he had no doubt that his government, as the Germans had already predicted, would have been forced to sue for peace within a matter of months.[18]

On 10 April President Wilson's naval representative, Rear Admiral William Sims, arrived in England. Sims, whose role was to foster naval co-operation between the two countries, was a good choice. He was a known anglophile and had a long-standing friendship with Admiral Jellicoe. But when he arrived in Whitehall a shock awaited him. Up to that point, all the evidence available to him had seemed to indicate an Allied victory. But what Jellicoe frankly told him, as he handed Sims the tonnage losses for the preceding few months, revealed a very different state of affairs. Sims later wrote:

> It is expressing it mildly to say that I was surprised by this disclosure. I was fairly astounded; for I had never imagined anything so terrible...
>
> 'It looks as though the Germans [are] winning the war,' I remarked.
>
> 'They will win, unless we can stop these losses – and stop them soon,' the Admiral replied.
>
> 'Is there no solution for the problem?' I asked.
>
> 'Absolutely none that we can see now,' Jellicoe announced.[19]

On 14 April Sims cabled Washington these unpalatable facts. He recommended that base personnel and the maximum possible number of destroyers be dispatched to Queenstown from where patrols could be instituted to the west of Ireland. He also requested sea-going tugs be sent to the war zone, and throughout the conflict he urged that more be sent, stressing they would 'save valuable tonnage by rescuing torpedoed and stranded transports',[20] showing he was an early, and influential, supporter of a rescue tug organisation.

Sims' advice to send destroyers was promptly taken and the first six arrived at Queenstown on 4 May 1917. But despite his characterisation of the United States as 'the country of tugs',[21] it seemed that few were available, and by August 1917 the US Navy Department had only managed to purchase twelve. By October seven of these had arrived in Europe and were assigned to French territorial waters, and to Genoa, Gibraltar and Queenstown. The British situation was no better and in November 1917, when the TDC reviewed the number of rescue tugs available, only forty-seven were in service in home waters and just four in the Mediterranean.[22]

Perhaps it was Sims' influence that persuaded the Admiralty, on 27 April, to order a trial ocean convoy from Gibraltar, and when three more arrived in May/June without a single loss the sceptics were confronted with irrefutable proof that convoys worked, and that far fewer escorts than anticipated were needed to protect them effectively. Ship owners added to the mounting pressure by insisting that the 'death traps' be abandoned to free up escorts for more convoys. This also meant transferring more destroyers to the Atlantic, but Jellicoe's mindset, as Lloyd George pointed out in his memoirs, was rooted in large fleet actions like Jutland, and he still refused to allow his Grand Fleet to be stripped of its destroyer protection.

It was therefore not until the middle of August that westbound Atlantic convoys, escorted by American destroyers from Queenstown, were started, eastbound ones having been instigated earlier. From a high of more than 545,000 tons lost in April 1917, British tonnage losses now began to decrease and by December had been reduced to just over 253,000 tons.[23]

EARLY OPERATIONS

In addition to Queenstown, Falmouth and Buncrana, rescue tugs were to be stationed at Berehaven, Milford, Scilly Isles, Portland and Plymouth, and elsewhere when new builds became available. In May 1917, it was decided to keep at sea fifty per cent of rescue tugs based at these ports, and in wireless touch with their SNOs. This arrangement, it was thought, would not only ensure more rapid assistance to damaged vessels but would help strengthen patrols in the area.

There are few records of the activities of these early rescue tugs, but Archibald Hurd relates how in September 1917 the 184-ton *Flying Falcon* and the 283-ton *Milewater* left Lough Swilly (Buncrana) with sealed orders to meet a homeward-bound convoy.[24] The weather was bad, but the next morning both tugs reached the convoy and took up positions behind it. By midnight a full gale was blowing and *Flying Falcon* was labouring badly. Off the Oversay Light (Islay) a tremendous wave broke over her, sweeping away the top of the companionway and sending water down below. A second smashed the hawser grating and washed the towing hawser overboard, which wrapped itself around the propeller. The engine stopped, leaving the tug wallowing helplessly. Another wave shifted the bunker coal to leeward so that she lay on her beam ends and nearly capsized.

One of the boats was lowered, prior to abandoning ship. As this was being done, another wave swept the tug and washed the captain, some of the crew, and the boat into the water. Three of the crew and the captain managed to climb back aboard, but three others were drowned. *Flying Falcon* was now drifting helplessly towards the land and though the captain dropped both his anchors, their cables snapped, and the rescue tug was driven ashore. Luckily, all those on board were saved, but it showed the kind of savage weather these small vessels were expected to brave.

Perhaps it was this incident that made the Admiralty change its mind, as the following month, October 1917, it advised the commander-in-chief (C-in-C) Devonport that in future he should use his discretion about sending out rescue tugs to meet homeward-bound convoys, and that in some cases, depending on the U-boat threat, it was better to keep the tugs in harbour until they were needed.

A first-hand account by Captain TH Bull, serving in the Rescue Tug Service, in 1918 shows that tagging on behind convoys was the normal tactic. He joined the 1916-built 294-ton *Sonia* at Loch Ewe, then a base for convoy vessels, after she had been hired by the Admiralty as a rescue tug:

> Our duty on the Rescue Tug consisted in sailing in a
> position well astern of a convoy so as to take in tow
> any ship damaged or torpedoed and try to beach her.
> A sandy foreshore near Buncrana in Lough Swilly was
> used and temporary repairs could be made to enable
> the stricken ship to get to the shipyards at Belfast for a
> permanent job. The outward convoys were assembled at
> Lamlash, Arran, and we followed them out to longitude
> 20° West where, in turn, we met inward convoys
> following them in through the North Channel until
> they dispersed for their various destinations.[25]

It was *Sonia* that tried to save the 32,234-ton British troopship *Justicia*, while the rescue tug was escorting a westbound convoy off Lamlash in July 1918. The three-funnelled *Justicia*, which had no troops aboard, remained afloat after the first torpedo struck her, and *Sonia* started to tow her towards Lough Swilly where it was intended to beach her at Buncrana. But the next morning, after several more torpedoes hit her – some sources say six in total – she sank. 'It was a sad moment,' Captain Bull recorded, 'that after towing for so long, to watch the great ship slide down into the depths of the sea funnel by funnel and to realise our efforts were to go unrewarded.'

THE SCILLIES AS A RESCUE BASE

The Scilly Isles were close to the Atlantic convoy routes, but at first their strategic position seems to have been overlooked, as a list of the disposition of rescue tugs on 28 May 1917 only shows the 197-ton *Sun II*, built in 1909, being based there,[26] and she was by all accounts totally inadequate. Later, it was realised that more rescue tugs were needed there before the winter, and by August 1917, *Sun II* had been joined at St Mary's, the archipelago's largest island, by the 214-ton *Bramley Moore*, the 154-ton *Joseph Constantine*, the 577-ton *Atalanta III*, the 283-ton *Blazer*, and by the 218-ton steel trawler, *Zaree*. Built in 1904 and recently purchased by the Admiralty and converted to towing, *Zaree* was to play a significant role in making the Rescue Tug Service a viable concept.

The Scillies was part of Rear Admiral William Luard's Falmouth Command and it was under him that the Rescue Tug Service was primarily developed. Their position made them the ideal location for the nascent organisation to hone its skills, experiment with new methods and test untried equipment. Because so many damaged ships were towed to St Mary's, or beached nearby, the Admiralty's Salvage Department based a large contingent from its Devonport dockyard workforce there.

One resident's memories of this time is recorded in *The Scillonian War Diary, 1914–18*, a fascinating if labyrinthine source for, among other things, the types of ships and cargoes that the rescue tugs brought in:

> They were towed in just under Samson [a nearby
> uninhabited island] where the deep water is and the
> dockyard men mended them; everybody in Scilly had
> to take in these dockyarders [as we called them], we
> couldn't refuse; if we had one bedroom and they had to
> share a bedroom, that was all there was to it, you had
> to take as many as you could take. They went out, they
> took their lunch and went out on the ships, carpenters
> and the lot, and mended the ships.[27]

Once a ship had been made watertight she either made her own way, or was towed, to Devonport or other dockyards where she was repaired and returned to service. The Rescue Tug Service and the Salvage Department often worked hand in hand to salvage ships, and their responsibilities sometimes overlapped, especially if a vessel were stranded. Both organisations were entitled to salvage money, an age-old concept that if men risked their lives to save a ship and her cargo it was only right that they be compensated for doing so, and this was continued during the Second World War.

How much compensation was due was adjudicated by the courts and was based on the percentage of the value of the ship and what she was carrying. In the First World War, the crews of warships were also entitled to salvage money, as they were initially during the Second World War – though payment was confined to those ships damaged by the enemy (war risks), not by stress of weather or other natural causes (marine risks). Later in the war this, too, was stopped.

Nearly all the vessels assisted by the rescue tugs based at St Mary's would have been damaged by war risks, and the base saw plenty of them. Some of the stories surrounding these casualties are amusing or dramatic; others are tragic. In the latter category was the 5525-ton British steamer *Great City* that was torpedoed thirty miles west of Bishop's Rock, west of the Scilly Isles, on 16 June 1917 while en route from the US port of Newport News, Virginia, to London. She was loaded with wheat so it is not surprising that, remembering the acute shortage of food in Britain at the time, the C-in-C Devonport described her cargo as 'valuable' when ordering the rescue tugs *Bramley Moore* and *Sun II* to her estimated position.

She was brought in safely and beached at St Mary's, and was then made watertight and refloated by the 'dockyarders', but on 31 August an entry in *The Scillonian War Diary* records a horrific incident aboard her:

> Four men gassed on steamer *Great City* lying in the
> Roads. This dreadful happening cast a gloom over the
> Islands; for a week or two the smell of rotting grain
> from the cargo of the *Great City* had been distressingly
> apparent and if the breeze was in any way from the
> north it spread through the town and windows had to be
> shut to exclude the terrible odour of decaying grain.[28]

Some of the salvage men were below as there was still a lot of water in the holds that had to be pumped out. One of them bent over to pick up a piece of floating debris – a necessary precaution to avoid the pumps being blocked – and was immediately overcome. Others, thinking he had fainted, rushed to his rescue, only to meet the same fate. One would have thought anyone aboard from then on would be warned to keep clear of the lethal water-sodden cargo, but, astonishingly, the diary records that men also died from the fumes when the ship was later towed to Holyhead, and then to Liverpool.

An antidote to *Great City*'s noxious fumes was the cargo carried by the 4277-ton British steamer *Eastgate*. She was en route for New York from Le Havre when she was torpedoed a hundred and twenty miles south-west of Bishop's Rock, and was brought in to St Mary's while the *Great City* was still there. According to *The Scillonian War Diary*, 'she turned the Islands into a bouquet of flowers', as she was carrying a cargo of medical requisites, perfumery and also, it was said, Paris model fashions. The torpedo struck her, as the Diary put it, 'in the perfumery department'. Bottles of scent were washed up on the beach along with cough mixture and hair dye, bundles of silk stockings and yards of lace, and the town, and the townspeople, reeked of perfume for weeks after the steamer had been beached there.[29]

INADEQUATE VESSELS

Once the United States entered the war, the increased numbers of ships arriving in British waters meant rescue work was unrelenting, and emphasised, as the year wore on, the continuing shortage of rescue tugs. Additional ones were requisitioned from their civilian owners but, initially at least, the Admiralty allowed some to keep control of their vessels, provided they gave satisfactory service. All the crews were volunteers, but using civilian crews and management in wartime was far from ideal. Nor were the tugs, with one or two exceptions, even remotely adequate for the task that faced them, as a Court of Enquiry into the loss of the 8557-ton British steamer *Condesa* revealed.[30]

On 7 July 1917, while bound for Liverpool with a cargo of frozen meat from South America, the *Condesa* was torpedoed about a hundred miles west of Bishop's Rock. She had been zigzagging correctly while steaming at eleven knots, but this did not save her, and her escort immediately sent out an SOS. This brought several ships to the scene, including *Joseph Constantine*,

Sun II and *Atalanta III*, as well as the Falmouth-based *Triton*, which was still under the management of her owners. The weather deteriorated as efforts were made to save the damaged steamer. Indeed, it became so bad that the court decided that *Sun II* and *Atalanta III* had been justified in turning back on account of it, an all too frequent occurrence.

The court's first witness was the captain of the Scilly-based armed trawler *Whitefriars*. He was early on the scene, and he described his failure to tow the sinking *Condesa* in the high winds and a rough following sea, as the trawler was not properly equipped for towing. He therefore handed the task to *Joseph Constantine* when she arrived from St Mary's, and she and the armed yacht *Ravenska* managed to tow the crippled steamer to within about thirty miles of the Scillies. But at 1.30pm on 9 July 1917 she sank, some forty hours after being torpedoed.

When the trawler's captain – an RNR officer – was cross-examined, it soon emerged that if more suitable help had arrived earlier the ship might have been saved.

'Do you know these tugs *Joseph Constantine*, *Sun II*, *Triton* and *Atalanta*?'
  'Yes.'
  'Which do you consider the best for sea-going purposes?'
  'The *Triton* is the best boat.'
  'Is the *Sun II* a sea-going tug, would you say?'
  'No, absolutely useless as a sea-going tug.'
  'What do you think of the *Atalanta*?'
  'I think she is worse than the *Sun II*. Not meant for a tug boat. She is a ferry boat or tender.'
  'And the *Joseph Constantine*?'
  'She is not an ocean tug.'
  'What is the *Bramley Moore* like as a tug?'

'Not what you would call an ocean tug, but she is the best of the lot at the Scilly Isles.'

'Is she better than the *Triton?*'

'No, better than the *Joseph Constantine*, *Sun II* or *Atalanta*. She is a river tug and not a sea-going tug.'

Another witness, the Senior Naval Officer (SNO) of the Scilly sub-base, Commander Oliver RN, was even more damning. When asked if any of the four tugs stationed at the base were sea-going tugs, he answered:

'No, not in my opinion, sir.'

'Were they suitable for the work required of them?'

'Certainly not.'

He explained to the Court that if a vessel were damaged in the Atlantic, a Scillies-based rescue tug typically had to cover about one hundred and twenty miles to find it, and that this required 'both speed and power. These vessels are quite incapable of dealing with it. I have an order for next Monday, a secret one, where vessels have to go as much as 600 miles, 6 degrees [of longitude].'

It was, he said, a bitter disappointment to him when given such an order to find that when the time came the weather was too bad to send them out, or they were forced to return because of it. Besides, the tugs were not fitted out for ocean work – they didn't even have sextants or chronometers to find their position at sea – and he always preferred to send trawlers if he could, but never had enough of them.

After asking if any of the tugs' commanding officers may have turned back unnecessarily, and received a negative reply, the Court asked about the Falmouth-based *Triton* which Commander Oliver had specifically requested to help the sinking steamer. Her tug master, though experienced, was sixty-one years old and his crew were not exactly youngsters. Time was lost when the tug master argued it was his Sunday off and that *Victor*, another of the company's tugs, should be sent. However, he eventually agreed to go – once the crew's dinner of pasties had been delivered on board.

More time was lost when the tug master took *Triton* into St Mary's. His W/T (wireless telegraphy which used morse code) operator was too seasick to function, but he wanted to know if the *Condesa* was still afloat. However, he agreed with the court when it was suggested to him that the best way to have found out would have been to follow his orders, though he had also decided the weather was too bad to continue. Commander Oliver had disagreed. He had the W/T operator replaced and ordered *Triton* back to sea. Finding the weather even worse as he headed westwards, the tug master returned to St Mary's. Again, Commander Oliver sent him back to sea, and told the court he had never been 'more astonished in my life' when *Triton* had returned a second time. *Triton* eventually reached the stricken *Condesa*, but had been too late to save her.

The Court of Enquiry then asked if there had been anything more he could have done, and Oliver replied:

'I do not know of anything. It was simply a series of accidents. The vessels returned, and we practically lost 24 hours in coming and going without any assistance being rendered by them. I did not know they were coming back half the time.'

'The accidents you refer to [are] the coming back on account of the weather?'

'Yes, and the means I had. I do not think the boats are suitable for Scilly.'

In submitting the findings of the Court of Enquiry to the Admiralty, the C-in-C Devonport, who was in overall command of Falmouth, pointed out that the only tug really at fault appeared to be *Triton*, but nothing could be done about it as her master and crew were not under naval discipline. He suggested both Falmouth-based tugs should be requisitioned and commissioned into the Royal Navy, and to the annoyance of their owners this was done the following March. New officers and crews were recruited under the T.124T Agreement (see below), and *Victor* and *Triton* were renamed *Ictor* and *Plunger* respectively.

MERCHANT NAVY AND T124.T AGREEMENT

These accounts, extracted from contemporary documents, show clearly the inadequacy of the vessels in which their crews had to operate, and says much for their skill and bravery. Many were recruited from the Trawler Reserve[31] and some of them, wrote Archibald Hurd, 'did so well that in five months they were promoted to second mate, and then to mate. Such men had before the war been skippers of sailing smacks with no experience of steam, but owing to their practical knowledge of sea-lore they made excellent officers.' It was, he quite rightly emphasised, no easy task to find a sinking vessel in the Atlantic in foul weather, and to bring it to safety. 'Such efforts demanded seamanship, daring, patience, and coolness of the first order. The Rescue Tug Service paid for itself many times over in the value of the ships and cargoes which were saved.'[32]

But the Merchant Service was a civilian organisation only answerable to the Board of Trade so, in 'a military sense, the Merchant Navy was an undisciplined force. While the great shipping firms maintained a regular body of officers, they drew upon the labour market as necessary for manning the ships, men in the overseas trade signing on for the voyage and then being discharged.'[33]

This may have worked in peacetime, but in war it meant that if a seaman's ship was sunk under him, or he was made a prisoner of war, his pay ceased immediately and he did not even receive any compensation for the loss of his belongings, an iniquitous state of affairs that continued until 1941.[34]

The solution was for the Rescue Tug Service to recruit volunteers under the T.124T Agreement. This was a variation of the T.124 agreement that the Royal Navy used to recruit Merchant Navy personnel in wartime for auxiliary vessels that the Royal Navy did not have the personnel to man. For instance, T.124X was the agreement for recruiting personnel into the Royal Fleet Auxiliary. Recruits signing the agreement agreed to serve for the period of hostilities and were subject to naval discipline, but they retained their Merchant Navy pay, which was higher than the naval equivalent, a cause for grievance in the Second World War, as will be seen.

If Merchant Navy officers held certificates as master or first-class engineer they were given temporary commissions as lieutenant or lieutenant (E) in the Royal Naval Reserve (RNR). Those not holding certificates were given the rank of temporary sub-lieutenant RNR. Later, T.124T was corrupted into 'Tattie' by those who served in rescue tugs. They became known as 'the Tattie Lads', and the nickname stuck. But rescue tugs in both world wars also had naval gunners aboard, as well as naval signalmen and W/T operators, so the crews came from both services.

The two cultures did not always mix easily, for merchant seamen were, and are, fiercely independent and, as will be seen in later chapters, not always amenable to discipline. Misunderstandings in terminology also arose as a Court of Enquiry in January 1918 revealed, when the master of the tug *Victor*, still managed by her civilian owners at that time, admitted he was unfamiliar with the naval method of giving a true bearing, and had therefore been unable to find a freighter that had been torpedoed just twenty-five miles off the Lizard.[35] No wonder the Admiralty requisitioned *Victor* two months later.

EVELYN GEORGE MARTIN

The early development of the Rescue Tug Service was largely due to Lt Evelyn George Martin RNVR. A scion of the banking family of that name, he was educated at Eton and then at Oxford where he studied medicine, though he never qualified as a doctor. He was born in Worcestershire, and spent much of his time with relations in the Devon fishing port of Brixham as his father was in the Indian Army. A very tall, shy man – a life-long bachelor – he was a first-class yachtsman, had a golf handicap of two, and played cricket for Oxford and Worcestershire. He also possessed many artistic talents. *The Isis* magazine remarked that 'on the ski and on the piano, with the paint-brush and with the dissecting knife, he is equally at home'.[36]

He sounds just the sort of upper-class gentleman amateur the public school system and Oxbridge was so good at breeding at that time. But there was nothing amateur about Martin. He was not a man who objected to getting his hands dirty, and before going up to Oxford he worked with Brixham's fishing fleet and in local shipyards. What he didn't know about working boats wasn't worth knowing, and this knowledge was to serve him well in both world wars.

In November 1914 he joined the Motor Boat Reserve[37] as a sub-lieutenant RNVR, and was given command of the *Mayfair*, a 55-ton motor yacht that would have been too small to be employed anywhere but in the most sheltered waters. Unfortunately, one dark night while there was a hunt for a suspected U-boat, one of the hunters rammed the *Mayfair* and she sank in thirty seconds, luckily without any loss of life.

Martin, who was at the wheel at the time, later wrote about this unnerving experience in a yachting magazine,[38] and put it to good use to explain how best to avoid a full-on blow that sliced through the *Mayfair* 'as a knife slices a melon'.

He was then appointed to the stone frigate HMS *Excellent*, for a gunnery course, and later served in the monitor HMS *Prince Rupert*. While aboard her, he showed such technical ability that his service record noted: 'Appreciation expressed for zeal and ingenuity in working out design of fuze setting device.'

At some point his peacetime knowledge of working boats must have come to the notice of higher authority, for on 10 June 1917 he was appointed to HMS *President* (the London depot ship for RNVR and RNR personnel) as an inspector of tug equipment. The following month, he was lent to the RA (Rear Admiral) Falmouth as 'Inspector of Rescue Tug Equipment' and put under the direct orders of the SNO of the Scilly base. He arrived at St Mary's on 12 September 1917, with the Scilly base weekly report noting 'that yacht *Venetia* [*II*] arrived with Lieutenant Martin RNVR. Yacht proceeded on patrol.'[39]

Martin had a gift for writing, and he later vividly described his wartime work in equipping and handling rescue tugs:

> Many months were spent in finding out what gear
> was necessary and could be handled by small crews
> in rough water; in providing suitable hawsers, wires,
> swivels and shackles – all of which had to be specially
> made, tested to destruction, and proved at sea. Besides
> this, the right class of seaman had to be collected, a
> very difficult matter, for only the very best sailors are
> of any use in handling huge hawsers in small craft in
> bad weather; and guns, wireless, depth charges, smoke
> apparatus, line-throwing guns and many other things had
> to be arranged.

For every class of ship in the Navy there is an 'establishment' – in other words, an official inventory, and the dockyards are able to supply ships accordingly. Those who have experience of naval dockyards may guess the difficulty of fitting out complete a fleet of tugs for which there was no 'establishment'. For a long time the writer had little chance of getting to sea, but at last things were more or less in shape, he was given an assistant, and a ship of his own with charge of all rescue work at sea in the Western Area.[40]

From this description, and from the few surviving official reports relating to his wartime work, Martin probably spent the rest of 1917 and the early part of 1918 chasing round dockyards for what he needed, and going to sea for short periods to test equipment. But by the spring of 1918 documents show that progress was at last being made.[41] 'The tug *Woonda* is now being fitted as a rescue tug in readiness to be appropriated for that Service,' the captain of dockyard and deputy superintendent, Devonport, informed the admiral superintendent on 2 March 1918; and on 18 March the C-in-C Devonport, in commenting on how rescue work would be controlled, informed the Admiralty that the rescue tugs in the Plymouth Command now totalled eleven: five at the Scillies, four at Falmouth and two at Plymouth, though he added that the latter 'can scarcely be classed as capable of ocean work, or for work with convoys', which makes clear that even the most unsuitable vessels continued to be used as rescue tugs.

On 6 April 1918, the R-A Falmouth submitted to the C-in-C Devonport reports from the Inspector of Tugs, Lt-Cdr EG Martin RNVR [he had been promoted the previous November], regarding the tugs now operating in the area. The printed forms, filled in and signed by Martin, recorded his comments on the equipment aboard each of them, including the condition of the tow ropes, W/T set, life rafts, depth charges and hydrophones. General quarters and fire practice had to be carried out at regular intervals on all the tugs as did practice at firing the guns now mounted on them.

On 8 April 1918, the SNO Scillies reported the routine the five rescue tugs based there followed. On returning from sea they would immediately take aboard coal, water and stores. Two of them would then be at immediate readiness and two at half an hour's notice. When a damaged ship had been reported, the duty trot boat would give five blasts on her whistle to summon the tugs' crews who all lived nearby. It then took them to their ships that lay about half a mile off the pier at St Mary's, where they would await their orders to proceed to sea, and after doing so would communicate their position, course and speed by W/T every four hours.

This was all very well, but as Martin pointed out to the R-A Falmouth, rescue tugs often had to try to find torpedoed ships beyond the range of the primitive ¼ kW Marconi sets they all carried. It was also not unusual for as many as six tugs to be at sea (it had been decided that, where possible, tugs should work in pairs) and these might not only be out of touch with land but with each other. It was also a common occurrence to search for ships that had already sunk, or had been taken in tow by other ships, so this lack of co-ordination was a huge waste of time and effort – and sometimes lives.

MARTIN'S PLANS AND PROPOSALS

To counter this drain on precious resources, Martin submitted that one vessel should be detailed for the following duties: to maintain W/T communication between shore stations and all rescue tugs operating in the area; to relay information to other rescue tugs received from shore or elsewhere; and to ascertain the positions and circumstances of the damaged vessels being sought, together with such instructions as may be issued from the shore. This vessel would transmit the position of each rescue tug to the shore, render additional towing assistance where needed, and carry additional stores such as spare W/T equipment. It would operate from Falmouth or the Scillies, have a 'rescue tug officer' in overall command, and a leading telegraphist to cope with the extra W/T load. In fact, once his plans were approved, Martin recruited four additional telegraphists for the W/T sets he had had installed, thus enabling a twenty-four-hour watch to be maintained.

Martin suggested that the converted trawler *Zaree*, though not powerful enough to be a good rescue tug, would be ideal for the task. She was an exceptional sea boat, with a large steaming radius, and there was room aboard for a W/T office, ancillary equipment and stores. The more powerful Marconi set with which she was equipped was expected to have a range of between two and three hundred miles.

> The tugs could not spread proper aerials and were
> always getting out of touch. So the trawler was specially
> fitted. She had preposterous topmasts – and she felt
> them too with a beam sea – but her aerial was over
> 70 feet from the deck, and she was the connecting link
> between the shore and the ships working with her.[42]

Martin proposed 'that I may be allowed to carry out the duties of Rescue Tug Officer mentioned, observing that I have had opportunity during the last nine months, of going to sea in rescue tugs and that I am well acquainted with the personnel and sea-going abilities of all the tugs, and with the localities in which they operate. I would suggest that these last two points are of great importance when considering the movements of tugs in rough weather.'[41]

He also requested that his present appointment be changed from Inspector of Rescue Tugs to 'a sea-going appointment as Rescue Tug Officer for Devonport Command', and that he be appointed to command *Zaree* for control of all rescue work in the area. If he had to be at sea for prolonged periods, he wanted to appoint a junior officer to take over his shore duties.

Attached to this correspondence was a detailed drawing of the proposed alterations to *Zaree* to accommodate an enlarged W/T office. Neatly captioned, it was obviously drawn by a skilled draughtsman, since Martin, who was to become a talented water colourist between the wars, was an accomplished artist.

Martin's proposals swiftly passed through the chain of command, and on 18 June the Admiralty approved them. Martin then issued details of the future W/T organisation of Rescue Tug Service in the Falmouth area when at sea, and made it clear that while *Zaree* would always be ready to proceed to sea if any rescue operations were launched, she would not normally be employed on convoy or any routine duties. Then on 27 August he made a further, and very important, proposal:

I have the honour to submit that: hitherto no attempt
to keep vessels afloat while being towed has been
made. The reason being, that the Admiralty Salvage
organisation does not deal with any vessel until the
Rescue Tugs have beached her or brought her into
port. Tugs employed in towing can carry neither the
extra men, nor the gear required for first aid salvage at
sea; and are fully occupied in the work of towing alone.
    I am of the opinion that vessels which have sunk
after many hours towing, might in several cases have
been saved, had it been possible to put men and gear

on board. This is particularly the case when an engine room is being slowly flooded through a leaky bulkhead, so that it has been impossible to keep the engine room clear of water. The same applies to the stokehold.[41]

He suggested *Zaree* should be supplied with an electric pump 'together with a phase generator, and the necessary piping, switchboard starters and flexible lead; 2 sets of Tangye Tackles [differential pulleys] to lift about one ton; and diving plant'. The generating plant could be fitted to a rescue vessel and the pumps run on board the torpedoed ship through an electric cable slung from a hawser. This had not been done before, but the Admiralty Salvage Adviser with whom Martin had discussed it had thought it perfectly feasible:

> It is submitted that *Zaree* will, in addition to her W/T duties, be able to give most valuable assistance in this way, and that I shall be able to spare an Executive and an Engineer officer, and a working party for this work, which cannot be done by a Rescue Tug when towing.[41]

He wanted the W/T store with which *Zaree* was to be fitted to be big enough to house a lathe, a drilling machine and a motor for the lathe: 'If these were installed the efficiency of the ship would be considerably improved. If they are not available from Admiralty Supply, I would supply them myself,' but would like to know if he would be compensated if these items were lost or damaged. 'The tools are stored,' he added, 'as I took them ashore when leaving my last ship, in which I had rigged an armourer's workshop.' There was, it seemed, no end to his talents.

After the necessary alterations to the *Zaree* were approved, it took a couple of months for them to be completed, but on 11 October she was reported as having arrived at Brest where

Martin, a fluent French speaker, was to discuss with the French authorities the co-operation between the French tugs based there and the British ones based at Falmouth and the Scillies.[43]

On 26 October he reported to the R-A Falmouth that the telegraphists were working well and there had been no difficulty in transmitting to land stations. However, communication with the tugs was not as good as expected, though the Stoic class *Cynic*, now based at the Scillies, had received his signals at a distance of one hundred and twenty miles. He thought this could be improved upon, as the previous month the *Zaree* had been able to contact the torpedoed Norwegian steamer *Thomas Krag* being towed by the *Cynic* some three hundred miles from the Scillies. As a result, the *Zaree* had been able to assist in towing the damaged steamer to Brest.

Martin obviously relished his new command. 'It would be difficult to imagine any work which could be more interesting or exciting,' he wrote after the war, and went on to explain the intricacies of taking another ship in tow, especially in heavy weather:

> The best plan is to cross the disabled ship's bow at right angles, or nearly so; and whether she should be approached from the weather or the lee side depends greatly upon the way in which the towing ship handles, the way she cants when going astern, and whether she lies naturally head or stern to the wind when drifting herself. The chances of getting a heavy line across are better when approaching from the windward side, and if the ship will answer her helm readily when going dead slow or with the engines stopped, this is probably the better plan. Taking a vessel in tow in bad weather is a very severe test of seamanship, and the safest method can only be decided upon at the moment, for in no two cases are the conditions really similar.[44]

He also had some interesting insights into the handling of an ocean-going tug:

> [Anyone looking at one] might think that she would stand any amount of hard driving, and hard driving was the essence of the job, for no time [should] be lost in reaching the ship in distress. But no greater mistake could be made. A tug is literally built around her towing hook, which, for purposes of handling the vessel, must be practically amidships. As a consequence, boilers, bunkers and all the superstructure must be crowded into the forward half of the ship.[44]

A tug would behave well enough when moving at about four knots, but:

> Drive her all out into a head sea and you will see something you will never forget. She takes the first sea all right – the water just rushes through the hawse pipes. Up goes her head, hovers a moment, and then crash she goes into the next, a cataract pours over the fo'c'sle, solid chunks of water dash against the wheelhouse windows and the sea rushes aft knee deep and leaps out over the taffrail.[44]

He then explained why life on board during long passages to find a damaged ship was so hard:

> Put it at 360 miles at 6 knots, and this is very good going against a head sea in the Western Ocean in winter – 60 hours – and then perhaps a long and heart-breaking tow afterwards. Thirteen, fifteen, and in one case, from memory, seventeen days out with eleven days'

towing. That ship was brought safe to Queenstown at last in tow of five or six tugs – one end of her was in the air, the other under water; she wouldn't tow and she wouldn't steer, but they saved her. It was no wonder that sick returns were heavy and the accidents numerous.[44]

RECOGNITION

On 19 February 1919 the Admiralty issued a notice to the Fleet:

The Board of Admiralty desire to record their high appreciation of the work performed during the war by the Rescue Tugs, the Foreign and Coastal Towing Tugs, and the Tug Service generally, and to express their thanks to the officers and men who rendered such efficient service in saving life, in salving valuable tonnage, and in many other directions...

[After describing the work of the Rescue Tug Service, the notice continued:] From the inception of the Rescue Tug Service, in the early part of 1917 up to November 1918, some 140 damaged vessels were safely towed into harbour by these tugs. In addition to these vessels the tugs have also assisted over 500 ships,[45] which had become disabled either by enemy action or marine risks...

Throughout a long period of arduous labour the officers and men of the various tug services have shown promptitude, courage, and resources, and the thanks of the whole nation are due to them for the magnificent work which they had established.[46]

On 11 June 1919, *The London Gazette* announced that Martin had been awarded the OBE (Military) 'for valuable services as Officer in Charge of Rescue Tugs, Plymouth', and he was allowed to retain his rank of Lt-Commander RNVR.

NOTES

1. Conan Doyle A. 'Danger! Being the Log of Captain John Sirius', *Strand Magazine* (July 1914): 1–22.
2. May ER. *The World War and American Isolation, 1914–17.* Cambridge, MA: Harvard University Press; 1959. p.115.
3. Tug Control: Work of the Tug Distribution Committee, 25 May 1917, in ADM 116/1739.
4. Report of the Tug Distribution Committee, 15/11/17, in ADM 116/1739.
5. Indicated horse-power is a reciprocating engine's theoretical power assuming it to be frictionless. A rough rule to estimate a tug's pulling power is one ton of 'pull' for every 100 ihp, but in the higher horsepower tugs this 'pull' is less, e.g. a 4000 hp tug develops a 'pull' of about 32 tons. A seven-ton 'pull' will tow a ship of 5000 tons displacement about four knots in good weather. See AFO P.600/43 in ADM 1/13096.
6. Brown B, Hancox D. 'Tugs and Salvage Craft of the Royal Navy', part manuscript in the DSRTA archive. Courtesy Buster J Browne.
7. All First World War rescue tugs are listed in www.naval-history. net/WW1NavyBritishShips-Dittmar5Support.htm
8. Commander RGH Henderson RN, who organised the successful French coal trade convoys, proved these figures were based on inaccurate statistics.
9. Grove E, editor. *The Defeat of the Enemy Attack on Shipping, 1939–45.* London: Navy Records Society; 1997. Chapter 1.
10. Lloyd George D. *War Memoirs.* Vol. II. London: Odhams; 1938. pp.681–82.
11. Hurd A. *The Merchant Navy.* Vol. III. London: John Murray; 1929. p.371.
12. Still WN. Jr. *Crisis at Sea: The US Navy in European Waters in World War I.* Gainesville: University of Florida Press; 2006. p.350.

13. Halpern PG. *A Naval History of World War I*. Annapolis: Naval Institute Press; 1995. pp.344–45.
14. Grove E. *The Defeat, op. cit.* p.4.
15. Hurd A. *The Merchant Navy, op. cit.* p.40.
16. Halpern PG. *A Naval History, op. cit.* p.342.
17. French D. *The Strategy of the Lloyd George Coalition, 1916–18*. Oxford: Clarendon Press; 1995. p.70.
18. Lloyd George D. *War Memoirs, op. cit.* pp.676–77.
19. Sims WS. *The Victory at Sea*. Annapolis: Naval Institute Press; 1984. pp.9–10.
20. Still WN. Jr. *Crisis at Sea, op. cit.* pp.165–66.
21. *Ibid.*, p.166.
22. From Appendix II TDC meeting, 15/11/17 in ADM 116/1239.
23. Fayle C. *Official History of the Great War: Seaborne Trade.* Vol. III. London: John Murray; 1924. p.465.
24. Hurd A. *The Merchant Navy, op. cit.* pp.64–65.
25. Bull TH, article from unknown journal in DSRTA archive.
26. Tug Control: Work of the Tug Distribution Committee, 28 May 1917, in ADM 116/1739.
27. Osborne J. *The Scillonian War Diary, 1914–18*, Vol. II, Appendix C, unpublished manuscript. Memories of Mrs Katie Thompson. Courtesy Isles of Scilly Museum, St Mary's.
28. Osborne J. *The Scillonian War Diary, op. cit.*, Vol. II, Appendix O, pp.xiv–xv.
29. *Ibid.*, p.xxv.
30. Court of Enquiry into *Condesa*'s loss in ADM 137/3287.
31. Officially known as the Trawler Section of the Royal Naval Reserve (RNR). It was formed in 1910 and recruited from fishermen. After the First World War it was absorbed into the RNR.
32. Hurd A. *The Merchant Navy, op. cit.* Vol. III. pp.40–41.
33. *Ibid.*, Vol. II. p.227.
34. Lane T. *The Merchant Seaman's War*. Manchester: Manchester University Press; 1990. pp.30–31.
35. Court of Enquiry in ADM 156/169.
36. Dear I. *The Royal Ocean Racing Club: The First Seventy-Five Years.* London: Adlard Coles Nautical; 2000. pp.18–20.

37. Formed from privately owned small steam and motor yachts whose owners offered their services in an emergency to the Royal Navy. In July 1915 it was amalgamated with what became the Auxiliary Patrol.

38. Martin EG. 'Cruising', *Yachting World & Marine Motor Journal* (20 November 1926): 1208.

39. The Scilly base weekly report dated 14 September 1917 in ADM 137/2209.

40. Martin EG. 'Cruising', *Yachting World & Marine Motor Journal* (20 December 1924): 1141–2.

41. ADM 131/96.

42. Martin EG. 'Cruising', *Yachting World & Marine Motor Journal* (20 December 1924): 1142.

43. Falmouth weekly diary of 14/10/18 in ADM 137/949.

44. Martin EG, 'Cruising', *Yachting World & Marine Motor Journal* (20 December 1924): 1141.

45. A more recent source puts the figure at over 800. See Booth T. *Admiralty Salvage in Peace and War, 1906–2006*. Barnsley: Pen & Sword Maritime; 2007. p.78.

46. This tribute was published in many British newspapers in February 1919.

2

CAMPBELTOWN

THE ADMIRALTY'S RESCUE Tug Service was just getting into its stride in 1918 when the Armistice brought an end to hostilities. The Service and the TDC were disbanded the following year, and during the 1920s the dire economic situation forced the Admiralty to dispose of the Stoic and Frisky class rescue tugs, one of the Resolve class and twenty-seven of the Saint class, the balance being retained in various capacities.

Frisky and *Saucy* were two of the Frisky class sold abroad. In 1930, *Frisky* was acquired in Hamburg by a Canadian salvage firm, Foundation Maritime Ltd. She was renamed *Foundation Franklin* and did useful work during the Second World War.[1] *Saucy* was purchased by the Admiralty from the Shanghai Tug & Lighter Company soon after the start of the war. In September 1940, while in the command of Lieutenant A Paton RNR, she towed to safety a Dutch ship that had been set on fire by German aircraft in the Firth of Forth. But she was then sunk by a German mine with the loss of her entire crew of twenty-eight, eighteen of whom came from the Devon fishing port of Brixham. When the new Assurance class was built (see Chapter 5), two of them were named *Frisky* and *Saucy* after their First World War predecessors.

The loss of *St Genny*, which foundered off Ushant in January 1930, had shown the Saint class was not really suitable for the open ocean, although that didn't mean they didn't go there. But when the war started in September 1939, they were mostly employed in coastal waters, in the Mediterranean or in the more sheltered parts of the North Sea.

The prompt revival of the Rescue Tug Service and the TDC[2] – the latter before war had even been declared – and the appointment of a CCRT, was proof that EG Martin's ideas, given the serious limitations of the vessels at his disposal, had worked and had not been forgotten. Despite being fifty-nine years old, he was one of the first to be recalled for duty, and on 11 October 1939 he was granted the rank of Lieutenant RNVR and appointed 'for inspection duties outside Admiralty (Rescue Tug Section)'.[3] Later he was appointed Inspector of Tug Equipment, though there is no record of the date. Probably it was on 25 November 1939 when he was promoted to his First World War rank of temporary Lt-Commander, as later correspondence confirmed the appointment required someone of this seniority.

In October 1940, a base for rescue tugs was opened at Campbeltown, a small Scottish port on the Mull of Kintyre that was close to the Atlantic convoy routes. Martin was put in charge of it as Maintenance Officer Rescue Tugs[4] and was under the NOIC, Campbeltown, who commanded HMS *Nimrod*, the ASDIC [an early form of sonar] and mine detection base at the port.

In March 1941, he was promoted to the acting rank of commander, with the title Commander-in-Charge Rescue Tug Base, Campbeltown (CRTB, Campbeltown, for short). However, where appropriate, he continued to be addressed, and to sign himself, as the Maintenance Officer. Although the CCRT was responsible for recruitment, in practice Martin was in charge of recruiting ratings and the deputy CCRT recruited officers.

Martin remained at Campbeltown until the autumn of 1944, when the doctors judged his health too poor for him to spend another winter in the north. However, they said he was fit enough to take another appointment in the south, and he wrote to a friend that he would accept the post of CCRT if it were offered him – the present incumbent being 'a nice man personally, but in service matters an idiot. Quite hopeless as an organiser which is his job'[5] – but knew this was unlikely. He was right, and in October 1944 he took retirement when it was offered him. He died of a heart attack in April 1945, worn out, no doubt, as so many were, by overwork and the stress of a long and tedious conflict.

In private correspondence Martin wrote how he had been initially received at Campbeltown, and what his work during the previous three-and-a-half years had involved:

As an Admiralty officer, there was a lot of antagonism to my particular department: this has been gradually lived down and I, as one of the oldest naval people here, am taken as a matter of course... Almost the whole of my work here [is] dealing with hundreds of men from all our coasts: the Shetland and the Hebrides to the Scillies; big seaports like Hull, Tyneside and Glasgow; fishing ports like Lowestoft and Brixham; lightermen and bargemen from the Thames – taking them, unused to any discipline and helping them to find their feet in the Navy, and, so far as one can, in their personal troubles – and I think I may say that it has been successful.[6]

Even Martin could not have foreseen the importance the Rescue Tug Service was to attain, and its rapid expansion. It became so much part of the war at sea that in 1944 an American war correspondent was prompted to write of 'a new type of naval vessel – the British fighting escort tug', adding that no naval action or landing operation would have been attempted without it, and that it was 'as much a factor in winning the Battle of the Atlantic as the corvette or escort carrier'.[7]

Although Martin's plans for a Rescue Tug Service had taken wing, much had changed since he had started to develop it. By 1939, steam propulsion (coal- and oil-fired) was giving way to diesel, though the first British diesel-powered rescue tug was not launched until 1942 after diesel engines became available. This gave them greater endurance and increased power, so necessary with the Battle of the Atlantic being waged across the whole width of that ocean. Extra power was also needed, because the average size of merchant ships had doubled in twenty years, from 2300 tons to 5250,[8] though the average size of those in Atlantic convoys must have been much larger.

The conflict also became truly global, with rescue tugs being based wherever convoy routes attracted U-boats. By 1945, they were stationed in places as far apart as Newfoundland, Iceland, Gibraltar, South and West Africa, and the West Indies, and were part of the British naval contribution to the Pacific War. The geographical scene had changed, too. Most of Ireland had gained independence in 1922 and remained strictly neutral during the war, denying bases for rescue tugs. And once the Germans had overrun France, Belgium, the Netherlands, Denmark and Norway, the coastlines of these countries became the springboard for not only U-boats, but for hostile aircraft and the fast German torpedo boats, or *Schnellboote*, which the British called E-boats.

Schnellboote harassed the coastal convoys up Britain's east coast so frequently that the area became known as 'E-boat Alley'. The English Channel was even more dangerous, and commercial traffic ceased to transit it after a convoy passing through it in July 1940 was heavily bombed. From then on, all Atlantic convoys were routed to the north of Ireland, which was why Campbeltown was chosen as the rescue tugs' main base.

Iceland, a one-time Danish colony, now became an important Allied base for waging war against the U-boats and for assembling the Russian convoys to Murmansk. When the Germans occupied Denmark in May 1940, British and Canadian forces occupied the island before US Marines took over responsibility for defending it in July 1941. Stanley Butler, a rescue tug engineer officer, had some interesting comments about Iceland, and from his description it could not have been a popular place to be stationed, especially in winter:

> There was only daylight from mid-morning until
> mid-afternoon. The seas around there were awful,
> with bad weather being swept by a never-ending
> succession of gales. In winter these gales take the form
> of snow-laden blizzards cutting visibility to nil. The
> northwest of Iceland is just inside the Arctic Circle,
> so additional hazards are ice floes, icebergs, pack ice,
> and even other shipping can give a ship's captain
> some sleepless nights. To make matters even worse,
> compass needles could not be trusted on the approach
> to Reykjavik harbour, or south of the entrance to
> Hvalfjord. The high iron content of nearby mountains
> caused magnetic distortion.[9]

It was certainly the appalling weather and tricky navigation conditions that caused the loss of the Assurance class rescue tug

Horsa in March 1943. At the time she was towing to Seydisfjord the fore part of SS *Richard Bland*, a Liberty ship that had been cut in half by a torpedo while in convoy RA-53. Forced to abandon the hulk, which had become almost uncontrollable, she subsequently ran aground and became a total loss. The Court of Enquiry exonerated her commanding officer, Lt Ian Taylor RNR, and more will be heard of him later. The admiral commanding Iceland commented that Taylor had 'made a most gallant attempt' to tow the remains of the Liberty ship. This 'difficult operation was carried out in appalling weather conditions, but even so he hung on until he was certain that the tow would drift ashore on a beach where salvage would be possible'.[10]

MORE EFFECTIVE U-BOATS

By 1939, the U-boat had a much longer range than its First World War counterpart, and had more sophisticated weaponry and communications systems. Because of its superior range, the type VIIA and its later variants – the roman numerals defining the different types went up to XXIII – could remain on patrol much longer; and with the collapse of France in June 1940 were able to be based much closer to the Atlantic convoy routes.

U-boats also had more sophisticated help in guiding them to their targets. Aircraft could vector them on to convoys or individual ships; and 'wolf-pack' tactics – a number of U-boats co-ordinated by U-boat headquarters in France to attack a convoy simultaneously – were used with devastating effect. And though much has been quite rightly written about the brilliant work at the British government's Code and Cypher School at Bletchley Park in deciphering the U-boat's Enigma signals, it should not be forgotten that *B-Dienst*, the German naval cryptanalysis service, also had its successes, especially early on.

It broke both the British naval ciphers and the British Merchant Navy code, and this added to Allied convoy losses, and made the Battle of the Atlantic as much a battle of wits as it was of technological innovation and *matériel* superiority.

Although convoys were instituted immediately once the war began, stragglers and rompers – those that dropped behind a convoy, or ahead of it through failing to take evasive action with the rest of a convoy – gave the U-boats plenty of targets. So, too, did the independently routed ships, which relied on their speed, generally at least twelve knots, to keep them safe. In any case, early on there were not nearly enough convoy escorts, either in the air or at sea, and ASDIC (or sonar as the US Navy called it), a British anti-submarine device for detecting submerged submarines, did not initially produce the results expected of it.

In fact, so weak at first were the Royal Navy's anti-submarine measures, and the toll on Allied shipping so great, that U-boat commanders called the months between April and October 1940 'the Happy Hour', a description they were to use again when they attacked ships along the eastern seaboard of the United States after that country entered the war in December 1941. It was only the advent of more and better escorts; the use of anti-submarine devices such as centimetric radar and 'huff-duff' (high-frequency direction finding);[11] the efforts of Bletchley Park; and the closure of the mid-Atlantic air gap, that finally swung the battle in the Allies' favour.

OTHER THREATS

The U-boat was the principal threat to commercial shipping but not the only one. Aircraft, rarely a direct danger in the First World War, now proved to be a constant hazard, especially before the introduction of escort carriers, catapult aircraft merchantmen

(CAM) and merchant aircraft carrier (MAC) ships gave convoys some kind of air cover. But after aircraft were withdrawn to support the German invasion of the USSR (Operation BARBAROSSA) in July 1941, those that remained never posed the same threat to Atlantic and North Sea convoys, though they sank and damaged many more ships in the Mediterranean.

Mines, too, had advanced technologically and were a far greater menace in the Second World War, though degaussing did help protect ships from the German magnetic mine.[12] Nevertheless, mines only accounted for 6.5 per cent of Allied shipping losses and aircraft for 13.4 per cent, while U-boats were responsible for almost 70 per cent.[13] German surface ships, which had some success early in the war, would have accounted for the balance.

STARTING UP AGAIN

On 20 September 1939, the Director of Sea Transport, a member of the TDC, spelt out in a memorandum the paucity of resources available to it. On the day Britain had entered the war, there were only five commercial tugs in British ownership powerful enough to be used as rescue tugs: *Superman*, *Seaman*, *Englishman*, *Salvonia* and *Neptunia*. However, *Neptunia*, one of the country's most modern ocean tugs, had already been sunk by a U-boat,[14] and by 1944 only *Salvonia* was listed as being powerful enough to operate in the open ocean in any weather (see Appendix for the three different categories). It was not much to build on, and no one could have foreseen that the number of rescue tugs would rise to eighty-five by the end of the war in Europe, and that the personnel would have increased from fifty-four officers and three hundred and eighteen ratings in 1941 to six hundred and four officers and one thousand six hundred and two ratings in 1944.[15]

In the same memorandum, the Director of Sea Transport ruled that two of the four surviving tugs should be reserved for heavy coastal towage. If they were allocated to rescue work, 'it should only be on the understanding that they would be withdrawn at short notice for general towage requirements', showing that some of the lessons that had been learnt had been forgotten, and that the director appeared to have his priorities all wrong.

Ten days later, another memorandum was circulated within the Admiralty, which announced that the Rescue Tug Service was being reformed under the Director of Trade Division (DTD); laying out the duties of the CCRT, who until August 1942 was Captain the Hon. Walter Seymour Carson RN (ret.); and announcing that rescue tugs had been stationed at Falmouth and Campbeltown, and that one would be available for rescue work in the Thames.[16]

The same month, as a stop-gap until the Service was properly organised, flag officers and NOICs were instructed to make arrangements for tugs in their particular area to be ready to render immediate assistance locally, but this was soon cancelled as it was uneconomical to have hired tugs standing by all the time, especially as many were of limited range and sea-going ability. Instead, a scheme was started at the main ports for tug owners to pool their resources and keep a duty tug available. By doing this, tugs were used on a commercial basis and there was no waste of public funds.

During 1940, the situation did slowly improve. On 8 February a confidential Admiralty fleet order (CAFO) announced that a number of ocean-going tugs were being taken up from various sources and would be stationed at the ports closest to the areas where enemy submarines or aircraft were most active. In addition to Falmouth and Campbeltown, these were Milford Haven, Kirkwall, Rosyth, Humber, Harwich, Dover and Portsmouth. It also announced that two inspectors of rescue tug equipment had been appointed, one of whom would have been EG Martin. One was to be based at Falmouth, who would cover Plymouth and Portsmouth Commands; the other at Hull would be responsible for the Nore and Scottish Commands. They were to forward to the Admiralty monthly reports on the state and efficiency of the equipment of rescue tugs, and report on the progress of those being built and fitted out.[17]

The CAFO also confirmed that rescue tugs currently under commercial management would be eventually armed and commissioned by the Admiralty – in fact, some already had been. Once commissioned, rescue tugs would act as tenders to the depot at the bases to which they were attached. As in the First World War, they were not to be used outside harbour for anything but rescue work unless Admiralty permission had been granted; and only tugs fitted with W/T would be allowed to sea for rescue work.

The problem was that following the loss of *Neptunia*, civilian crews had become reluctant to go to sea unless their tugs were armed and escorted. This must have hastened the Admiralty's statement on 12 October 1939 that a proposal to start arming and commissioning suitable tugs had been approved. Escorts could not be guaranteed, but an armed trawler, equipped for anti-submarine warfare (ASW), normally accompanied a rescue tug, as they had done in the previous conflict. However, by January 1940, *Englishman* and *Seaman* had still not been armed.

Crews, all volunteers, were again engaged under the T.124T Agreement, but as it was drafted along the lines of the Merchant Navy form of a Ship's Articles of Agreement, war risk money was paid on top of Merchant Navy rates of pay. This gave T.124T ratings a higher rate than RN ratings serving in the same ship or base. This caused a lot of resentment and is still remembered today for the antagonism it caused. However, it does seem that RN ratings aboard the commissioned rescue tugs – specialists such as gunners, wireless operators and signalmen – did sometimes receive preferential treatment, as in some rescue tugs they ate in the petty officers' mess. Small compensation one would have thought, but of course if Merchant Navy rates of pay had not been offered there would have been precious few volunteers. In any case, according to the deputy CCRT in a post-war article (see below), this anomaly was later corrected.

There were other differences between the two services, insignificant in the larger scheme of things, but an irritant nonetheless. Being on Merchant Navy articles, T.124T ratings were the only branch of the Royal Navy not to carry a hammock and bedding, but were issued with bedding on joining a ship or barracks, which was returned on leaving. However, as T.124T rating Jim Williams discovered when returning to Britain in a naval troopship, there was no spare bedding for passengers; instead he had to sleep on a bare canvas bunk, using his kitbag as a pillow and his topcoat as a blanket, and once Gibraltar was reached he had to sleep fully clothed to keep warm.[18]

There were also complaints in the newspapers about the unfairness with which Merchant Navy personnel were treated compared with those serving in the Royal Navy. One letter writer said that though he had been in the Rescue Tug Service for nearly four years, and wore the uniform of a naval petty officer, it appeared that on his release from the Service, he would not be entitled to any of the gratuities naval ratings were entitled to. Nor did the Admiralty give a grant to buy civilian clothing, though there were so many complaints that this was later reversed. In the same newspaper, the wife of a member of the Rescue Tug Service and the mother of five children, with a sixth on the way, wrote: 'With reference to your appeal for an extension of privileges enjoyed by the regular forces to men of the Merchant

Navy, may I suggest that they be extended also to their wives?'
Her applications for a grant and child allowance had both been
turned down because her husband was in the Merchant Navy, not
the Royal Navy.[19]

There were sartorial differences, too, as Fred Radford recalled
when his rescue tug went to the assistance of a Royal Navy
frigate damaged by a mine:

> When we arrived on the scene our skipper, Tim Bond,
> stood on the wing of the bridge to take stock of the
> situation. He had an old woolly hat on, a thick-knitted
> jersey and a pair of clumpers, which are cut down
> sea-boots. This was normal for him, even though he
> was a Lieutenant-Commander RNR. On the bridge
> of the frigate the skipper, an RN lieutenant, was in
> full uniform plus a duffel coat and they began having
> a discourse about the situation; our skipper with his
> strong Hull accent and the RN skipper in clipped,
> cultured English. They were both using loud hailers and
> we could hear every word. There seemed to be some
> difference of opinion and the last thing we heard was
> Tim Bond saying, 'I'm running this bloody job, not
> you.' Anyway, we connected up without incident and
> towed her into Loch Foyle.[20]

A spat about an article by the commanding officer of a
minesweeper, HMS *Jason*, also raised hackles. It appeared in the
Admiralty's *Weekly Intelligence Report* (WIR) of 31 January 1941
and was called 'A Tiresome Tow'. It described the difficulties
the minesweeper had had the previous September in assisting a
British steamer, SS *Harpenden*, which had been broken in two
by a torpedo some three hundred miles west of Inishtrahull,
Ireland's most northerly island. The *Jason* had taken part of her

in tow, and when the rescue tugs that subsequently appeared refused to take over, the writer described one of them as 'haughty'.[21]

When the aristocratic CCRT – he was the son of an earl – read this, he leapt to the defence of the Rescue Tug Service:

> Many criticisms and gibes are made in this story
> at the conduct of two tugs which, it is known in
> the section, were HM tug *Marauder* and Dutch tug
> *Schelde*.
>
> The remarks made are not borne out by official
> reports received and in any case it is submitted that
> sneering remarks on the part played by other HM ships
> or any commercial ship taking part in any operation
> are undesirable in a document such as WIR, especially
> when the ships concerned are Merchant Service manned
> and therefore may need encouragement and education
> towards service standards.[21]

To which the Director of Naval Intelligence tartly replied:

> The remarks were bald statements of fact and were not
> intended to be construed as gibes or sneers, although
> it is agreed that the word 'haughty' was ill-chosen. It
> is regretted if the article has given offence, for it was
> intended to bring out the good seamanship, persistence
> and courage displayed by many of the participants in
> the operation.[21]

TRAINING

Before induction courses were started at Campbeltown, training for ratings was on a 'learn as you go' basis. Captain FJ Thompson

OBE RNR, who worked in the Admiralty's Convoy Section before becoming the deputy CCRT in November 1942, gave details of the training in an article[22] he wrote after the war:

> Training of the seamen took place at the rescue tug base, Campbeltown, Argyllshire, which was established in October 1940 with a commander, RNVR, as base commander. This able officer had been in the Rescue Tug Service in the First World War and was supported by a gunnery officer and gunner's mates. At the end of 1942 a signal class was started under a yeoman of signals.
>
> All new recruits were given instruction in seamanship (which included ocean towage), wire splicing, gunnery, and signalling, the most suitable men being selected as gunners and signalmen. The Campbeltown base thus became self-contained. A second base was established at Harwich where a number of tugs of the smaller class were operated with East Coast convoys between Southend and the Tyne. In the early months of the war Royal Navy signalmen and gunners had been drafted to rescue tugs but this proved unsatisfactory as the difference in pay packets of the RN and T.124T ratings was considerable and caused ill feeling. This difference in pay was subsequently eliminated when RN rates were increased and other emoluments taken into account.

The selected T.124T recruits were in the charge of ex-chief petty officers and petty officers, and after passing the two-month course were rated as ordinary seaman (OS) signalman or OS gunner, and were then drafted to a rescue tug.

Equivalent ranks of RN and Merchant Navy ratings

Merchant Navy	Naval Rating
Carpenter	Chief Petty Officer
Boatswain	Chief Petty Officer
Quartermaster	Leading Seaman
Able Seaman	Able Seaman
Ordinary Seaman	Ordinary Seaman
Engine Storekeeper	Petty Officer
Donkeyman	Petty Officer
Greaser	Leading Stoker
Fireman	Stoker
Steward	Chief Petty Officer
Assistant Steward	Leading Steward
Cook	Petty Officer
Assistant Cook	Leading Cook

All ratings engaged in Britain were ordered to Campbeltown to report to the C-in-C, Rescue Tug Base. On arrival, irrespective of any previous examination that they may have had, they were medically examined to make sure they were fit for sea service. If passed they went to the Mercantile Marine Office at Campbeltown where they signed the T.124T Agreement for HM rescue tug *Minona*, though *Minona* was in fact a handsome Edwardian steam yacht, permanently moored to the harbour quay as officers' quarters.[23] From August 1941, the ex-Scottish fisheries vessel *Vigilant* was also used as an accommodation ship. Renamed *Ixiom* in April 1943, she was then moved to Glasgow[24], where Commander Parker ran administrative offices for the Rescue Tug Service on one of the floors of the commandeered St Enoch's Hotel.[25]

Until they were appointed or drafted elsewhere, both officers and ratings were borne on the books of HMS *Nimrod*. Like the ratings, at first there was no formal training for rescue tug officers, but as most of the commanding officers were ex-tug masters, the officers under them quickly learnt what was required of them. Later, Merchant Navy officers with foreign-going and Home Trade certificates, and those who had served in small ships, became the chief source of supply, but a number of uncertified junior officers were also recruited. Commanding officers were granted the temporary rank of lieutenant RNR or RNVR, while navigating and engineer officers were granted the temporary rank of lieutenant or sub-lieutenant RNR or RNVR.

In July 1941, six senior commanding officers were granted the temporary rank of lieutenant-commander. With the rapid expansion of the Service, their numbers were further increased in August 1943 when an additional six commanding officers, who held foreign-going masters' certificates and had held a command for two years, were given the rank of temporary lieutenant-commander RNR. All personnel (ratings as well as officers) not embarked were retained as spare crews at Campbeltown, or at the Rescue Tug Service's North Sea base at Harwich. Later, T.124T reserve pools were established at Gibraltar, St John's in Newfoundland, Algiers, Malta and Colombo. From May 1943, T.124T officers were given a two-week officers' divisional course at Portsmouth. This proved of great benefit for new entries from the Merchant Navy who had no previous knowledge of naval procedure and customs.

Once the Campbeltown base began training courses, and as the section expanded, teenagers from the Sea Cadet Corps in different parts of the country were recruited as deck hands and galley hands, and ordinary seamen. The idea for recruiting them came from EG Martin, who wrote in March 1943 that he was 'very much pleased today with the results of the examination of the first batch of sea cadets I took on, as an experiment, for special training – a shot in the dark which has hit the mark'.[26]

Although young – sometimes very young – the Sea Cadets knew their knots and splices, and port from starboard, and some were already proficient in handling the smaller defensive armaments with which the rescue tugs were equipped. Jim Williams was in no doubt that it was his Sea Cadet experience that got him on to a gunnery course at Campbeltown. He passed out joint top and, when he was drafted to the Assurance class *Eminent*, he was given the job of manning the rescue tug's starboard Oerlikon.

When D-Day came and a German bomber attacked *Eminent* off Gold Beach, it was Jim's crippling burst that sent it heading south with its starboard engine and wing on fire. Jim was rewarded with a carton of cigarettes and a tot of rum, though at sixteen he was too young to draw his own rum ration.[27]

Jim was still aboard *Eminent*, and still the youngest member of the crew, when she was dispatched to the Far East. He wrote, recalling how he spent the first hours of 1946:

In addition to the officers serving Christmas dinner to the crew, another naval tradition was that the youngest crew member took command of the ship at midnight on New Year's Eve, for four hours. Our skipper, Lt-Commander Charlie Stanford, being the kind of gentleman he was, entered into the spirit of the occasion, sent for me at five minutes to midnight, presented me with his officer's cap and two bottles of whisky to give the lower deck a dram. He wished me 'all the best' and discreetly disappeared until breakfast the next morning. Everything went well and the cap was returned to the skipper, minus the empty whisky bottles, little realising that the future would see me in command of my own ship. But that would be nearly 20 years later.[28]

Recruiting from those with a knowledge of the sea would have been almost obligatory – there were exceptions – for a rescue tug was no place for landlubbers, as this extract from a book by two of the volunteers for the Service showed:

> On leaving port [to find a damaged ship] it was almost invariably a case of pushing on as fast as possible, irrespective of sea conditions, to the aid of a disabled vessel. A design feature of any tug is a large power to weight ratio and this is essential in a rescue tug – i.e. the engine power of such vessels is out of proportion to their size to give them the necessary towing power required. This, allied to the vessels' shape, made them very uncomfortable in any sort of rough sea. Add to this the need to make all speed with an Atlantic gale blowing, and conditions on board [became] abysmal…
>
> Once the casualty had been located there then came the task of getting a tow rope on board in sea conditions which, in the 50-foot waves of an Atlantic gale, often meant the tug and the ship going up and down in opposite directions. Aside from those cases where the actual condition of the vessel made salvage impossible a further two important factors now came into play. These were whether or not enough crew remained on board to connect the tow: if not crew had to be put on board from the rescue vessel. Also, if the vessel still had sufficient power to operate her own winches; if not then the heavy towing hawsers had to be manhandled onto something strong enough to stand the strain of the tow – this with the two vessels heaving and pitching. Even the successful passing of the first towing rope was not necessarily the end of the operation since

it was not unknown for the ropes to part two or three times during the tow. Then the whole procedure had to be undertaken again. This meant the passing of lines of increasingly greater size until the final tow rope was reattached and the tow could resume.

With the tow successfully attached the long journey back to port could begin, usually without any sort of escort since such vessels were in short enough supply even for a large convoy. There would be little or no respite for the crew of the tug during this period. Not only did the tow require constant attention – in spite of being wrapped around with cowhides and coated with grease where it passed over the towing horses at the stern of the tug – but the constant vigilance of lookouts and the gunners was needed in case of enemy attack. These were in addition to the watch-keeping duties required to navigate the ships to safety and keep the tug's machinery fully operational.[29]

NAVAL DISCIPLINE

Perhaps one of the hardest lessons that had to be learnt was the naval discipline all T.124T recruits signed up for. Having to wear uniform – at least ashore, informal crew photographs show this was far from the case at sea – was bad enough, but having to learn who to salute and when, and how those in authority were to be addressed, must also have been difficult for some T.124T personnel to swallow, particularly those who had already served in the Merchant Navy and were used to a less formal way of life. Nor would the Royal Navy's quaint and rigid class-driven regulations have always been received with equanimity. But at Campbeltown naval discipline was strictly maintained, with any serious offender being dealt with by the RN captain commanding HMS *Nimrod*.

The recruits at Campbeltown were housed in an old Army drill hall, Victoria Barracks, which had been vacated by the Argyll and Sutherland Highlanders, though their large wooden crest still decorated the building. Recruit Ed Gardner remembered it like this:

The main hall was filled with rows of bunks, two and three high, with metal lockers around the outer walls. We all were allotted one of each and that became our home for our stay. The petty officers' quarters were at the far end and upstairs. They looked over the balcony and kept an eye on the shenanigans that went on in our section...

[There was] 'a lot of activity in the town and the harbour. Ships were continually entering and leaving as the North Atlantic was right on our doorstep, handy for joining or leaving convoys. Often we would be ashore and hear ships sounding their recall signals, and see sailors running through the streets to board the boats taking them out to their ships at anchor. Each crew knew their own signal, so many blasts, long and short, on the ships' sirens. Everything stopped in the town bars, cafes, restaurants, etc. while everyone listened to identify whose signal it was, and then either relax or start running like hell for the harbour. No excuse was accepted, if you didn't make it in time you were AWOL (absent without leave), a very serious offence in wartime, and shore patrols (naval police) would round you up and throw you in the clink until your case came up or your ship returned.

Once we had been issued our uniform and kit we had more medicals, got our shots, and were detailed off into Messes and groups: seamen, stokers, gunners, etc. and settled into our training routine. A petty officer or chief petty officer was allotted to each group and he became our instructor and basically controlled our lives until we left to join our ships.

The daily routine was being rudely awakened by a recorded bugle call over the Tannoy system at 0600 hours, and our days were taken up with work parties, drills, route marches, parades, boat pulling, sculling, rope work, seamanship, rifle drill and unarmed combat against the physical training instructors. They were all Bruce Lee wannabes and manhandled us unmercifully. Often we were hauled out of our beds at four in the morning to catch the lines and tie up the submarines that were based at Campbeltown and coming in from Atlantic patrols. They appeared out of the mist like ghosts and the only welcome they got was from us guys who caught their heaving lines. Brave men.[30]

Jack Close, a T.124T W/T officer who joined in 1943, remembered his first sight of Campbeltown after a tedious trip from Glasgow:

A neat little harbour in the shape of a square; a few fishing boats nestled up to the quay and a steam yacht with graceful lines was moored at the farthest arm of the harbour. The bay stretched out towards Davaar Island, nestled under the shadow of Beinn Ghuilean, rising steep and austere to the south. From the harbour a pleasant promenade stretched away into the curving distance and was lost in the evening mist. The main street climbed gently towards a couple of hotels and a scattering of shops. It all seemed pleasant, picturesque and agreeable enough to two weary travellers.[31]

The officer in charge of training at the base was Lt RD Robinson RNVR. He had begun his own sea career aged twelve, attending the Naval Training College at Hull before becoming a cadet in the Humber Pilot Service two years later. 'Part of the induction training,' he later told a journalist, 'was to keep the cabins and saloons clean and to assist in the preparation of meals around the clock, for thirty pilots. The life was hard, discipline was strict and often involved physical punishment.'[32]

After six years he studied for his second officer's certificate, and at the outbreak of war was serving as first officer on a small tanker. Soon afterwards he joined the Rescue Tug Service as a Sub-Lt RNVR aboard the Saint class *St Cyrus*, which was sunk by a mine off the Humber in January 1941. He was one of only three survivors, and was in the water two and a half hours before being rescued. He spent three months in hospital recovering from his injuries, but these made him unfit for sea service. Instead, he was promoted to lieutenant and put in charge of rescue tug training.

During his time at Campbeltown, Robinson was awarded the Royal Humane Society Medal for rescuing two men from drowning who, on a dark and stormy night, had fallen into the water from the quay. He jumped in after them and kept them afloat until help arrived. The police constable who made notes of the incident wrote that 'while in conversation with Lieutenant Robinson he seemed to treat the whole affair as a matter of course, making very light of his brave action.'[33]

He also received no less than four Admiralty commendations for his wartime work, one of them for his courage and skill in helping to refloat HMS *Nyasaland* which had been stranded during a severe gale on a lee shore in Campbeltown harbour. In May 1945, he moved with the Rescue Tug Service to Harwich (HMS *Badger*) when the Campbeltown base was closed, and later transferred to the Royal Navy. By the time he retired in 1954, he had attained the rank of commander.

Robinson is an example of how tough tug men were in those days. They had to be able to manhandle eighteen-inch manila tow ropes in extreme weather. But sometimes they were more than that. In the first few months of the war, the crew of one rescue tug, *Marauder*, were so unruly that their commanding officer had to alert any UK port she was about to enter, and in early 1940 the entire crew was dismissed and replaced. Ed Gardner tells the story of a crewman refused entry to the Campbeltown cinema because he was too drunk. He returned to his ship, loaded the bow gun and fired at the cinema. But he wasn't a gunner and hadn't laid it properly, and the shell passed over the cinema and landed in the parade ground of HMS *Nimrod*. The man was caught, court-martialled and sent to prison.

This story sounds unlikely, but it does reflect the general attitude of the Rescue Tug Service, which Jack Close summed up well:

A dislike of authority and a grudging adherence to law and order characterised the service, the officers being no exception. We conformed when necessary in order to placate the Admiralty, otherwise we went our own way, quietly proud of the job we did, which, by its very nature, was often carried out in the worst of conditions and in the knowledge that we were frequently somebody's last hope. This approach to life I absorbed gradually, though it had been evident early on that HM Rescue Tugs was far from being a quiescent branch of [the] Admiralty. There was usually an air of truculence bubbling away below the surface, even among ourselves sometimes, as witness the ditty directed at some luckless tyro issuing orders from the bow, which begins:

They stand on the fo'c'sle and shout,
They shout about things they know nothing about...
(substitute own words)[34]

Though it is doubtful if anyone took a pot-shot at the
Campbeltown cinema, on one occasion another T.124T rating
did produce a loaded pistol in a pub when he was refused a
drink – the most frequent offence among T.124T personnel
was drunkenness. This applied to officers as well as ratings
as the following memorandum from the deputy CCRT made
clear. Dated 18 January 1943, it was addressed to all rescue tug
commanding officers:

> A number of reports of disciplinary courts and
> court-martials held on officers in the Rescue Tug
> Service have recently been received at the Admiralty.
> CCRT is much concerned regarding these reports which
> not only reflect on the discipline and self esteem of the
> officers, but such reports tend to give a bad name to
> the Rescue Tug Service, which is certainly not desired
> and would be deplored by all concerned.
>
> It is not desired to interfere with the amenities
> and general comfort of the officers in the Rescue
> Tug Service as a result of these few cases of
> drunkenness and misbehaviour by the issue of
> drastic regulations and it would be preferred that
> Commanding Officers exert their authority and use
> every endeavour to check insobriety and its attendant
> results.[35]

When dealing with a miscreant, a warning was sometimes
sufficient, the memorandum added, especially in the case of a
young and inexperienced person. But where this did not apply

a procedure should be swiftly adopted that would end with the officer in question being reported to the appropriate Naval Authority for disciplinary action. 'CCRT relies on Commanding Officers in upholding the standard of the Rescue Tug Service in which there is no room for anyone who lets the "side" down,' the memorandum concluded, 'especially when the "side" is composed of members of the Mercantile Marine of which our country is so proud.'[35]

This was followed on 5 April 1943 by a memorandum from the CCRT himself, warning all commanding officers about the mismanagement of duty-free goods: 'Pay careful attention to the regulations concerning duty-free stores, and the great privileges given by this provision, thus misunderstandings need not occur which may, on occasion, lead to the withdrawal of such privileges.'[36]

From these pronouncements, and another about ensuring all ranks wore the correct uniform, one can infer that it was taking time for Martin to instil the required level of naval discipline. But at Campbeltown, the punishment for ratings of such a minor misdemeanour as drunkenness was hardly draconian. Often it involved an old ship's wheel. This was hung in the water from a bollard to accumulate barnacles and rust, and was hauled out for the offender to clean and polish like new. It was then put back in the water to await the next defaulter. Confined to barracks, extra rifle drill with full pack and spud bashing, as it was called, were also regular punishments.

More severe was the punishment meted out to Fred Radford. After a boisterous evening at the pub, he had a *contretemps* with the regulating petty officer, not noted for his benevolence. To Fred's surprise, the next morning he was told he was on a charge, which his commanding officer, Lt Robinson, told him was too serious for him to deal with, and that he would have to go before the NOIC Campbeltown:

I was taken before this officer who had about a half a yard of gold braid on his sleeves. He asked me a few questions about the previous night and decided not to hang me. However, he did sentence me to fourteen days cells with three days' low diet and no bed.

I spent the next fourteen days in a cell about nine feet square. It had a grilled skylight and a solid door with a small observation hatch in it. I had to clean the floor every morning. At one side facing the door was a wooden bench, about three foot wide, which served as a bed, but for the first three days there was no bedding and after that I was only allowed one blanket. I was marched out every morning by a sentry to the wash-house to wash, but no shave, and if I needed the toilet at any other time I would have to bang on the door and ask the sentry and he would march me to the toilet and stand by the door and then march me back. Also, for the first three days my food consisted of sixteen ounces of ship's biscuits, called hard-tack, and water. After that I would get a few potatoes and gravy; sometimes with a trace of meat in it.

A naval padre came to see me after about four days to see if I wanted any spiritual guidance. I told him to get lost. The experience didn't bother me a lot but I was pleased when it was over and I went back to the hall and the cheers of my mates. My sentence obviously was not too detrimental for me because shortly after I was released I applied for, and got, a promotion to the job of cook. On a big tug like the *Bustler* [in which Fred was serving at the time of his incarceration] there were three people in the galley so the first cook was in charge of a small team. I was therefore promoted to petty officer cook. Probably one of the very few teenaged petty officers in the Royal Navy.[37]

IN ACTION

No sooner had he sewn on his badges than Fred was transferred to *Mammouth*, a French rescue tug with a British T.124T crew. She was based at Harwich and escorted convoys up and down E-boat Alley. The rescue tugs were always positioned astern of a convoy 'but we saw plenty of action and the *Mammouth* towed quite a few damaged ships in'. One he remembered assisting was a 'Woolworths carrier' – naval slang for an MAC ship. She had hit a mine and *Mammouth* towed her into the Humber Estuary. Fred lived at Hull and thought he might get a night at home, but was foiled by the standard procedure of harbour tugs taking over a damaged ship from the less manoeuvrable rescue tugs to take it into port.

While serving aboard *Bustler*, Fred was involved in a lot of rescue work at a critical time in the Battle of the Atlantic. In August 1942 she searched for, and found, the 5661-ton *City of Cardiff* torpedoed and abandoned off Lisbon while in convoy SL-119 from Freetown:

> She was down by the stern and there were two dead men with their feet trapped in the rail hanging over the side with their heads dipping in the water as she rolled in the swell. It was presumed they had been blown out of the after accommodation alleyway by the explosion which killed them. We towed the *City of Cardiff* for half a day but then she reared up, practically stood on end, and sank. We had to quickly chop our wire then return to base.[37]

In January 1943 *Bustler* assisted two American Liberty ships in three days. Both the *William M Stewart* and *John Marshall* were on passage from Swansea to the Clyde to join a Mediterranean-bound convoy when the former developed mechanical trouble north of the Isle of Man, and *Bustler* towed her to Belfast. Two days later, the *John Marshall* ran aground south of Portpatrick on the south-west coast of the Scottish mainland. *Bustler* managed to refloat her and towed her to Kames Bay at the southern end of the Isle of Great Cumbrae, a sheltered spot where rescue tugs often left damaged ships to be picked up and taken to the nearby Clyde repair yards.

Fred's last ship was *Director*, a wooden Lend-Lease rescue tug, whose sea trials had not been auspicious. She was steam-powered and at inconvenient times lost power due to a loss of condenser vacuum. On one occasion, it occurred during a Christmas dinner of ham sandwiches while beam-on to a heavy swell off Cape Cod, with predictable results:

> On another occasion she would not go astern when
> berthing and instead of going alongside the wharf
> ploughed straight into it causing the foreman in
> the shed immediately above the wharf to sing out:
> 'Come right in folks!' She also leaked continuously
> and eventually had to be dry docked at Bermuda
> where it was found that only wooden dowels inserted
> where ten keel bolts should have been had prevented
> her from sinking as soon as she had been launched.
> A hurricane force wind en route for Newfoundland
> to join an eastbound convoy proved her subsequent
> seaworthiness.[38]

On the afternoon of 23 April 1945, she helped one of the last U-boat victims of the war when the 7345-ton British freighter

SS *Riverton*, in ballast and bound for Bristol, was torpedoed while in convoy TBC-135 near Land's End:

> [The torpedo] completely demolished the stern and
> flooded the ship as far as the forward holds. HMRT
> *Director*, commanded by Lt CA Hire RNR, was in the
> vicinity, and proceeded to her assistance immediately
> and took off 46 survivors. The vessel was sinking
> slowly; nevertheless, it was decided to attempt salvaging
> her. A tow rope was connected and the sinking and
> waterlogged vessel towed to the nearest sheltered bay
> [St Ives], where salvage pumps were put aboard her.
> Pumping continued throughout the night, and on the
> afternoon of the following day the vessel was again taken
> in tow, and after covering a distance of over 100 miles
> the badly damaged ship was brought into port and saved.[39]

The last operation of the war involving a rescue tug was on 27 April 1945, when the frigate HMS *Redmill* was hit aft by a U-boat's gnat torpedo,[40] killing twenty-eight of her crew. At the time she was hunting U-boats with the Twenty-first Escort Group north-west of Ireland. Another frigate took her in tow until the Assurance class *Jaunty* – whose valiant rescue work during the famous Operation PEDESTAL convoy to Malta is described in Chapter 8 – arrived the next morning and connected up with the damaged frigate.

There was now a heavy swell and a northerly gale, force 7–8, and the tow parted twice before the *Redmill* was passed that evening to harbour tugs off Moville, on the north coast of Ireland. The frigate's commanding officer later reported that 'the success of the tow in very unpleasant weather was entirely due to the superb seamanship and ship-handling of the commanding officer, HMRT *Jaunty*'.[41]

DISCIPLINARY ISSUES

The matter of discipline sometimes surfaced when official reports were submitted on a rescue tug's operational efficiency. One such case was the French steam tug *Mastadonte*, a sister ship of *Mammouth*. After her escape from France, she was manned by a British crew, who appeared to have a somewhat happy-go-lucky attitude. At the time, June 1941, she was stationed at Greenock and employed in target towing, an important but hardly exciting role, and tedium may have had a role in their behaviour.

On 5 June her chief engineer wrote to the CCRT, ostensibly to submit details of the repairs that were being carried out. After pointing out the difficulties of finding spare parts that would fit a French tug, he wrote that his main problem was 'fireman trouble' (stokers). In his opinion, this was due to lack of discipline of long standing where the men, the majority from Glasgow, had unlimited leave so that they 'come and go as they please. While coaling at Greenock they disappear for two or three days and nothing can be done to punish them. The naval authorities refuse to crime the men, the civil police cannot interfere, I have tried Merchant Service methods with use of force but to no effect.'[42]

The problem of discipline also taxed the new CCRT, Captain CC Walcott OBE RN, when he was appointed in July 1942, and was one he immediately raised with all rescue tug commanding officers:

> It is most essential that Commanding Officers of HM Rescue Tugs realise in every way their responsibilities with regard to the personnel under them, their guidance and comfort, and also the responsibility of the Commanding Officers regarding all Government stores and the

observance of privileges, especially those that affect the provision of duty-free wines, spirits and tobacco. It is also essential Royal Naval procedure be understood by all concerned. The Commanding Officer only is entitled to deal direct with the appropriate Naval Authority (FOIC, NOIC, or RNO), and only when circumstances arise where there is no appropriate Naval Authority he may deal direct with the CCRT at the Admiralty...

The efficiency of the Rescue Tug Service very largely depends on the Commanding Officers of the Rescue Tugs. They will have every possible support to effect this efficiency. CCRT is anxious that the Rescue Tug Service shall be second to none. There is no room for malcontents, neurotics or weak-minded characters who, cowardly at heart, only show a pretence of bravery under the influence of alcohol, and generally let the side down on shore and afloat. Such characters must be weeded out if they exist, and Commanding Officers will bear in mind that personnel, removed as no longer required in the Rescue Tug Service, will not be employed by the Pool, and will have no alternative but to be conscripted for the Army. From my short experience of the personnel I have already met, I have great confidence in the loyalty and future efficiency of the Rescue Tug Service...

In conclusion, I would like a portion of Lord Nelson's last letter, which was written in his cabin on board HMS *Victory* immediately before the battle of Trafalgar on October 21st, 1805, to be a guidance to all the personnel I have the honour to be in charge of, and I am endeavouring to promulgate this prayer by the provision of a framed copy to be hung in every HM Rescue Tug in a suitable position where all can see.

The portion of this letter reads as follows: 'May the great God whom I worship grant to my country and to the benefit of Europe a great and glorious victory, and may no misconduct in anyone tarnish it.'[43]

One wonders how the hard-bitten readers of this unusual missive reacted to its sentiments, and what provoked them. One wonders, too, why it was necessary in December 1942 for the CCRT to recirculate a letter first sent out in December 1940 to all flag officers-in-charge and NOICs at home and abroad. This began: 'I am to state that examination of reports on the loss of one of HM Salvage Vessels and other recent incidents in HM Rescue Tugs, indicates the necessity for greater supervision of the administration of these vessels, and of the welfare and discipline of their personnel, by Flag and Naval officers-in-charge.'[44]

The letter was promulgated as a CAFO, and spelt out the obligations the naval authorities had to rescue tug personnel:

[Although rescue tug officers and ratings] are drawn from the Merchant Service, and in particular and as far as possible, from those normally employed on towing duties, nevertheless, they are subject to naval discipline; and the fact that these officers and men have little or no knowledge of naval routine, procedure and discipline, makes it all the more important that they should be assisted and led with care, tact and foresight under the constant supervision of senior officers...

The work of Rescue Tugs is generally arduous and exacting, although there may be unavoidable periods of idleness, which are bad for morale. Only by careful supervision of the welfare of the personnel, and thorough understanding not only of prevailing conditions but also those under whom they have been accustomed to serve, can discipline and efficiency be retained.[44]

In short, tread carefully.

It is impossible to know what sparked all this and why it was felt necessary to quote Nelson; and it may, or may not, have been a coincidence that Captain Walcott received another appointment in August 1943, though by then, as will be seen, there had been a number of complaints, from the C-in-C Western Approaches downwards, on the way the Service was being run. He was replaced by Captain GS Holden RN, who remained CCRT for the rest of the war.[45]

PILFERING, LOOTING AND MUTINY

If Captain Walcott was reacting to a serious offence, such as looting or mutiny, very little has come to light in official documents. Looting was, quite rightly, strongly condemned, but pilfering was not uncommon, especially in ports where damaged ships were taken in by harbour tugs after a rescue tug had handed the wreck over. But working with damaged and abandoned ships at sea presented temptations and opportunities, and all officers were on the alert to make sure it did not happen on their watch.

However, there is an amusing anecdote where the officers knew exactly what was happening. It occurred after the North African landings in November 1942 when a rescue tug, investigating a merchant ship aground and abandoned by her crew, discovered part of her cargo was sugar. The crew 'rescued' some of it, but after returning to Algiers, or perhaps it was Bône or Oran, they heard that the local custom officials were making spot checks on all recently arrived vessels. Panic ensued, and in the middle of the night they threw the lot overboard, only to find the next morning that a barge had been moored alongside, and was now covered in sugar. Quick action had to be taken with hoses to clear it. The customs officers never appeared.

'Acquiring' government stores that had been abandoned was one thing; taking someone's personal belongings was quite another. The only hard evidence of this happening occurred when the 8,457-ton Dutch freighter *Mangkalihat* was torpedoed and badly damaged off the Mozambique coast on 1 August 1943, while en route from Beira to Durban in convoy BC-2. Eighteen members of the crew were killed and, with the ship's engine room and boiler room flooded, the rest took to the boats, and were eventually taken aboard one of the convoy's escorts, the South African corvette *Freesia*. The next morning, the captain wanted to reboard his ship, but was not allowed to when he refused to sign a document stating that he had abandoned her. Instead, the corvette put a party aboard and began to tow her towards land, presumably under the assumption that the corvette's crew would be entitled to claim salvage.

The freighter's captain later wrote that the tow 'proved very cumbersome', and they did not get far.[46] On the morning of 3 August, the rescue tug *Prudent* appeared and *Mangkalihat*'s crew was transferred to her from the corvette. The captain and some of his crew were then allowed back on board the damaged freighter, while the rescue tug's deck crew rigged a pump on board her to tackle the flooding, which had made the ship settle further into the water.

What happened next is not entirely clear, but *Mangkalihat*'s crew went to and fro gathering what they could of their personal belongings, and they also gave some items – including a canary – to the crew of *Prudent*. The ship's captain went to his cabin, retrieved some of his belongings and took them across to *Prudent*. When he returned to collect a few last items, he found that some shirts he had wrapped in a parcel were missing. He went to the officers' quarters and found two men from the *Prudent* there. He told them to clear out and when they passed him he noticed, too late, that one had a suspicious bulge under his shirt. He drew his revolver and took a shortcut to the deck to prevent them leaving the ship, but was only in time to stop the second man, who was about to board the rescue tug. The captain then saw that he, too, had a bulging shirt, and levelled his revolver at him.

At this point one of the corvette's officers who was aboard the crippled freighter intervened. He reminded the Dutch captain, rather forcefully one would imagine, that the man was not under his command. *Prudent*'s captain was called and made the culprit – the young second steward – empty what was under his shirt on to the deck, and the *Prudent*'s captain later listed them in his report of the incident: 'Small items of clothing, two or three small rupee notes, an ink pad, a belt, and a carton of cigarettes which I have found out since was given to him by an officer of the wreck.'[47] The shirts, of course, had been taken by the other crew member who had escaped on to the rescue tug. The *Prudent*'s commanding officer, Lt CT Atkinson RNR, wrote:

> I informed the captain that the boy was doing his first
> trip to sea and that I would punish him as heavily
> as I could and would try and find the other culprit
> and his shirts. Remaining on board the wreck I gave
> orders to my lieutenant on my bridge to inform the
> men remaining on board that a paper parcel containing
> shirts had been taken and was to be placed on deck.
> About half an hour later these were found on deck and
> returned to the captain, but despite questions the other
> culprit has not been found and a comprehensive search
> of the ship has revealed nothing...
>
> The captain's actions definitely prevented any chance
> of finding the other culprit and any stolen property
> and, with my own knowledge and those of my officers,

I am firmly convinced that only two men entered the accommodations, the rest including the officers had far too much work to do.[47]

This was a rather different version from the Dutch captain's, who reported 'wholesale looting', but then he had just lost his ship and could be excused some hyperbole. The *Prudent*'s commanding officer concluded:

I personally was on the decks all the time. It is an impossibility in the circumstances and conditions to keep every member of the crew under supervision and proceed with the essential job of trying to salvage the vessel. The rating in question has been punished by 14 days No. 11 and 12 [extra work and stoppage of leave] and been severely warned. His statement that the room he was in had everything of value taken from it and he thought the rest was left being, I think, the truth on account of the value of the articles on him.[47]

Reports of the whole episode was sent to the Admiralty, but from the correspondence it seems their Lordships were far more concerned about the corvette captain's irregular behaviour in forbidding the ship's captain to return to his ship, and that he should have known that HM warships no longer claimed salvage on a vessel damaged by war risks. He was therefore acting entirely without authority and the C-in-C South Atlantic had been asked to point this out to him. 'If this officer had been serving in the Royal Navy,' the Admiralty informed South Africa's High Commissioner in London, 'he would have incurred an award of their Lordships' displeasure.'[48]

When the South African naval forces authorities received this information, they passed the buck and suggested the

Admiralty take any necessary disciplinary action. So almost a year after the incident, the Admiralty wrote to the C-in-C Eastern Fleet, under whom *Freesia*'s commanding officer was then presumably serving, 'to request you to convey to this officer an expression of My Lords' displeasure'. One would have thought that the officer would not have lost any sleep over this quaint admonishment.

Another *Prudent* story illustrates the naval habit of 'acquiring' anything that appeared to have been abandoned and could come in useful. At the time, the rescue tug was on her way home from Addu Atoll in the Maldive Islands:

> On the voyage she called in at Aden to take on fuel, water, and stores. Arriving in the morning they tied up to an oil tanker in the middle of the harbour and were set to sail in the late afternoon. In the early afternoon some of the crew were able to watch an elderly gentleman sailing about the harbour in a very smart skiff. He is reported as 'making a very professional job of it considering he was three sheets to the wind'. He did, however, manage to pass a line to the tug and make his way onto the tanker. At sailing time the Second Mate Rolf Andreasen reported to the bridge that the sailing boat was still tied alongside and was told by the skipper (Tom Pickering) to use his own discretion about it, and the *Prudent* duly set off to the next port of call, Port Said. After transit of the Suez Canal they received a signal: 'Request whereabouts of the Harbour Master's Sailing Skiff', and it soon transpired that the skiff had been firmly stowed on board *Prudent*. Fortunately another tug was in Port Said on its way to Aden so the transfer of the boat was made with suitable apologies.[49]

As for mutiny, well, as will be seen, the behaviour of some of
the crews of the Dutch rescue tugs could have been construed
as such, but was not, probably because the Admiralty knew
they were too valuable to lose. However, the incident witnessed
by Cliff Hubbard, a petty officer aboard the Assurance class
Assiduous, initially looked as if it might develop into something
more serious than a drunken confrontation:

> We had many long slow trips, with heavy tows across
> the Indian Ocean and beyond, so were at sea for long
> boring periods. Consequently when we were able to go
> ashore with pay built up in our pockets and plenty of
> pent up energy, and we always had a good time. On
> one such occasion we arrived at Trincomalee, Ceylon,
> and off we went on shore leave. We had a good time
> and my pal and I were on our way back, along the
> long winding road to the jetty, when we were nearly
> mowed down by a speeding jeep driven by a Naval
> Patrol. We briefly described their parenthood, and
> carried on back to the ship.
>
> On arriving at the *Assiduous*, there was the offending
> jeep. It had been sent to sort out an incident involving
> some of our crew who in a merry state had tried to
> steal the local fire engine. The patrol went straight to
> the only officer on board, who was in his usual state
> soaked in gin (the others were all merrymaking ashore)
> and gave the patrol permission to arrest and take ashore
> some of our crew. The lads were having none of this,
> so the patrol was thrown off the ship.
>
> Next a truckload of rifle carrying sailors had arrived
> and were lined up facing the *Assiduous*, so it must
> have been classed as a mutiny. The crew was in high
> spirits facing up to them from the ship, offering to

take them all on. My pal and I in our petty officers' uniforms now arrived on the scene and were allowed on board, where we learned all about the incident and as the officer was not available senior crew members were wondering what to do. Then a staff car arrived and some bigwig got out in his 'Whites' as he had come straight from an official engagement. He and his minders went without a word straight to see the officer. Shortly afterwards he returned, spotted my uniform, came to me, and said quietly: 'Let them quieten down and encourage them to go below and get a good night's sleep.' The shore party finally left and the mutiny was over.[50]

NOTES

1. See Mowat F. *Grey Seas Under*. Michael Joseph; 1959.
2. Records of the Tug Distribution Committee meetings, 1939–45, are in MT 163/152.
3. EG Martin's service records, 1939–45, show that he was borne on the books of HMS *President*, the London base ship for RNR and RNVR officers. The Navy List lists him as being attached to the Admiralty's Trade Division but on the establishment of HMS *Nimrod*, which was the address he used when he ran the Rescue Tug Office at Campbeltown. See also correspondence of CCRT and Second Sea Lord in ADM 199/1238, dated 13/3/41 and 20/3/41.
4. ADM 1/16594.
5. Letter to HE West, 16 July 1944. Courtesy of the Martin family.
6. *Ibid.*, 13 March and 17 April 1944. Courtesy of the Martin family.
7. Davidson B. 'Warships in Dungarees', *Yank* (6 February 1944): 9.
8. Van der Vat D. *Stealth at Sea*. London: Weidenfeld & Nicolson; 1994. p.189.

9. Butler S. *Not For Davy Jones*. Bound manuscript, p.22. Courtesy of Peter Butler.

10. ADM 1/15032.

11. 'Huff-duff', or HF/DF (high-frequency direction finding) equipment, could pinpoint a U-boat's position by measuring the distance and direction of its radio transmissions, however brief.

12. A process, known as 'wiping', that neutralised the magnetism of a ship's steel hull by momentarily discharging an electric current through a copper cable wound round it. As this had to be repeated at regular intervals, cables were later wound permanently round a ship's hull, either inside or outside it.

13. Milner M. 'Battle of the Atlantic' in Dear I, editor. *The Oxford Companion to World War II*. Oxford: Oxford University Press; 2005.

14. The *Neptunia*, launched in 1938, was lost on 13 September 1939. A U-boat fired a round across the bows of the unarmed *Neptunia*. When she failed to stop, the U-boat began to pump shells into her. The civilian crew abandoned ship and the U-boat, after failing to torpedo the tug, sank her with gunfire. See www.uboat.net

15. ADM 199/2165, marked 'Rescue Tug Section of Trade Division' and 'Trade Division History', and letter to Admiral Sir Eldon Manisty, 30 November 1945.

16. *Ibid.*, marked 'Trade Division History'.

17. CAFO 174 in ADM 182/137. See also ADM 1/10654.

18. Williams J. *Swinging the Lamp*. Hull: Riverhead; 2013. p.77.

19. *Hull Daily Mail*, 17 February 1943 and 5 November 1945.

20. Courtesy of Fred Radford, from manuscript of his memoirs.

21. ADM 199/1238.

22. *Sea Breezes*. Vol. 30, July–December 1960. Liverpool: Charles Birchall & Sons; 1960. pp.448–51.

23. The *Minona* was owned before the war by the Coates family. In the 1960s she was acquired by Richard Burton and Elizabeth Taylor, who renamed her *Kalizma*.

24. Warlow B. *Shore Establishments of the Royal Navy*. Liskeard: Maritime Books; 2000.

25. AN 109/304.

26. Letter to HE West, dated 20 March 1943. Courtesy of the Martin family.

27. Williams J. *Swinging the Lamp*, *op. cit.* p.41.

28. *Ibid.*, p.69.

29. Williams J, Gray J. *HM Rescue Tugs in World War II*. Privately printed. pp.18–21.

30. From a letter written by Ed Gardner to John Wilson whose father served with Ed in HMRT *Destiny*. Courtesy of John Wilson.

31. Close J. *Beyond the Horizon*. Hull: Riverhead; 2010. p.105.

32. Clipping from unknown newspaper in DSRTA red file marked HRMT.

33. Williams J, Gray J. *HM Rescue Tugs, op. cit.* p.115.

34. Close J. *Beyond the Horizon, op. cit.* p.105.

35. ADM 1/15548. See also Lane T. *The Merchant Seaman's War*. Manchester: Manchester University Press; 1990. p.137, where he remarks: 'Drunkenness was as common amongst officers as it was amongst ratings and it rankled that only officers were allowed alcohol at sea.'

36. ADM 1/15548.

37. Courtesy of Fred Radford, from manuscript of his memoirs.

38. Williams J, Gray J. *HM Rescue Tugs, op. cit.* pp.95, 97, who state the information came from Lt Tom Hepworth's memoirs *Failed Sea Trials*.

39. Courtesy of Fred Radford, from manuscript of his memoirs, and unidentified newspaper clipping.

40. German acoustic torpedo. GNAT came from the initials 'German Naval Acoustic Torpedo'.

41. ADM 199/2071.

42. ADM 199/1239.

43. ADM 1/15548.

44. Confidential Admiralty Fleet Order in ADM 1/15548.

45. TDC meeting 26 August 1943 in MT 63/152.

46. ADM 1/15051.

47. ADM 116/5301.

48. ADM 1/15051.

49. Williams J, Gray J. *HM Rescue Tugs*, *op. cit.* pp.65–66.

50. *Towrope*; 2009 (winter issue): 14–15.

3

SAINTS AND BRIGANDS GO TO WAR

O<small>N</small> 11 S<small>EPTEMBER</small> 1939, the First Lord of the Admiralty, Winston Churchill, informed a meeting of the Shipping Defence Advisory Committee that the enemy had already begun to make serious inroads into British commercial shipping: 'In the first five days of the war we lost 11,000 tons a day by sinking. Well, that is just a little more than half the [daily] losses in April, 1917, which of course was the peak month in the Great War, the month in which we were forced to envisage extremely ugly possibilities.'[1]

The first British U-boat casualty was the 13,465-ton liner SS *Athenia* with one thousand, four hundred and sixteen passengers aboard. On 3 September 1939 she was en route for Montreal from Liverpool and was some sixty miles south of Rockall when she was torpedoed. One hundred and twenty-eight people died, including twenty-eight American citizens. The British interpreted her sinking to mean that Hitler had abandoned the 1930 London Naval Treaty that stipulated submarines had to abide by certain rules, which included safeguarding the lives of the crew. Though these had been altered in favour of the submarine – a merchant ship could now be sunk without the crew and passengers first being taken to a place of safety if it actively resisted or persistently refused to stop – this had not been the case with the *Athenia* as she had been attacked without warning.

In fact, all U-boat commanders had been expressly ordered to obey the treaty's rules. So Hitler could not have been best pleased to hear the *Athenia* had been sunk, and the following day he issued an order specifically barring attacks on passenger ships, even if they were escorted. At the same time the German propaganda machine accused the British of sinking the *Athenia*, a propaganda lie it took a year for the neutral American government to officially rebut.

The sinking of the *Athenia* emphasised the urgent need for rescue tugs, but the few vessels suitable for conversion were also needed for harbour work and coastal towing, and could not be released until they could be replaced. So, in late 1939, the Admiralty co-operated with the Ministry of War Transport to institute a new building programme to produce what were essentially commercial tugs. More than a hundred were built, modelled on a dozen different types of existing harbour and coastal tugs, and they all had 'Empire' as a prefix to their names, but they should not be confused with the many merchant ships that had the same prefix.

They were controlled by the Ministry of War Transport, which delegated their management to civilian companies. Because of the acute shortage, a number were commissioned as rescue tugs, and were T.124T manned and flew the White Ensign. The rest flew the Red Ensign and had civilian crews, though the masters and other officers, depending on their qualifications, were normally commissioned into the RNR or RNVR. Their complements also included naval W/T operators, gunners for their armament – mostly an Oerlikon and two Lewis guns – and fifteen-year-olds to act as deck, steward or galley boys, who would have been too young to sign a T.124T Agreement or enter the Royal Navy.

The largest type was modelled on the 135 ft, 487-ton *Englishman*, which the Admiralty had requisitioned at the start of the war. Clelands of Willington and Goole Shipbuilding yards built thirteen of this type, and the earliest ones had full *Englishman* specifications, but later ones depended on what was available. This also applied to the other types for it was impossible to standardise the machinery or boilers and the wartime scarcity of materials meant that scantlings were reduced to a minimum, and a strict check was kept on modifications.

The first of the *Englishman* type to be launched, in January 1941, was *Empire Larch*, followed by *Empire Oak* on 15 March 1941. By that time, the shortage of rescue tugs was so acute that *Empire Oak* was immediately equipped as one, as by the time she joined convoy OG-71 in August 1941 she was armed with a twelve-pounder gun and two Hotchkiss machine guns. The Gibraltar-bound convoy comprised twenty-two merchant ships and eight escorts. Later called the 'Nightmare Convoy',[2] it left Liverpool on 13 August 1941 and was first attacked off the coast of Portugal six nights later by several U-boats, which had been homed in on the convoy by shadowing Focke-Wulf bombers. They torpedoed three ships and one of the escorts, and *Empire Oak*, at the rear of the convoy, picked up seventeen survivors. 'We got all the men on board without mishap,' the master, Captain FE Christian, later wrote in his report, 'although there was a big sea running and it was a dark night. We used white cotton heaving lines to pick up these men, so that they could see them in the darkness, and they remarked later how useful this had been.'[3]

Three nights later, the rescue tug was herself torpedoed, and only six of her crew of twenty, and eight of the seventeen survivors from the earlier attack, were rescued. Altogether ten ships were sunk, including two of the escorts, the rest of the convoy being ordered into Lisbon by the Admiralty, which some thought an ignominious retreat. Altogether nearly four hundred lives were lost, including twenty-two Women's Royal Naval Service (WRNS) personnel and a nursing sister from the liner SS *Aguila*, sunk on the first night. As a result of this tragedy, the Admiralty immediately reversed its orders forbidding female naval personnel from travelling aboard HM warships, and from that time they were only transported in them.

EARLY LOSSES AND SUCCESSES

A possible source for purchasing large ocean-going tugs was Holland, which had a worldwide reputation for ocean salvage, but early on it was neutral and intended to remain so if it could. Instead, the TDC started negotiations to charter Dutch tugs with their civilian crews for use outside the war zone – which would have released some British tugs for war work – but these came to nothing when Holland was overrun in May 1940.

The TDC had better luck when it scoured British shipyards, for it discovered two tugs had been laid down for the South Africa Railways and Harbour Administration Board: the 620-ton, 156 ft sister ships *Theodor Woker* and *TH Watermeyer*. These were requisitioned with the approval of the South African government, the former after she had already started on her delivery voyage. They were given T.124T crews and flew the White Ensign, but were returned to South Africa in 1941/42.

An early assignment for *Watermeyer*, as she was renamed, was to assist Lord Louis Mountbatten's destroyer HMS *Kelly*, after she had been torpedoed by an E-boat in the North Sea on 9 May 1940. She was towed by another destroyer until *Watermeyer* arrived just after dawn on 12 May to take her to the Tyne, arriving there that evening. By then the *Kelly* had been towed or hove-to for ninety-one hours,[4] and had been under constant air attack the entire time. For the crew of *Watermeyer*, it must have been an interesting introduction to rescue work.

This was not the only time Lord Louis needed the assistance of a rescue tug – though undoubtedly brave, he was rather accident-prone. In November 1940, he was aboard the destroyer HMS *Javelin* as Captain 'D' of Fifth Destroyer Flotilla when she had her bow and stern blown off by an encounter with German destroyers in the South-Western Approaches. Forty-six of her crew were killed. Her remains – just 155 ft of her original length of 353 ft – were towed into Plymouth by the rescue tug *Caroline Moller* (ex-*St Mabyn*). The operation was also harassed from the air, and took more than thirty hours.[5]

Theodor Woker had an even earlier initiation into rescue work. Launched on 25 May 1939, she answered the *Athenia*'s distress signals while on her way to South Africa. She helped pick up survivors, and returned with them to the Clyde, where she was promptly requisitioned and renamed *Stalwart*.[6] She then took part in the Dunkirk evacuation of May–June 1940 and, along with two Saint class rescue tugs, *St Olaves* and *St Clears*, survived the hazards of towing lighters to the beaches to pick up troops. But German aircraft sank two others of the Saint class, *St Abbs* and *St Fagan*.

Several more of the Saint class were lost during the war. *Caroline Moller* was sunk by an E-boat off Cromer in October 1942; *St Breock* and *St Just* were sunk by Japanese aircraft in February 1942, the former off Sumatra, the latter off Singapore; as already mentioned, *St Cyrus* was mined off the Humber in January 1941; and *St Issey* was mined off Benghazi in December 1942 while supporting the seesaw battles in Libya. She sank with all hands, and in reporting the incident the C-in-C Mediterranean signalled that *St Issey* 'had done noble work with Inshore Squadron throughout every Western Desert

Campaign; her loss is much regretted'.[7] Others were lost due to stress of weather: *St Sampson* foundered in the Red Sea in March 1942, and *St Olaves* was wrecked off north-east Scotland in September 1942.

The loss of *St Olaves* made the newspaper headlines, not because such a misfortune was exactly good propaganda, but because the authorities must have decided that the bravery of one man definitely was. Headed 'Drama of the Dark Sea',[8] the newspaper reported the courageous action of Chief Petty Officer Alfred Kennar, of Brixham, Devon, when the *St Olaves* was caught in a storm while towing a water barge around Duncansby Head, Scotland's most north-easterly point. A vicious ebb tide had just set in, and it was pitch black and raining heavily, and wartime blackout meant there were no lights to show where the land was. At the height of the storm the tow parted, not once but twice. In a desperate effort to save the barge – and the men on it – the attention of the commanding officer, Lt AT Lewis RNR, must have been diverted, for just after the line had been reconnected for a third time the lookout shouted 'breakers ahead', and moments later the *St Olaves* hit submerged rocks and stuck fast.[9]

Lewis ordered the barge, which drew a good deal less than the *St Olaves*, to be brought alongside, and her crew clambered aboard. The tow was then cut and the barge was blown ashore, some two hundred yards from the rescue tug. An attempt was now made to launch the *St Olaves'* lifeboat, but this failed when the rescue tug's violent motion smashed it against her superstructure. Four of the crew volunteered to take one of the two Carley floats and row ashore with a rope. But the rope parted and the Carley float disappeared into the darkness. Luckily, all four managed to get ashore.

The ebb tide drove the tug deeper on to the rocks until they holed her and flooded her engine room. Everyone aboard was now in a very dangerous situation indeed, and Kennar, who was twenty-seven years old and a strong swimmer, suggested he swim to the barge with a rope. The other Carley float could then be used to ferry the crew, four at a time, by hauling themselves to the barge. This was agreed, and Kennar told his friend Jack Gardiner to stand by the line and be ready to haul him back if he got into trouble. Jack said he would.

'I had full confidence that Jack would keep his promise,' said the young Kennar, in an interview with the newspaper.[8] 'I was lowered over the starboard side of the *St Olaves*. It was the coldest sea dip I had ever had.' But he made it to the barge and hauled himself on board. He then saw the lights of rescuers descending to the beach, but each time they fired a rocket over the rescue tug, the attached line broke. Eventually, the commanding officer ordered the second Carley float to be launched and the crew ferried themselves to the water barge, leaving just the commanding officer, a signaller and one able seaman on the stranded *St Olaves*.

At first light the local lifeboat was seen approaching and took off the entire crew, including the ship's dog. The weather was so bad that the newspaper reported the lifeboat coxswain was in line for a lifesaving medal, and Kennar received the British Empire Medal (BEM) for his bravery. But there was no saving *St Olaves* and she became a total loss.

St Mellons had a more successful war. Although launched just before the 1918 Armistice, she wasn't commissioned until 1939 and was the only Saint class still named as a rescue tug in a February 1944 CAFO, which named and categorised the rescue tugs then operating (see Appendix). In November 1939, she was stationed first at Kirkwall, the Orkney Islands' capital, and later at Falmouth, and was almost constantly at sea. In January 1940, when the Pink List shows her to have already been armed,[10] she rescued twenty-two members of the crew of the 3161-ton

Greek cargo ship *Tonis Chandris*, which, after being chased by a U-boat, ran aground in fog near Unst, the most northerly of the Shetland Islands.

Then in February she was dispatched to bring in the 4996-ton British freighter *Loch Maddy*, a straggler from convoy HX-19, which had been torpedoed near Copinsay, one of the Orkney Islands, and abandoned by her crew. A few hours later, before *St Mellons* could reach her, the ship was torpedoed again, and broke in two. *St Mellons* towed the stern section to Inganess Bay, near Kirkwall, and beached it, saving more than 200 tons of her cargo.

In March, she attempted to bring in an abandoned Norwegian merchant ship, the 1267-ton *Svinta*, damaged during an air attack while outward-bound from Kirkwall to join the Norway-bound convoy ON-21. As the rescue tug was towing the *Svinta* to Kirkwall, there was an explosion – probably a mine as there is no evidence she was torpedoed – and the *Svinta* sank a few miles off Orkney.

After moving to Falmouth, *St Mellons* was damaged in an air raid. While under repair she acted as a depot ship, before moving to Sheerness in September 1940 where her armament was increased by the addition of a twelve-pounder gun and a two-pounder pom-pom, these being fitted for unspecified special duties. When the special duties did not materialise, the pom-pom was removed, as its position prevented her from towing normally. In November 1940 she made good use of her armament by shooting down one German bomber and damaging another. The same month she fought off an air attack while towing into Harwich the V class destroyer HMS *Vega*, which had been badly damaged by a mine.

Perhaps it was this prowess at downing German aircraft that led to discussions in early 1941 for her to have her pom-pom refitted – in a position that would not restrict how she towed – and for her to be used as a decoy for the four-engined Focke-Wulf bombers that were harassing British shipping.[11] This never materialised either, and she later became part of the Rescue Tug Convoy Escort Service on its formation at harwich in August 1942, and then towed parts of the prefabricated harbours to France after D-Day. By January 1945, she was commanded by Lt Arthur Godfrey Hawkins RNR of *San Demetrio* fame, and ended the war stationed in the Scheldt Estuary. For a vessel that had been launched in 1918, she gave a good account of herself.

Hawkins was second officer of the tanker *San Demetrio* when, on 5 November 1940, the German pocket battleship *Admiral Scheer* attacked her in mid-Atlantic and she was soon on fire. She was carrying 9000 tons of petrol and the crew abandoned ship, but when by some miracle she did not explode, Hawkins returned. He and the men from his lifeboat dowsed the flames and, without any navigational aids except the sun and the stars, managed to bring the tanker to the west coast of Ireland.

By then her presence had been reported and *Superman* soon appeared with orders to take her to Londonderry or the Clyde. Hawkins, who was later reported as refusing a tow because it was too expensive, asked the rescue tug what speed she could make. 'Nine knots,' came the answer, to which Hawkins immediately replied that he could still make ten, and that he'd prefer to make the Clyde under his own steam. A destroyer then arrived which, with *Superman* standing by, escorted the tanker to Rothesay Bay.[12]

Superman, as she was entitled to do, later made a claim for escorting the tanker from Clare Island to the Clyde,[13] but the courts ruled that Hawkins and those with him had salvaged the ship themselves – and all but two hundred tons of her precious cargo – and were awarded substantial sums of money for doing so. In what must have been a unique case, the tanker's owners, the Eagle Oil and Shipping Company, guaranteed the men's Court costs and not only did not contest the court's decision, but strongly supported it. A book was published about the incident, which was later made into a film called *San Demetrio, London*, one of the few wartime films featuring the courage of the wartime Merchant Navy. For his bravery and leadership, Hawkins was awarded the OBE and in a nice piece of irony joined the Rescue Tug Service shortly afterwards.

BUCCANEER'S TRIALS

Realising the Saint class were getting rather long in the tooth, during the 1930s the Admiralty had ordered five 840-ton, 174 ft Brigand class tugs: *Brigand* (the first to be commissioned, in 1937), *Buccaneer* (1937), *Bandit* (1938), *Marauder* (1938) and *Freebooter* (1940). Their oil-fired triple expansion steam engines produced 3000 ihp, which gave them a speed of fifteen knots. They had twin screws, and were armed with a three-inch gun forward, two Lewis guns and an Oerlikon, and had a complement of forty-three. Primarily built as fleet tugs – towing targets and the larger warships where necessary – they all acted as rescue tugs during the war, though by 1941 *Buccaneer* and *Bandit*, based at Scapa, had reverted to their original use.

The Brigands were powerful but far from perfect, and their faults showed that the Admiralty still had some way to go in understanding what was needed in a rescue tug. When Jack Philip-Nicholson and his commanding officer went aboard *Buccaneer* for her commissioning trials in 1937, they both agreed she was well built but left a lot to be desired. Jack later put it this way:

> The trouble with the new class was that it had been designed by a committee. So by the time the designers

had tried to satisfy the Board of Trade, the Admiralty, Lloyd's, and a few other authorities, the result was a camel, a camel of course being the direct result of a committee trying to design a superior horse.[14]

It seemed the stipulations made by one authority had negated those of another, so they set about altering the tug to suit purely Royal Navy requirements.

The faults were numerous, some of them seemingly insurmountable. Firing the gun at a target was pure guesswork. It had been designed about 1914 and was supposed to be able to fire at eighty-knot aircraft, or slow cumbersome Zeppelins, as well as enemy ships, but actually did neither very well. An old-fashioned log was towed astern, and the officer of the watch had to take the helm while the helmsman ran aft to read it. The depth sounding was equally dated, and the tug's boats looked useless. 'I think that in any real emergency, they would have gone down with the ship,' Jack noted. 'The design of the davits was pure Harry Tate at its worst.'[15]

It was impossible to use a chart on the bridge as the bridge was open, and was continually washed by walls of spray 'that poured from a bow apparently specially constructed to throw water vertically'.[15] The chart house was directly below the bridge, and the only means of communication between the two was for the helmsman to stamp his feet. The twin screws, 'by a mistake of the first magnitude', would unexpectedly move the tug off course.

George Corke, who served as first officer on the *Buccaneer*, added that the class 'were poor ships for ocean work because of [the] twin screws which, having only a single rudder, could not hold the course required in a strong wind on the bow and were designed with the towing winch right aft for target towing'.[16] With rescue tugs having to go out into the Atlantic as far west as 25 degrees to pick up a torpedoed ship, another drawback was that the class could not always carry sufficient fuel to complete the task.

'The rudder was of the same shape as the rudder on the old paddle tugs of the time of Turner's *Fighting Temeraire*,' Jack wrote. 'There were times when, at certain speeds, and certain helm angles, it made you believe you were riding a roundabout.'[14]

By far the most dangerous fault was the obsolete system of chain and rod steering. According to Jack, this method had been condemned by every navy in the world and by most shipping companies as well. On one occasion, during rough weather in the Bay of Biscay, the chain came off the rudder cross-head:

> Steering became impossible. Great waves struck the rudder and the rudder brake proved useless. We looked to the boats, recalling that a Saint class tug [*St Genny*] had gone down a few years before in this area due to stress of weather.[14]

By a mixture of courage and skill, the chief engine room artificer (ERA)[17] reattached the chain and the tug was brought back on course, but it sounds as if it had been a close call.

But it wasn't all bad news. The engines worked beautifully, and the boilers, under the expert eye of the chief ERA, were excellent. The wireless, too, worked well; the coxswain was a good sailor, and a good seaman, and though one of the crew was a drunk, he remained sober at sea. 'The ship,' Jack concluded, 'was reasonably happy. No-one went sick, no-one deserted in my two years', and some good work was done which included keeping 'a bright eye on Franco's large cruisers off Gibraltar with our pop-gun loaded'.

When the trials were over Jack composed a long report on the ship's shortcomings and sent it to the Admiralty. As a mark of appreciation, or perhaps not, it sent him to the naval training establishment at Shotley as a teacher.

IMPERIAL TRANSPORT

Presumably, the *Buccaneer*'s faults had been ironed out by the time the war started, for she was soon in action when, on 11 February 1940, the 8022-ton tanker *Imperial Transport*, sailing alone and outward-bound in ballast for Trinidad, was torpedoed two hundred miles north-west of the Butt of Lewis. Her captain later related:

> We were struck by a torpedo about nine o'clock at
> night. It got us on the port side just underneath the
> bridge. A terrific explosion was followed by a mountain
> of spray, which enveloped the whole ship. In less than
> five minutes the tanker broke in two. The bridge on
> which I was standing crumbled beneath my feet as
> it was carried away by the bow half. I managed to
> scramble on to the stern half just in time.[18]

That night the captain decided to abandon ship in case the after part sank. In doing so, two of the crew were drowned, but when the ship remained afloat, the crew returned. They managed to start the engines and began steering her to the nearest land, but they had no means of sending out a distress signal, though they painted an SOS on the deck:

> All my navigation instruments went with the bridge, and
> I had to set a course with the aid of a school atlas.

> I reckon we steamed about 110 miles before we were
> picked up by a British destroyer [other reports said
> there were four of them]. We were asked if we wished
> to abandon the ship, but I said I thought we could
> carry on.[18]

The destroyers signalled for assistance and one was detached
to escort the remains of the tanker, but on 15 February the
weather began to deteriorate. The forward bulkhead was also
showing signs of stress, and when an attempt to sail stern
first failed, as did the destroyer's attempt at towing, the
crew decided to transfer to the destroyer until the weather
improved. At daylight on 16 February, the *Buccaneer* arrived
with a destroyer escort, and towed the remains of the tanker
to Kilchattan Bay on the Isle of Bute, and beached them.[19]
This was another sheltered area used by rescue tugs to leave
damaged ships to be dealt with by the Liverpool & Glasgow
Salvage Association, which was based on the island during the
war. The bow was never recovered, but the after part was
later taken to the Clyde, where a new bow was fitted, and
the tanker returned to service the following year. She was
torpedoed again in 1942 but again survived. A remarkable
story.

After she was commissioned, the *Brigand* was based in the
Mediterranean to tow targets, but when war broke out she
was recalled from Malta and stationed at Kirkwall where
she was kept busy salvaging the casualties of U-boat attacks
on Atlantic convoys. As so often happened, she sometimes
arrived too late to be of assistance, or the damaged ship was
beyond saving. For instance, in July 1940 a U-boat attacked
an outbound convoy, OB-188, and torpedoed the 10,364-ton
tanker *Thiara*. The *Brigand* found her and took her in tow,

but the *Thiara* sank south-south-west of Rockall with heavy loss of life.

The *Brigand* was more successful when the 8016-ton British tanker *Alexia*, part of Convoy OB-191, was shelled and then torpedoed in the Moray Firth on 2 August 1940, and the *Brigand* was able to tow her into Greenock despite her stern being almost submerged.

SALVAGE CO-OPERATION

The Rescue Tug Service often co-operated with the Admiralty's Salvage Department, just as it had in the previous war. One such operation, in which *Brigand* was involved, showed how much money could be saved from salvaging a ship that would otherwise have been lost. On 23 August 1940, German aircraft attacked the 10,119-ton British freighter *Beacon Grange* off the Scottish coast. At the time she was carrying 2500 tons of general cargo and was en route from London to Rio de Janeiro. She burst into flames and twenty-six of the crew lost their lives. The *Brigand* and two salvage vessels doused the fire, but after the freighter was towed to Kirkwall, fire broke out again and she had to be beached well away from the town. It took another two days to control the blaze, but she was eventually refloated and towed to Dundee, where her cargo was unloaded.[20] According to the chief salvage officer, the ship was only two years old, cost £750,000 to build, and had a general cargo worth about £450,000. The total damage to the ship and cargo probably did not exceed £150,000, representing a saving of over £1 million.[21]

Another of the Brigand class, *Marauder*, was officially classed as defective for the first few months of the war, though it may in fact have been her crew who were faulty, as a note in one of the Rescue Tug files by a baffled naval officer reveals – and it also reveals another of the differences between the two services:

> The position is a rather curious one. It seems that an officer or man T.124T can commit quite serious offences against Naval Discipline, without offending under the Merchant Service Act. It is not a technical offence, as I understand, for a M.S. (Merchant Service) officer to be drunk and disorderly out of his ship, or in fact at anytime when he is not on duty, as far as being drunk goes. The standard discharges are 'V.G.', which in effect does not mean 'V.G.' in our sense. It means merely satisfactory; 'g' has the implication of unsatisfactoriness [sic]; and 'D.R.' (decline to report) means damned bad and will prevent a man getting further employment [as did 'g' normally]. There is a strong feeling among M.S. Officers against doing this [with good reason, considering the terms of employment under which merchant seamen worked], and some of the original scoundrels in *Marauder*'s crew, who were discharged at Plymouth in Jan '40, got 'V.G.s'.[22]

After her crew was replaced, the *Marauder* was stationed at Campbeltown. It was from there on 6 June 1940 that she went to the assistance of HMS *Carinthia* – a Cunard White Star Liner converted to an armed merchant cruiser (AMC) – that had been torpedoed west of Galway Bay. The signals that followed,[23] passed through Malin Head on the emergency wireless to naval authorities, give some idea of the kind of emergencies that rescue tugs, and those they were attempting to assist, had to cope with:

'Torpedoed by submarine in vicinity in position 53 degrees, 13 minutes N, 10 degrees, 39 minutes W,' the *Carinthia* signalled at 14.20. 'Unable to proceed. Submarine in vicinity.

If planes can be sent to keep submarine away I think ship can be got in.'

The response was no plane could reach them before about 18.15, but destroyers and a rescue tug had also been dispatched. A periscope was sighted and fired at, and at 1435 the U-boat again tried to sink the *Carinthia*. The torpedo missed, but her crew spent four anxious hours waiting for the U-boat to attack again.

Then at 18.23 the first aircraft appeared and signalled: 'Do you need help?'

'Help is being sent,' the *Carinthia* replied. 'Am glad to see you. Last saw submarine at 1430.'

'How long can you float?'

'We hope to be towed into harbour as we are not making any more water.'

For the next five hours, one or more aircraft kept watch on the crippled ship, and at dawn the next day the first of four destroyers arrived. By that time the ship was beginning to fill aft, and the captain decided that the majority of his crew should be transferred to the destroyers, leaving a skeleton crew on board. 'As most of the ship's company wished to remain,' the captain reported later, 'the working party was in reality a hand-picked one.'

The transfer was completed at 10.35 and soon afterwards the *Marauder* appeared.

'What possibilities of salvage may I report?' she signalled the *Carinthia* at 11.11.

'Fifty-fifty if weather holds,' was the reply.

There was trouble connecting the tow rope, but at 12.12 the *Marauder* began the tow, working up a speed of about four knots, with a course being set for Tory Island, off the north-west coast of Ireland.

At this point, though water was slowly rising in the compartments abaft the engine room, the *Carinthia's* captain still had hopes of saving his ship. However, he realised that if the water reached

'C' Deck, or near it, the position would become critical and he had three of his officers constantly monitoring the situation. One of them 'visited the boiler room at intervals to keep in check by pumping the foot or two of water that was passing through engine room bulkhead at the electric cable glands. At one time, to obtain tools from a store room, he had to break down the door with an axe, and wade up to his waist in water.'

But it must have been obvious to the rescue tug that their efforts were not succeeding, for at 12.30 she signalled: 'Should you fear she is going, endeavour to slip my rope before abandoning [ship].'

'We cannot slip,' the *Carinthia* replied. 'You must make preparations to slip in an emergency.'

At 13.00 the trawler *British Honduras* arrived to render assistance.

'Act as submarine screen at your discretion,' the *Carinthia* signalled the trawler. 'I should like you to remain fairly handy so that in case of emergency you could come alongside and remove the balance of crew I have left on board.'

The weather must then have started to deteriorate, for at 16.20 the *Carinthia* signalled the *Marauder*: 'I think the position will arise when I shall have to temporarily abandon the ship without abandoning the tow. Should the ship stand the altered conditions, it may be possible to return. In any case I shall not be able to steer very many hours as emergency engine will be giving out. I will ask you to slow down when we leave.'

At 19.25 dense fog enveloped the area. *Carinthia*'s captain must then have realised he had no alternative but to abandon ship, for at 19.57, after requesting the *Marauder* by megaphone to slow down, he ordered the trawler to come alongside and take off the remaining crew, which she did. The *Marauder* continued to tow the crippled ship – perhaps hoping to beach her at the nearest suitable spot – but at 21.40 she broke up and sank in a matter of seconds in sixty fathoms of water. The *Marauder*'s crew would have been standing by with axes to sever the manila tow rope, and they must have acted with commendable speed to escape the tug being dragged under. At 20,277 tons, the *Carinthia* was one of the largest merchantmen to be torpedoed during the war.

The *Marauder* seems to have been one of those ships with constant problems. In May 1941, she attracted the wrath of the base engineer officer at Campbeltown who was also acting, on a trial basis, as engineer officer, rescue tugs: 'As some three months have now passed since I was appointed Base Engineer Officer Campbeltown and additional for duty with Rescue Tugs,' he wrote to the NOIC Campbeltown, Captain Addis RN, 'I feel it a duty to urge that Rescue Tug Service efficiency is susceptible to considerable improvement.'[24] He went on to claim that the *Marauder*, in particular, was a waste of valuable resources, 'which amounted to adversely influencing the war effort'. This was, perhaps, over-egging it a bit.

The problem was a lack of guidance by a responsible engineer officer. It was a matter that 'calls for urgent remedy or the whole of the rescue tug new construction may tend to suffer a similar fate. The *Marauder*'s condenser trouble, boiler salting, general piston rod condition, rusted-in tunnel door, savage treatment of towing winch ratio gearing screw, the absence of spare gear for fan engines, the casual abandonment of oil for stern tubes, and the disgraceful condition of spare gear generally, are conclusive evidence of long continued neglect of reasonable engineering practice.'

That wasn't all. 'The Rescue Tug Engineers, in spite of their RNR rank, are of the type known as working engineers, that is to say those who, customarily, are expected to carry out running repairs without the aid of artificers.' They had to be given the opportunity to carry out routine examinations and repairs. Instead, the writer seemed to be implying, they went on leave, and that this had to be looked into as well.

The situation was obviously unsatisfactory, and the CCRT agreed that the trial showed it was essential to have two separate posts. However, as there was an acute shortage of engineer officers, there was no alternative but to leave things as they were.

FREEBOOTER

The last of the Brigand class to be launched, *Freebooter*, was the only rescue tug to be equipped with ASDIC and depth charges, and so carried two additional crew, an ASDIC rating and a torpedo rating. Although she had a pennant number painted on her bows, which all warships of the same class had to differentiate one vessel from another, *Freebooter* also displayed a skull and crossbones on her bridge.

Freebooter's commanding officer, Lt Lionel Greenstreet RNR, wore the white ribbon of the Polar Medal, a rare distinction Greenstreet had earned when serving as first officer aboard the *Endurance* during the 1914 Shackleton Expedition to the South Pole. After commanding *Freebooter*, Greenstreet was sent to Washington, DC in January 1942 as rescue tug equipment officer in charge of the US shipbuilding programme of rescue tugs for the Admiralty, which were acquired under the Lend-Lease Act the US Congress had passed in March 1941. Later he worked as an adviser to the Admiralty at Henry Kaiser's shipyards on the West Coast, which built many of the famous Liberty ships, before returning to the UK in July 1944. That October he replaced EG Martin as Commander Rescue Tug Base, Campbeltown, when Martin retired, and was awarded the OBE.[25]

The prominent journalist and war correspondent Godfrey Winn described a voyage aboard *Freebooter* while she was helping to tow a 20,000-ton Admiralty Floating Dock (AFD) from one unknown port to another – no names, of course, it was wartime – and his book is an interesting example of propaganda.[26] It is also interesting that the authorities decided rescue tugs were a suitable subject for Godfrey Winn's expert pen. It certainly included some unusual facts: for instance, *Freebooter*'s eighteen-inch manila tow rope – one hundred and twenty fathoms long and costing £400 new – stretched an extra nine feet in the first two days of the voyage.

Towing an AFD was a tricky business. Towing a massive block of concrete – which Winn graphically described as like being pursued by Tower Bridge – and controlling it in any kind of heavy weather, needed impeccable seamanship and a cool head. Throughout the war, it was one of the more exacting tasks of the rescue tugs to deliver these essential pieces of kit wherever they were needed. That included the other side of the world, and *Brigand* and *Marauder* were two of the five rescue tugs and two escort ships to take a massive 978 ft, 98,000-ton AFD from Bombay to Malta as soon as peace returned. The whole operation was aptly described, because of the number of ships employed, as 'Snow White and the Seven Dwarfs'.

Winn wrote:

> 'I was thinking of the other trip I had done in one
> of these ocean-going tugs, far out into the Atlantic; of
> all the trips that these rescue tugs have performed in
> the war, salvaging hundreds of thousands of tons of
> shipping. I was thinking of the German aircraft that
> the skipper of one of the other tugs in our tow had
> destroyed by holding everything, including his fire, until
> the last moment. I was thinking of the tug, suitably
> named the *Englishman*, which gallantly went down with
> all its crew, in the course of its duties.[26]

The first incident Winn was referring to above was when the *Seaman* was bombed and strafed by a four-engined Focke-Wulf

Condor bomber south of Rockall in January 1941. The bomb missed the *Seaman*, but the strafing wounded the second mate. The aircraft circled, and this time attacked from ahead. According to one newspaper,[27] Mate Jimmy Ryan kept a watchful eye on the bomber while carefully rolling a cigarette. When it began its run in, Ryan lit his cigarette, opened fire at just the right moment, and knocked the huge aircraft into the sea.

A more recent description of this incident is less dramatic but gives an assessment of its importance:

> By the end of January 1941, the surge in Condor attacks had sunk 17 ships of 65,000 tons and damaged five others. In return, the British had destroyed only a single Condor – the Fw 200 C-3 flown by Oberleutnant Burmeister – who incautiously decided to conduct a low-level strafing run on the rescue tugboat *Seaman* on 10 January. Although only 369 tons, the *Seaman* was extremely well armed against low-level attack with one of the few available 20mm Oerlikon guns, a 12-pdr and two .50cal machine guns. Burmeister was surprised to run into a wall of intense flak that holed his plane and forced him to ditch near the tugboat. He and two other survivors of the crew were captured and revealed under interrogation a great deal about Condor operations, which allowed the British to begin developing effective countermeasures. The tiny tugboat *Seaman* had not only struck the first blow against the Condor, but it had accomplished what larger warships had failed to do, and thereby set the Royal Navy upon the path of reversing the Condor's ascendancy.[28]

One of the interesting facts that Burmeister revealed under interrogation was that German aircraft had 'orders to single out ocean-going tugs for attack'.[29] Unfortunately, these orders were carried out only too successfully when, in the second incident Winn mentions, the rescue tug *Englishman* was bombed on 22 January 1941 and sank with the loss of all hands. The day before the attack, she had been accompanied by one of the new Assurance class rescue tugs, *Restive*, but the two had lost contact during the night as the weather was bad. Stanley Butler, who was an engineer officer aboard the *Restive*, remembers that 'about mid-morning the next day our wireless people picked up a message from *Englishman* that she was being attacked by enemy aircraft. The message was not finished, and nothing more was ever heard of the *Englishman* or her crew.'[30]

In fact, the *Englishman* did turn up again. German records reported her as having been sunk near Tory Island off the north-west coast of Ireland, and the Admiralty accepted this without further investigation. However, during the 1980s, while a survey was being carried out on a U-boat sunk in the North Channel in 1945, the remains of the *Englishman*, including her bell, were found nearby, some six miles west of the entrance to the Mull of Kintyre.

AWARDS AND DECORATIONS

For his bravery under fire, Ryan was subsequently awarded the George Medal; and for his seamanship *Seaman*'s captain, Lt-Commander Owen Jones RNR, received the OBE.

There was, as the war progressed, considerable dissatisfaction about awarding civilian decorations to Merchant Navy personnel. In 1916, Merchant Navy officers had been made eligible for the Distinguished Service Cross (DSC), awarded for 'gallantry during active operations against the enemy at sea'. However, when the Order of the British Empire was introduced in June

1917, and later divided into civil and military divisions, King George VI, in June 1940, approved that the civilian division be used to decorate Merchant seamen for acts of bravery, but not in the face of the enemy. In the case of the *Seaman* this was obviously nonsense – as it was in many cases – and Churchill, for one, strongly disagreed with this policy. While First Lord of the Admiralty, he minuted:

> It is idle to suppose that civilian decorations
> are not regarded as inferior to military decorations
> or that newly instituted decorations [which had been
> mooted for the Merchant Navy] can have the same
> prestige as those which have a long succession of
> brave deeds associated with them. I regret very much
> that the DSO [Distinguished Service Order] and the
> DSC cannot be gained for acts of equal courage
> by the Merchant Service. The awards should be
> proportionate to the action and not to the status of
> the actor.[31]

However, for various reasons, including the case of Captain Fryatt,[32] he agreed to continue with the existing policy 'for the time being'.

Aware of the inconsistencies in the granting of awards, both the C-in-C Western Approaches and the C-in-C The Nore pressed for changes, and it is interesting but probably a coincidence that they commanded areas where the Rescue Tug Service was most active. However, the Admiralty chose to prevaricate, being reluctant to abandon the idea that as the Merchant Navy was a civilian organisation and the Royal Navy a military one, they should not be awarded the same decorations – despite the fact that the Merchant Navy was serving under the Royal Navy and the Rescue Tug Service was part of it. The Admiralty's illogicality became even more apparent when it was pointed out that the Distinguished Service Medal (DSM), the lower deck equivalent of the DSC, had already been awarded to twenty-four merchant seamen during the evacuation of Dunkirk.

In April 1941 Churchill, now Prime Minister, showed he was also dissatisfied with the number, as well as the type, of awards being made to the Merchant Navy. Having asked for figures, he scribbled in red ink on the memo: 'Aim at doubling the number of awards and report to me when this is achieved, in order that a further advance may be made.' In June, an increase was submitted and Churchill circled the number allotted to July 1941 and scribbled: 'Good, but more are needed. Press on.'[33]

In September 1941, one correspondent involved in the ongoing debate also highlighted the discrepancies between the number of awards for the two services, pointing out that during a recent, and successful, operation involving six merchant ships, fifty-two awards had been made to Royal Navy personnel and only ten to merchant seamen:

> It is true that the Royal Navy did the fighting, but
> the Merchant Navy personnel, under the orders of
> the Navy, took, I think, more than a 'civilian' risk.
> However that may be I feel that the above is the line
> of criticism we may expect to have, and if it is made
> publicly, it can only be harmful to the feeling between
> the Merchant Navy and Royal Navy, and that is what I
> am concerned about.[34]

Eventually, the Admiralty was forced to concede, and it also agreed that Merchant Navy personnel could be 'mentioned in despatches'. Later in the war, several DSCs were awarded to rescue tug officers and a number of officers and ratings were mentioned in despatches.

NOTES

1. ADM 199/2165, minutes of the meeting held on 11 September 1939.

2. Lund P, Ludlam H. *Nightmare Convoy*. London: Foulsham; 1987. The title comes from a quote by Nicholas Monsarrat who was an officer aboard one of the escorts, and he based his novel *The Cruel Sea* on some of the incidents and personalities of this disaster. 'Whenever I think of war, I don't remember the happy things, but this convoy. It is my particular nightmare.'

3. ADM 199/1708.

4. ADM 199/905.

5. Williams J, Gray J. *HM Rescue Tugs in World War II*. p.37 (privately printed) and the wartime operations of HMS *Javelin* on www.naval-history.net

6. Williams J, Gray J. *HM Rescue Tugs*, op. cit. p.44.

7. ADM 358/1157.

8. *Western Morning News*, 17 March 1943.

9. This was not the first time *St Olaves* had run aground. In April 1941 while on passage from Holyhead to Bangor she bounced off several sand banks in the Menai Straits before grounding in Friars Bay. See ADM 199/1239.

10. ADM 187/5. Pink lists recorded the stations and movements of Allied and RN ships, and were issued every three or four days. Red Lists (ADM 208) recorded the disposition of minor war vessels in home waters and was printed weekly.

11. ADM 199/1238.

12. Tennyson J. *The Saga of San Demetrio*. London: HMSO; 1942. pp.40–62.

13. ADM 199/1238.

14. 'HMS *Buccaneer*' by Jack Philip-Nicholson, *Towrope* 2008 (Xmas issue):23–27.

15. Harry Tate's navy was the name given to the trawlers of the Royal Naval Patrol Service (RNPS) manned by reservists. Harry Tate was one of the best-known comedians of the era, so the RNPS, which did invaluable service during the war, was presumably regarded as comical by the regular navy.

16. George Corke memoir, courtesy of Mrs Joanna Barron. Before the war Corke had been a professional yacht skipper.

17. Engine room artificers were skilled in engineering repairs, making new parts if necessary.

18. Interview with Captain Smail in *The Buteman and West Coast Chronicle*, 29 March 1940.

19. *Sea Hazard (1939–1945)*. London: Houlder; 1947. pp.12–14. There is a photograph of the tanker's beached remains, and a Pathé News clip about her, on www.bute-at-war.org/vimage. shtml?/gallery/imperialtransportkb.jpg

20. *Lloyd's War Losses in World War II*. Vol. II. London: Lloyd's of London Press; 1989.

21. Booth T. *Admiralty Salvage in Peace and War, 1906–2006*. Barnsley: Pen & Sword Maritime; 2007. p.104.

22. ADM 199/1238.

23. ADM 1/10806.

24. ADM 199/1237.

25. Greenstreet's wartime career partly comes from his diary in www.enduranceobituaries.co.uk/greenstreet.htm

26. Winn G. *The Hour Before Dawn*. London: Collins; 1942. p.61.

27. *Dundee Courier*, 9 August 1943.

28. Forczyk R. *Fw 200 Condor vs. Atlantic Convoy, 1941–43*. Oxford: Osprey Publishing; 2010. p.49.

29. Memorandum from CCRT dated 25/1/41 in ADM 199/1238.

30. Butler S. *Not For Davy Jones*. Bound manuscript, p.9. Courtesy of Peter Butler.

31. ADM 116/4546, 12 February 1940.

32. The British responded to the first unrestricted U-boat campaign in 1915 by instructing merchant ships to turn towards a surfaced U-boat if they were attacked by gunfire, forcing it to dive to escape being rammed. The Germans regarded this as a hostile act, which indeed it was, making the perpetrator a combatant, subject to the rules of war. In March 1915, Captain Fryatt, the master of the railway packet *Brussels*, almost rammed a U-boat with this manocuvre, and the Admiralty duly awarded him a gold watch suitably inscribed to commemorate his bravery.

Unfortunately for him, the *Brussels* was captured the following year by German destroyers and taken to Zeebrugge. Fryatt's watch was found on him and he was put on trial as a *franc-tireur* (illegal combatant), found guilty, and executed by firing squad. The Admiralty was therefore understandably wary of decorating non-military personnel with military decorations.

33. T335/2, 14 April and 14 July 1941.

34. ADM 116/4546. The writer has only initialled the memo.

4

REINFORCEMENTS AND THE REMARKABLE *SALVONIA*

THE TDC's EFFORTS to acquire tugs from Holland had proved fruitless, but when the Germans overran the Netherlands and France in May–June 1940, some suitable ones escaped to England, and were leased on a time-charter basis. The largest ones, all owned by the famous towage company L Smit and Co., were *Roode Zee* and *Thames* – built in 1938 – *Lauwerszee* (1930), *Schelde* (1926), *Witte Zee* (1926) and the very powerful, 4000 hp *Zwarte Zee*, built in 1933, which arrived towing an unfinished Dutch destroyer. They were all requisitioned by the Admiralty, but continued to fly the Dutch flag. They were managed by a civilian company, Messrs JD McLaren Ltd., of Dorking, on the Admiralty's behalf, so the civilian crews – and this is an important point – were never subject to naval discipline.

Holland's most modern tug, the *Hudson*, built in 1939, was not in Europe when the country was overrun. She worked briefly for the French authorities, and from June 1940 was based at Freetown before arriving in England in December 1942.

The Admiralty did not list her as a rescue tug, although the work she did when at Freetown and later in the Mediterranean certainly merited this description, and she was often described as such. In October 1943, her managers wrote of her that since arriving in England she 'has made two voyages to the Mediterranean, assisting fleets of landing craft outward bound, taking them in tow during repairs in mid-ocean, and casting them off again, which you will appreciate required a very high standard of seamanship'.[1]

Some French tugs had also escaped, and the largest were acquired for the Rescue Tug Service. They were: *Mastodonte*, *Mammouth*, *Attentif*, *Champion* and *Abeille IV*, and they were all requisitioned and given British crews. The Belgian tug *Goliath* also escaped. Initially this had a Belgian crew, but in December 1940 they were replaced by a Dutch one, and from then on she flew the Dutch flag until her master refused orders two days before the Normandy landings in June 1944.

A mission to the United States in 1940 was only able to purchase two suitable tugs: *Sabine* and *Sea Giant*. Both were given British T.124T crews and flew the White Ensign. A third, *Bascobel*, was transferred in 1941 to the Ministry of War Transport under the Lend-Lease Act and was renamed *Empire Bascobel*. *Sabine*, incidentally, was the tug aboard which the movie star Marie Dressler made her film *Tugboat Annie* in 1933. *Sabine* was elderly (1917), but had a modern towing winch and a speed of thirteen knots. She did much useful work, bringing disabled vessels back to the Humber where she was stationed. *Sea Giant*, the former USS *Contocook*, was based at North Shields. She was on permanent one-hour notice, as there was a lot of enemy activity – particularly coastal bombing and minelaying – and most of the casualties brought in were coastal ships. Her second mate, Bill Stewart, later described her as being only suitable for coastal towage, though she had first-class accommodation.[2]

These reinforcements should have eased the shortage until some of the new Assurance class were commissioned. If it did, it did not last long, for when, in March 1941, the First Sea Lord, Admiral Sir Dudley Pound, suggested, in a distinctive green handwritten note, that Nore Command needed more rescue tugs, his request had to be turned down. As a memorandum from the CCRT to the Director of the Trade Division pointed out: 'Requests for further Rescue Tugs are being continually received from all the Commanders-in-Chiefs [except Portsmouth] ... these requests cannot at present be met.'[3]

The distribution of rescue tugs at that time shows only Western Approaches Command had adequately powered T.124T-manned rescue tugs suitable for work in the North Atlantic, and by February 1941 thirteen commissioned, Red Ensign and Dutch rescue tugs were based at Campbeltown for work in the North-West Approaches.[4] A high percentage stationed elsewhere were still civilian-manned and too underpowered to operate in anything but sheltered waters. Naturally, the distribution list continually changed, and on 4 April 1941, the CCRT made alterations because of attacks on shipping in St George's Channel, and because he intended to make more use of Iceland as a rescue tug base. This meant towing more salvaged ships to the UK for repair, which could only be done by rescue tugs.

SUPERMAN'S CENTURY

Two of the most experienced rescue tugs attached to Western Approaches were *Seaman* and *Superman*, and they often operated together out of Campbeltown. In June 1941, they tackled a particularly awkward tow, and one that did not end as happily as had the resurrection of *Imperial Transport*. While anchored in

Lough Foyle, Northern Ireland – a convenient jumping off place for the Atlantic convoy routes – *Superman* received a signal from FOIC Greenock to proceed with *Seaman* to the assistance of the 2491-ton British merchantman *Gravelines*. A straggler from convoy HX-127, she had been torpedoed off the northern Irish coast north-west of Bloody Foreland. They arrived at the ship's estimated position at midnight, but the search was delayed until dawn as the visibility was poor.

Gravelines was eventually sighted at 07.30, with the ASW trawler HMS *St Kenan* standing by her. She had been struck amidships and the whole of her midship section was awash. All the surviving twenty-five crew members [the master and ten of the crew had been killed] had already been transferred to one of the convoy's escorts, so the trawler put some of her own crew on board to make fast the rescue tugs' tow ropes. The hook-up was completed at 09.50, but by evening the stern half of the ship was starting to list to port and the fore part to starboard. Later the stern half broke away, but remained afloat with about thirty feet of it sticking out of the water. 'After this,' the skipper of *Superman*, Lt H Tarbottan RNR, drily commented in his report, 'the fore half towed moderately well.'[5]

The following morning, when abreast the Mull of Kintyre in a freshening east-north-east wind and a choppy sea, the tow took a heavy list to starboard and lost much of its deck cargo of timber. Half an hour later, it laid over on its side with the masthead in the water, preventing any further headway. After some hours using various tactics to try to bring it upright, the hulk righted itself but retained a twenty-five-degree list to starboard, and both rescue tugs recommenced towing. It was heavy-going and Kames Bay was not reached until 23.00, where the hulk was moored to a buoy. However, unlike *Imperial Transport*, nothing could be done with the remains of *Gravelines* – the stern was never recovered – and the following year the hulk was broken up for scrap.

Just retrieving part of *Gravelines* would presumably not have counted as one of the hundred successes with which *Lloyd's Shipping Gazette* credited *Superman* while commanded by Tarbottan, Lt Ernest Jones RNR, a Bristol Channel skipper in peacetime, or one of the Rescue Tug Service's most successful commanding officers, Lt JEL Brice RNR. Under the headline '*Superman* gets a century', the article eulogised *Superman*'s record of escorting one hundred convoys without losing a single ship she had been sent to save:

> The fact that the *Superman* operated in that
> stretch of the North Sea known as 'E-boat Alley'
> during the peak of enemy activity is a measure
> of her performance. Her contribution to the total
> of salved shipping is very large. She has enabled
> millions of pounds' worth of vital cargoes to reach
> these shores when they would otherwise have gone
> to the bottom of the Atlantic or the
> North Sea...
> As a fighting ship also, *Superman* has something
> to be proud of. She claims one enemy aircraft
> destroyed and one probable. Her guns have joined
> in beating off air and E-boat attacks, and three of
> her crew have been wounded in combat by attacking
> aircraft...[6]

Superman also played a valiant part in the Battle of the Atlantic, achieving something of a record by bringing four stricken ships to safety in five days. The closest of many close shaves she experienced occurred when she went to the rescue of a rammed ASW trawler. The incident was described by Sub-Lt

Brian Murphy RNVR, who joined the *Superman* as a stoker eight years earlier and was now her second engineer:

> We had made fast the tow rope and were just getting under way when the trawler's full load of depth charges came adrift and went over the side. I still don't know exactly what happened after that except that there was the biggest all-time record in explosions, and I found myself extricating myself from the galley stove. Another ship, which had a grandstand view, told us afterwards that they didn't know whether the *Superman* was coming down keel or funnel first! All that happened to her was a twenty-eight-degree list caused by the shifting of the coal in the bunkers.[6]

The 'probable' to which the article was referring was almost certainly the attack on *Superman* by a Heinkel bomber on 4 March 1942, when the rescue tug was commanded by Brice, and was helping to shepherd a convoy along 'E-boat Alley'. As Brice later wrote in his report:

> The first attack was made from the port quarter along the fore and aft line of the ship. Sub-Lt Mackay RNVR, who was on the bridge at the time put the helm hard to port, as three bombs left the plane. This avoiding action saved the ship as the bombs only missed by about twenty feet on the starboard bow. This ship answers her helm very quickly. The Oerlikon gun opened fire and got in several hits on the plane. The rear gunner of the plane opened fire. Several shells from the Oerlikon

hit and the rear gunner did not open fire again during the course of the action.

The plane appeared to lose height for a moment and then banked to renew the attack from ahead.
The .5 gunners were then able to bring their gun
to bear. There was quite a period of manoeuvring
for position; *Superman* was trying to bring both
.5 [machine guns] forward and Oerlikon aft to bear
and make him attack down wind to increase his leeway.
He then attacked from ahead at about 1000 feet. The
.5 gun hit him with a good burst, [as] he swept over
our mastheads, [but] the .5 gun was hit and jammed,
and both gunner and loader were wounded. The men
remained at their posts and attempted to clear the gun
even though wounded.[7]

The plane flew off and, keeping at a good distance, began circling around, sometimes out of sight:

He then attacked from the port quarter with canon
gun and machine guns. The Oerlikon got in a good
burst right into the plane and he swerved away. He lost
height but was climbing again before he disappeared in
the mist. Very shortly afterwards the sound of a plane
diving steeply was heard, then a thud; no more was
seen of the plane.[7]

For helping to achieve *Superman*'s century record, and 'for good services in action against enemy aircraft', Brice and Mackay and three ratings, Deckhand Edwin Lamswood, Able Seaman George Tilney and Fireman William Johnson, were all mentioned in despatches.[8]

One of the most exciting incidents in her career [*Lloyds Shipping Gazette* concluded] was when the convoy of which she was part escort was attacked by 18 E-boats. Two torpedoes fired at the tug missed their target. Her guns helped to smash up the attack and she picked up 37 survivors from a ship, which had been sunk. In fact, the saving of life is as much her charge as the saving of ships. Her biggest life-saving feat was to take off 58 survivors from a whale factory ship. On another occasion she saved the crew of an Iceland trawler which a Dornier attacked after making an unsuccessful attempt against the *Superman*.[6]

SALVONIA'S WAR

Of the commercial ocean tugs with which the Rescue Tug Service began the war, only the 150 ft, 571-ton *Salvonia* was classified by 1944 as being capable of operating in any weather (see Appendix). By then she was stationed on neutral territory, the Azores, and so was civilian-manned and managed, but at the start of the war she had been requisitioned by the Admiralty, and armed with a twelve-pounder gun, two Oerlikons and two Lewis guns. With 1350 ihp, she had a speed of ten to twelve knots and an endurance of at least fourteen days.

As will be seen, she had a remarkable career and was the model for the Assurance class, the Rescue Tug Service's backbone during the Second World War. From the start she had a busy time of it. Notices of the distribution of naval salvage money in *The London Gazette* records that between the outbreak of war and the end of 1939, members of her crew received salvage money for SS *Tongariro* and SS *Stratford*,

Sketch by E.G. Martin of *Zaree* (courtesy Martin family)

Great City after being beached at St Mary's, Scilly Isles, by rescue tugs, June 1917. Her cargo proved lethal (courtesy Isles of Scilly Museum)

Roysterer, one of the First World War Resolve Class rescue tugs retained by
the Admiralty. She is seen here towing HMS *Eridge* into Alexandria after
the Hunt Class destroyer was torpedoed, August 1942 (IWM)

HMS *Minona*. She was used for officers' accommodation and
as the Rescue Tugs' base ship at Campbeltown

Harbour tugs taking the remains of SS *Imperial Transport* to the Clyde after
a torpedo had broken her in two, February 1940. The aft part was brought
to Kilchattan Bay, Isle of Bute, by *Buccaneer* (courtesy Bute Museum)

The crew of *Superman* watching their tow, an Admiralty Floating Dock
(AFD), September 1941 (courtesy Joanna Barron)

Heave Ho! This publicity photograph shows the massive size of the
18-inch towrope compared to the arms of those hauling it in

The more modern rescue tugs had towing winches.
This one belonged to *Freebooter*

The rescue tug, *Jaunty*, steaming full speed towards the sinking aircraft carrier, HMS *Eagle*, during Operation PEDASTAL, August 1942. She rescued over 200 survivors (IWM). Inset: A Malta stamp issued to commemorate PEDASTAL's 70th anniversary

St Day, one of the First World War Saint Class to operate, 1939–45. She was stationed at Gibraltar. *Inset:* Charlie Ghent served aboard *St Day*, one of 215 Newfoundlanders to volunteer for the Rescue Tug Service (photos courtesy Charlie Ghent)

Salvonia, one of the Service's most successful rescue tugs

Nimble, the only one of her class to operate during the war (IWM)

Masterful, a Lend-Lease Favorite Class rescue tug,
She undertook an epic tow off the African coast

The Dutch rescue tug *Zwarte Zee* towing *Flora MacDonald* into Freetown after the Liberty ship had been torpedoed in the Atlantic, May 1943. Her valuable cargo was saved but she continued to burn for several weeks and became a constructive total loss (IWM)

Lt JEL Brice MBE RNR, commanding *Prosperous*, distributing sprigs of lucky heather to celebrate her first anniversary of commissioning, November 1943. She had just returned to port unharmed after three days of constant air attacks (IWM)

Cdr EG Martin RNVR. He did much to develop the Rescue Tug Service, 1917-18, and ran the rescue tug base at Campbeltown, 1941-44 (courtesy Martin family)

Lt-Cdr Owen Jones RNR wearing the OBE he was awarded after his rescue tug, *Seaman* downed a German Condor bomber, April 1941 (courtesy Hutton Press)

Lt 'Robbie' Robinson RNVR was in charge of training the T.124T recruits at Campbeltown

Destiny's football team, Gibraltar, May 1943 (courtesy Peter Sanders)

and in the first half of 1940 for SS *City of Roubaix*, SS *Ville de Bruges* and SS *Agia Varvara*. Some of these were standard peacetime tows, but valuable ships were saved that might otherwise have been wrecked or picked off by a passing U-boat. Perhaps because of this exceptional record, her commanding officer, Lt Reginald Chudleigh RNR, was gazetted for the OBE in July 1940.[9]

Then in August 1940, while stationed on the Clyde, *Salvonia* was dispatched to help the 15,434-ton Dutch liner, SS *Volendam*, of the Holland America Line. This ship had been crippled by a freak torpedo attack near midnight on 29 August, some two hundred miles north of Northern Ireland while part of an outward-bound convoy, OB-205. 'There was a terrific explosion,' the liner's master later wrote, 'a column of water was thrown up which splashed over the fore part of the ship and the bridge, flames were seen on port and starboard sides near No. 1 hatch, and later fragments of a torpedo were found on the fore deck and bridge.'[10]

The ship had been struck on the starboard side, sixty feet from the bow, the torpedo making a hole in the ship's side big enough to drive a double-decker bus through, and several smaller ones as well. The ship immediately took on a list to port, and it was found that No. 1 and No. 2 holds were filling rapidly. With the danger of the ship turning turtle and sinking, and with the weather worsening by the minute, the master decided to transfer his six hundred and six passengers, including three hundred and twenty children who were being taken to the safety of North America, to other ships in the convoy. Despite the deteriorating weather, all the passengers managed to get away in the lifeboats, and were picked up by nearby ships, though not without difficulty. Some of the children had to be hoisted on board one ship in a banana basket.

By 14.00 the next day, the wind had freshened to force 7 or 8, and the master of *Volendam* now requested assistance. At dawn on 31 August, the *Salvonia* was seen approaching. She made three failed attempts to shoot a line across, before the fourth was successful. The bows of the liner were too badly damaged, so the hawser was secured aft on her starboard side, and she was then towed stern first towards the Clyde.

The situation remained critical, but by late afternoon the wind and sea had decreased, and just after midnight on 2 September the *Salvonia* and her tow reached the Firth of Clyde. There they were met by harbour tugs, which helped beach the liner in Kames Bay, and the following morning a diver recovered an intact torpedo, without its warhead, lying on the starboard side in No. 1 hold. It was presumed at the time that two torpedoes had been fired in quick succession, and that the explosion of the first destroyed the warhead of the second.

But the torpedo could have been a dud, as U-boats were plagued by faulty torpedoes during the early part of the war. Admiral Karl Dönitz, the U-boat C-in-C, commented in his diary that at least thirty per cent were duds. The Norwegian campaign in April–May 1940 brought matters to a head, and the problems were eventually solved. Despite this, by the end of May 1940, early on in their 'Happy Hour', U-boats had sunk two hundred and forty-one ships amounting to 853,000 tons.[11] One wonders what the total would have been if their torpedoes had been more reliable.

Problems with their torpedoes did not prevent U-boats from causing havoc among convoy SC-7, which left Sydney on Nova Scotia's Cape Breton Island on 4 October 1940. SC was the designation for a 'slow' convoy, moving at six to seven knots, while the faster HX convoys, which left from Halifax, Nova Scotia, were expected to maintain eight to nine knots. SC-7 comprised an odd assortment of thirty-five old merchant ships of various nationalities that could never have kept up in an HX convoy, but they carried essential cargoes for the British war effort such as scrap iron, timber, pulpwood and steel.

Once clear of Canadian waters, the convoy only had a single escort, the sloop HMS *Scarborough*, until it was handed over to escort ships from the Western Approaches, which would shepherd them into Liverpool. By the time they reached Rockall Bank, the convoy had lost four ships to U-boats, three of them stragglers. But the convoy's luck did not really run out until the night of 18/19 October when, in an early, if rudimentary, use of the 'wolf-pack' tactics that caused such havoc during the Battle of the Atlantic, the convoy was attacked by five U-boats, which sank sixteen ships, making twenty in all, the highest loss a convoy suffered during the entire war. The 'wolf-pack' then went on to ambush an HX convoy coming up behind SC-7, and sank twelve more.

One of the ships torpedoed that night from SC-7 was the 4255-ton *Blairspey*, and her master later gave a graphic account of what happened.[12] It was very dark with no moon and the visibility was poor, half a mile or perhaps less. At 22.30, while about two hundred miles from land, a torpedo struck the ship on her port side by No. 1 hold about fifty to sixty feet from the bow. Unusually, there was no loud explosion, just a dull thud, and at first the master did not realise what had happened. A large column of water deluged the bridge, but there was no flame, smoke or smell. The ship staggered slightly and took on a small list to port before straightening up again. Then she stopped, as a steam joint had been broken in the engine room, which quickly filled with steam, but when an escort appeared the master reported he was confident he could get his ship into port, as his engineers were making the necessary repairs:

But while this was being done we were torpedoed again at 1am on 19 October, on the starboard side between No. 1 and No. 2 hold about 100 feet from the bow. We were all at our stations at the time. A column of water and some timber was thrown up. I gave orders to abandon ship. The explosion sounded like a dull thud and there was no flame. While abandoning ship we were again torpedoed on the port side amidships about 150 feet from the bow. There was about a 5-minute interval between these two torpedoes. I think there were 2 submarines firing at us, because the ship had stopped and was just drifting to leeward.[12]

Both lifeboats with all the crew got safely away, though there was a scary moment when a U-boat surfaced near them and someone in the conning tower demanded to know, in perfect English, the ship's name. But it then submerged and the lifeboats went their separate ways. The master set sail for the nearest land, while the mate decided there was better hope of rescue if he kept his lifeboat close to the crippled ship, which, despite having three torpedoes fired into her, miraculously remained afloat. This was where the *Salvonia*, dispatched from Campbeltown to find another damaged ship, came upon the mate's lifeboat on the evening of 19 October, and took the survivors aboard.

After closely inspecting the *Blairspey*, which must have resembled a giant colander, Lt Stanley Strowger RNR,[13] now the *Salvonia*'s commanding officer, decided there was a fifty-fifty chance of salvaging her. But the weather at the time was too bad to connect up so he stood off and waited until first light, hoping the weather would improve. It did, and on her way back to the *Blairspey* the rescue tug came across two more lifeboats filled with survivors from two other merchant ships, the *Sedgepool* and the *Clintonia*, and took the survivors aboard. All that day, Sunday 20 October, the *Salvonia* towed the wallowing *Blairspey*. On the following one, flares were seen in the water and the *Salvonia* went to investigate. She found yet another lifeboat full of survivors from two steamers, the *Port Gisborne* and the *Saint Malo*, which had been sunk from HX-77, the convoy in front of SC-7. The *Salvonia* took them aboard, bringing the total number of survivors to eighty-five.

It took until Friday 25 October for the *Salvonia* to tow the *Blairspey* into the Clyde, a full week after the freighter had been first torpedoed. Such was the damage she suffered that the engineers' accommodation protruded six feet out from her side. Remarkably, she was repaired and returned to service under a new name, *Empire Spey*, and saw out the war.[14]

The last boatload of survivors the *Salvonia* took aboard included a very brave man whose story cannot be passed over. Aged thirteen, he had run away to sea as a deck boy. He later returned to shore and became a prosperous businessman, and when the war came he chose to serve in the Merchant Navy. His name was Able Seaman Sydney Herbert Light, and his courage and determination before the *Salvonia* picked him out of the water subsequently earned him the George Medal and Lloyd's War Medal for Bravery at Sea. This is the citation from *The London Gazette* of 4 February 1941, which failed to name the *Salvonia* in its citation:

> Seaman Light's ship [*Port Gisborne*] was torpedoed at night. One boat was swamped in lowering, with the result that all hands except Able Seaman Light and a greaser were thrown out. Light released the forward fall, and with the greaser holding the boat off eight other men were got aboard. The boat then drifted

away from the sinking ship. As she lay broadside on
the seas swept over her and daylight found her still
afloat, but awash and with her crew worn out with
baling. Able Seaman Light, who had taken charge,
stepped the mast and set sail. Some ships were sighted,
but they failed to see the boat. Heavy rain squalls
caused the exhausted crew great hardship. Seaman Light
kept his men in good heart and they sailed on until
a lifeboat was sighted with no oars, sails or any sign
of life except a canvas tent amidships. This boat was
found to have sixteen men from a torpedoed merchant
ship [*Saint Malo*] on board. Seaman Light towed the
derelict boat in spite of rising seas and wind, which
made it necessary to bale the whole time. They sighted
an unknown rocky shore, and decided to lie off till
daylight, but the boats were driven out to sea again.
In a dead calm the men rowed all day till they were
worn out.
In the towed boat, men were giving up, and Seaman
Light went over into it and himself massaged two
men and gave them his stockings, and dressed their
wounds. Later, in his own boat again, he massaged
a deck boy who was in great pain, and bound up
his feet with blanket strips. Provisions and water
were placed in the towed boat and later the wind
rose again. After ten days of privation, weariness
and danger they sighted a British ship [*Salvonia*].
She answered a flare from the boat and came to the
rescue. In a steep sea the exhausted crews were with
difficulty transferred to the steamer, where every care
was given to them. Seaman Light's courage, leadership,
self-sacrifice and stout heart thus saved not only his
own crew but the sixteen men whose boat he had

towed and tended so well. This fine seaman kept a
log of the whole voyage.[15]

When the *Salvonia* landed the exhausted survivors at Greenock,
Light was asked where he might be found ashore. He asked
what was the best hotel in the town and was told the Tontine.
'Then that's my address,' said Light. His first stop was a naval
outfitter where he bought a new outfit, telling the outfitter to
send the bill to his banker. He then went off to enquire about
the survivors from the lifeboat he had towed, some of whom
had been sent to hospital to recover, and also about the men
from his own lifeboat. To his fury he was told that as they
were penniless they had been sent to the workhouse. 'His rage
at such an indignity being offered to the heroic seamen brought
forth such a torrent of invective that matters were soon put
right.'[15]

Unlike *The London Gazette*, Light remembered the *Salvonia*
and the last entry in his log, which he meticulously recorded on
the back of labels soaked off tins of food, read:

I will take this opportunity to express appreciation
on behalf of the survivors and myself for the
kind consideration and generosity offered
to us by the officers and men of HMS *Salvonia*,
and would suggest that a suitably worded letter
be sent them by the Directors of the Company.[16]

He was obviously so impressed with the Rescue Tug Service
that he joined it himself and in February 1941 one newspaper
reported he was the second officer in an unnamed rescue tug
based at Trinidad.

SOLO RESCUE

Though the practice of two tugs working together was implemented whenever possible, and the escort of an ASW trawler was supposed to be mandatory, the *Salvonia* often had to work alone. For example, on 11 February 1941 the FOIC Greenock signalled the *Salvonia*, then stationed at Campbeltown under the command by Lt. SF Strowger, that she was to proceed to the south end of Colonsay island and tow in the 2325-ton SS *Maclaren* that had eight hundred and fifty standards of timber aboard. The ship had struck the rocks off Ardskinish Point, Colonsay, during the early hours of 8 February, and had lost her rudder and stern frame. She had also damaged her propeller, and her bottom under her forepeak and No. 1 hold. She was anchored in twelve fathoms, but was in danger of hitting the rocks again when the tide changed.

Dense fog shrouded the damaged ship when the *Salvonia* arrived in the area, and she signalled the freighter to send her call letters at 1245 BST and afterwards to blow her whistle at frequent intervals. This enabled the rescue tug to take a bearing on the ship and she was eventually found with the Port Askaig lifeboat standing by. By now the fog had lifted slightly and SS *Maclaren* was instructed to have her anchor chain ready to connect with the towing hawser, which consisted of one hundred and twenty fathoms of eighteen-inch manila rope and a five-inch steel wire hawser.

The weather was moderate, with a force 4 wind. But progress was slow, two to three knots, as the damaged ship towed badly. She was down by the head and, without a rudder or propeller to steer her, sheered very badly. Soon she was reporting that her forepeak and No. 1 hold were leaking, and with night coming on, those aboard her were becoming increasingly anxious:

Eventually they signalled the *Salvonia*: 'Where are we going?' to which the *Salvonia* replied: 'Toward Point Greenock.'

Later, probably seeing her tow further down by the head, the *Salvonia* asked: 'What is your condition. Will you stand tow to Clyde?'

Maclaren: 'Why not take us to Oban.'

Salvonia: 'You will be unable to get repairs done there.'

Maclaren: 'No, but we can get water under control.'

Salvonia: 'If you cannot keep water under control we will take you to Islay Sound and pump you out.'

Maclaren: 'No. We will keep you informed about water.'

Fifteen minutes later, the *Maclaren* signalled, with perhaps a hint of panic: 'Can you take me to safe anchorage. It is not prudent to go to sea.'

Salvonia: 'I am increasing speed and altering course for Orsay Light. If necessary, will take you into Loch Indaal.'

Maclaren: 'OK, but at your own risk.'

Salvonia: 'Where are you leaking and by how much?'

Maclaren: 'No. 1 hold nine feet. Increase not yet known.'

Salvonia: 'Let us know increase.'

Maclaren: 'What lights shall we show tonight?'

Salvonia: 'Show no lights. Do not signal after dark unless in emergency and only use small light.'

Maclaren: 'Have one blade on propeller. Will try slow ahead.'

Maclaren: 'Have 11 feet of water in No. 1 hold. Pumps won't take it.'

> *Maclaren*: 'My DG gear [degaussing] is out of order.'
>
> *Salvonia*: 'Will take you by swept channel. No need to worry.'
>
> However, the ship's master had every reason to worry as he later signalled: 'Water port side No. 1 14 feet. Starboard side No. 1 11 feet. Forepeak full.'
>
> And a little later: 'Water 18 feet.'

But then: 'Water same', which must have come as a relief to Lt Strowger. However, there were other dangers now present and he signalled: 'Switch your lights out. Aircraft attacking shipping in vicinity.'[17]

It must have been a nail-biting few hours before rescue tug and tow reached the safety of Greenock, but such work was duly rewarded when in March 1941 the CCRT recommended awards to *Salvonia*'s crew:

> *Salvonia* has been employed in Western Approaches on Rescue work since the early days of the War, and has been instrumental in salving 13 ships with a total tonnage of 81,877 tons… [She] has spent long periods at sea unescorted and always subject to attack by enemy submarines and aircraft. She has worked with considerable determination and maintained great efficiency.[17]

Strowger was singled out for praise, the CCRT writing that he had 'displayed great courage, devotion to duty and has set a wonderful example of cheerfulness under trying conditions', and that he should receive 'substantial recognition' for his services. There is no record that he did so, but in the King's Birthday Honours List of July 1941, *Salvonia*'s chief engineer,

Sub-Lt GA Whittle, was awarded the MBE, one of her firemen, SH Gifford the BEM, and the chief radio officer, WE Sawnay, and one of the seamen, GM Foster, were mentioned in despatches.

Then, in August, the Director of the Trade Division forwarded to the Admiralty's Honours and Awards Committee a list of the names of the ships *Salvonia* had saved: two warships [HMS *Cheshire* and HMS *Taku*, a submarine] and seventeen merchant ships totalling 101,512 tons. He suggested such outstanding work was worthy of conveying to the rescue tug crew their Lordships' appreciation of this outstanding record. 'With the winter months before them, it is felt that some official encouragement would be an added incentive to continue their good work.'[18] Their Lordships agreed and a letter of congratulations was duly dispatched.

Even while this correspondence was being disseminated, the *Salvonia* was involved in another – and highly unusual – towing operation. She was at Reykjavik when she received a signal to sail immediately to the south coast, to a position near Thorlakshofn. Somewhat to the crew's surprise, when they arrived there it wasn't an Allied merchantman that had run aground but a German Type VIIC U-boat, *U-570*. This had been damaged by depth charges from an Allied aircraft on 27 August 1941 and had subsequently surrendered to naval forces, which had converged on the area to finish her off. Her crew had disposed of the U-boat's Enigma cipher machine and codebooks, but she was, nevertheless, a valuable prize, and the ships surrounding her were ordered to prevent her at all costs from being scuttled.

One of the ships approached the U-boat and, with considerable enterprise, signalled her crew: 'If you make any attempt to scuttle I will not save anyone, and will fire on your rafts and floats', to which the U-boat crew replied: 'I cannot scuttle or abandon; Save us tomorrow please.'[19] Saved they were and the U-boat was beached to ensure she did not sink. *Salvonia*'s second officer, Sub-Lt Louis Colmans RNR, later recorded:

> On arrival off Thorlakshofn, we found the U-boat lying broadside to the beach and rolling heavily in the surf. Anchoring as close as possible to the shore, our boat was lowered and rowed ashore with Lt-Commander Watchlin [the Salvage Officer from Reykjavik] and myself. We had some difficulty boarding the submarine due to the heavy rolling, but managed to do so with some of our crew members.'[21]

An initial examination revealed that while considerable damage had been sustained to some electrical gear, and there was water and flotsam sloshing around, it looked as if the U-boat had escaped major damage. It was then examined from a salvage point of view and it was decided to put a heavy five-inch wire strop around her hull. This proved difficult, but achievable. By the time the strop was in position a party of naval experts, flown out from Britain, had boarded the submarine, having finished their journey from Reykjavik by Bren gun carrier and finally by pony. They pumped out the surplus water, worked on the engines, and got the U-boat into a seaworthy condition. One hundred and twenty fathoms of eighteen-inch manila rope and fifty fathoms of five-inch wire were then connected by the *Salvonia*. Colmans reported that it was a rather heavy job but noted that the *Salvonia* had 'an excellent crew, consisting in the main of Brixham fishermen'.

There was a good tide and the U-boat refloated without too much difficulty, and *Salvonia* towed her round to Hvalfjord. 'To all of us on *Salvonia*,' the report ended, 'this was a great day entering the fjord with so many British and American warships at anchor there.'[20]

The U-boat was repaired and relaunched as HMS *Graph* and the following year took part in three operational patrols before being decommissioned in February 1944. The next month she was being towed to the Clyde to be scrapped when the tow broke in high winds and she was driven ashore and wrecked.

Colmans' report also recorded that on 6 September 1941 the *Salvonia* received yet another message of appreciation for her work with *U-570*, this time from the admiral commanding Iceland Command. It read: 'Hearty congratulations on successful completion of a difficult and important operation.'

DUTCH LOSSES AND PROBLEMS

The casualty rate for the Dutch rescue tugs was high. In October 1940, *Lauwerszee* was sunk by a mine near Plymouth with the loss of twelve of her crew, and the next month *Witte Zee* struck rocks near Port Eynon, South Wales, and became a total loss. *Zwarte Zee* was another early casualty when a bomb narrowly missed her in Falmouth harbour in August 1940 and she sank in shallow water. It took until February 1941 to repair her, after which she was stationed at Campbeltown. On 17 March 1941, she and one of the new Assurance class, *Prudent*, were ordered to assist ships from the eastbound convoy HX-112, which had been attacked by several U-boats. Many of the ships were tankers carrying precious fuel supplies, and the convoy was heavily escorted, but even though two U-boats were sunk, six ships were torpedoed.

The two rescue tugs found nothing at the co-ordinates they had been given. They were then directed to the north-east and contact was made on the morning of 19 March with one of the escort trawlers which was standing by the 8138-ton Norwegian tanker *Beduin*.

'Vessel apparently whole,' *Prudent*'s commanding officer, Lt Guy Quine RNR, later reported, 'although almost vertical with only portion of stern above water.' A message was sent to the FOIC Greenock saying the ship was not salvageable, and the two rescue tugs then proceeded to the assistance of another Norwegian tanker, the 9000-ton *Ferm*. When she was reached on the evening of 19 March, the outcome for any rescue attempt seemed equally bleak, for Quine later wrote that she 'had a very heavy list to port with main deck line under water with seas breaking over her'.

Valuable time was lost when a boat sent by the trawler escort was nearly swamped when it came alongside the *Prudent*. It was, anyway, much too small to take the extra men needed to connect up with the damaged tanker. The light was going fast and the commanding officers of both tugs agreed that any further attempts to board the *Ferm* must wait until morning.

During the night the wind freshened from westward, and at daybreak, with a heavy westerly swell running, it became impossible to board the *Ferm*. Seas were now breaking right over her and any boat trying to come alongside under her lee would have been swamped. It now looked to Quine as if the *Ferm* had been torpedoed aft as well as forward, as he could see she was now sinking by the stern. Another escort offered to try to board the tanker when the weather moderated. It failed to do so, and that evening the *Ferm* turned turtle and had to be sunk by gunfire from the escort. Both rescue tugs then returned to base.[21]

Perhaps that should have been the end of the matter. But there were undercurrents at work against the Dutch, and before long the British liaison officer aboard *Zwarte Zee*, having already criticised the under-manning of the Dutch tugs, submitted a report to EG Martin. In it he accused the Dutch of being commercially motivated. They regarded themselves 'as neutral victims of the war and are not actuated by any military or patriotic spirit'. If they weren't being paid what they should have been – and it seems they weren't – they didn't feel obliged to put themselves out.

The liaison officer reported that Quine had wanted to act to save the *Ferm* – he was probably aware that she was carrying thousands of tons of precious fuel – but had been dissuaded by *Zwarte Zee*'s more experienced master. The Dutchman had been equally negative about attempting to save the *Beduin*, saying the tanker would probably sink and he'd lose his towing gear.[21]

Martin forwarded this report to the CCRT and commented that he, too, had doubts about the morale aboard the *Zwarte Zee*, and about the *Thames* as well. It was impossible not to feel that their masters were 'always reluctant to take their ships to sea and welcome any excuse to delay sailing'. He did not think this was true of Captain Kalkman of the *Schelde*. 'He has, on occasion, been unable to sail punctually on receipt of orders owing to his men refusing duty; but has always been glad to do so immediately I have been able to complete his crew with British ratings.'

Such behaviour would surely have infuriated Martin, though he also wrote that he considered *Zwarte Zee* and *Thames* 'the two finest tugs afloat'. There is a suspicion that Martin did not think much of the *Zwarte Zee*'s liaison officer as he concluded his report by remarking: 'With regard to the opinion expressed that *Ferm* might have been taken in tow, I would observe that the weather was rough, and that Liaison Officers serving in rescue tugs have not enough sea experience to enable them to form entirely reliable opinions on highly technical questions of seamanship.'[21]

The Dutch certainly annoyed the FOIC Greenock, as he commented that 'experience of them at Greenock has shown that they only obey orders when it is convenient to themselves'. It appeared there was something seriously amiss with how the Dutch crews were being managed, and the matter continued to exercise the CCRT and the company managing the tugs. Then, in April, the liaison officer aboard the *Zwarte Zee* submitted another report. In it he pointed out that the 'system of higher pay and less men than on British tugs means a lot of difficulty over manning the armament and over leave and watch in harbour. The system of higher pay in harbour, i.e. 3s 6d extra "home port money" per day, cannot possibly make officers or men keen on going to sea'[21] and that the increased demands being made by the crew was already in the hands of the local union.

By then the *Zwarte Zee* was stationed at Iceland, as part of the CCRT's plan to make more use of it as a base, and the Director of Sea Transport commented that by posting her to the island, the crew would at least be removed from contact with union officials. The *Thames* was already there and in May her British liaison officer wrote an indignant report, strongly denying the crew had low morale, and described this accusation as 'astonishing'.[21] He listed the work the *Thames* had undertaken while stationed at Iceland – most of it was humdrum harbour work, quite unsuitable for a rescue tug – and added that the crew had recently donated £175 to assist in the Allied war effort, and had 'received the congratulations of the Base Accountant Officer'. Certainly, before being moved to Iceland, the *Thames* had already brought in a total of twelve disabled ships totalling 58,380 tons. This had included bringing in the 3292-ton SS *Baltara* to Rothesay Bay after the freighter had been torpedoed in mid-Atlantic on 9 March 1941, a tow of some eight hundred miles that took five days.

The *Zwarte Zee* also made at least two valuable rescues at that time. The 10,022-ton Norwegian tanker *Polarsol* was unloading at Liverpool in April 1941 when she received orders from the Admiralty that all ships capable of doing twelve knots or more were to proceed alone, a not unusual order as there was an acute shortage of escort vessels. The *Polarsol* sailed on 22 April for New York, and on 26 April, when about one hundred and fifty miles south of Iceland, she was attacked at dawn by a Focke-Wulf Condor bomber. It came from ahead and raked the ship with its machine guns before dropping its bombs, which hit the after part of the ship, including the engine room. The chief engineer later described how the door to the engine room was blown straight through his accommodation and out the other side.

The *Polarsol* was not adequately armed and could not prevent the bomber returning three times, machine-gunning the decks and dropping more bombs. The tanker was now burning fiercely aft and the crew abandoned ship, but after six hours in the lifeboats they returned, keeping well away from the aft part of the ship, which was still ablaze. Later that evening, the westbound convoy OB-318[22] appeared on the horizon and the *Zwarte Zee*, which was at the rear of it, steamed to the help of the tanker. After the fire had been brought under control, she took the *Polarsol* in tow. The fire continued to burn for twenty-four hours and it was three days before the crew could get into the remains of the engine room, which resembled a crater. Five days later, the *Zwarte Zee* brought the tanker into Rothesay, and she was eventually repaired and put back into service.

The *Zwarte Zee* then rejoined the convoy. On 10 May, this was attacked by a wolf-pack of several U-boats, south-east of Cape Farewell, Greenland's most southerly point, and one of them torpedoed the 4986-ton British freighter *Aelybryn*.

Her crew was taken off by a corvette escort and when the *Zwarte Zee* arrived on 12 May 'she found the ship abandoned and drifting helplessly with her engine room under water', as Leading Signalman George W Watson, one of the liaison team of six aboard the *Zwarte Zee*, later recorded.[23] 'The tug put some of her own men aboard the disabled ship: handling heavy towing cables in rough Atlantic weather is hard work... with the help of the trawler escort the towing tackle was secured. The stern of the *Aelybryn* had collapsed where she was torpedoed, but in spite of the immense risk of bulkheads giving way, the ship was towed all the way back to Reykjavik.'

TORPEDO ANNIE

In March 1943, the *Zwarte Zee* and two other rescue tugs, *Frisky* and the new American-built, Lend-Lease *Oriana*, towed an Admiralty Floating Dock (XXIV) from Louisiana, where it had been built, to Port of Spain, Trinidad, to refuel, and then on to Freetown, Sierra Leone. The passage was delayed at Port of Spain when the three rescue tugs were dispatched to assist the victims of a U-boat attack on the northbound convoy BT-6 (Bahia–Trinidad) off the coast of French Guiana. This consisted of twenty-nine ships, many of whose crews had no convoy experience, so they were 'frequently getting fouled up, showing lights, tooting whistles, sending up flares and even firing rockets, until the escort commander threatened to fire on any vessel that broke the black-out'.[24]

Security, it seemed, was also very lax at Brazilian Bahia, where the same impeccable source recorded that 'Torpedo Annie', 'a handsome redhead who consorted with nobody under the rank of master, was suspected of passing to the Nazis such confidences as she was able to extort during hours of amorous dalliance. This *La Belle Dame sans Merci* owed her unromantic sobriquet to the observed fact that her lovers, shortly after parting, were apt to go down with their ships.'[24]

'Torpedo Annie' certainly served her masters well as far as convoy BT-6 was concerned: one Liberty ship was picked off between Bahia and Recife, and in the early hours of 9 March four other Liberty ships and a British freighter were torpedoed about a hundred miles north of Cayenne. The British freighter sank, but with the help of a local tug, *George G Meade* was taken to Paramaribo and the others were towed back to Trinidad where the *Zwarte Zee* beached *James Smith* at Port of Spain.[25] *James K Polk*, whose master was said to have consorted with 'Torpedo Annie', and *Thomas Ruffin* were declared a constructive total loss, but the others were eventually repaired and returned to service.[26] Having delivered the AFD, the *Zwarte Zee* remained in Freetown, and in May 1943 she towed in another American Liberty ship, *Flora MacDonald*, which had been torpedoed and set on fire. *Zwarte Zee*'s decision to beach her in Freetown harbour saved her cargo of rubber, but the ship continued to burn for over a fortnight, and was declared a total loss.[27] Then, in July, the *Zwarte Zee* towed to Freetown the armed merchant cruiser HMS *Asturias*, torpedoed in the South Atlantic by the Italian submarine *Ammiraglio Cagni*. In three and a half years as a rescue tug, the *Zwarte Zee* saved 128,000 tons of Allied shipping.[28] Quite a record.

The immediate situation with the Dutch must have sorted itself out, for in July 1941 the FOIC Greenock reported that the *Zwarte Zee* had been transferred back to Britain, her liaison officer had been relieved of his duties, and in August the master of *Thames* was awarded an honorary MBE, for his salvage of SS *Baltara*.[29]

THE DUTCH *ANTIC*

Some of the Dutch tugs that had escaped from Holland were too small for the Rescue Tug Service, but the experience of their crews was put to use as soon as rescue tugs became available for them. In 1943, two of the new Assurance class, *Dexterous*[30] and *Antic*, were given Dutch crews, and flew the Dutch flag, but remained under Admiralty orders. It was not a simple transaction, and it exercised the minds of several occupants of the Admiralty for some months, involving as it did Orders in Council and a considerable correspondence.

But the Dutch, as will be seen, remained idiosyncratic to the end. They certainly gave Chas Stringer, an RN signalman, an unusual induction into rescue tugs. On completion of his training, he was assigned to HMS *Edinburgh Castle*, the depot ship at Freetown. This initially drafted him to HMS *Mercator*, a three-masted sailing ship. But as she never put to sea, he was then drafted to the *Antic*, the duty rescue tug at Freetown, as one of the liaison team, with the task of advising on naval radio (RT) procedures, and helping to decode signals. Unlike the UK-based Dutch rescue tugs, the *Antic* was managed by the South African branch of L Smit & Co., on the Admiralty's behalf, while she was based at Freetown, as probably was the *Hudson*. All this caused Stringer some confusion:

> I was, however, extremely encouraged when the skipper explained to me that although it carried a Pennant number, W.141, for all intents and purposes *Antic* was a merchant ship, which might at some point have to go into a neutral port. Because I was a naval rating (and therefore technically barred from neutral countries) it was necessary to sign me on as a crew member masquerading as an 'assistant cook'. For that

> I would be paid £15 per month, allowed a bottle
> of gin a month and a bottle of beer twice a week,
> but without having to carry out any cooking duties!
> This offer far exceeded my navy pay and entitlements
> so I was very happy to become a Deep Sea Rescue
> tugman, but not on T.124T terms, nor a radio
> officer, but just a very unusual, untypical, Ordinary/
> Telegraphist RN.[31]

Stringer stayed in the *Antic* until he was demobbed in 1946 at Chatham. At the RN barracks there he was viewed with some suspicion as they had lost all record of him. They were initially reluctant to pay him the three years' back pay he was entitled to as, thanks to the Dutch captain's generosity, he had not needed to draw it. However, what he didn't know until later was that the captain was drawing £30 a month from Smit's to pay him for being an assistant cook, but only giving him £15 a month!

> But finally and to my delight and surprise they told me
> that in addition to basic pay I was entitled to a shilling
> a day for serving on a foreign ship and sixpence a day
> 'hard lying' money because I slept in a bunk and not a
> hammock![31]

In the spring of 1944, the *Antic* received orders to return to the UK – for the Normandy landings as it turned out – but she was then dispatched to bring in an American destroyer, USS *Barr*, which had been torpedoed in the South Atlantic. The *Antic* towed her to Casablanca, and then helped tow the fighter direction ship HMS *Palomares* – damaged by a mine at the Anzio landings (22 January 1944) during the Italian campaign – from

Gibraltar to Liverpool. By the time she reached Liverpool, the Normandy landings had taken place, though she was in time to tow some replacement units for the artificial harbours constructed there.

In October 1944, the *Antic's* crew took over the *Dexterous* so that the latter's crew could rest after their D-Day exertions, and for the *Antic* to have her boiler cleaned. Later that month, the *Dexterous* was part of a salvage team that removed the *Ole Wegger*, a Norwegian whale factory ship that was blocking the River Seine and preventing the use of Rouen docks.[32] This accomplished, she returned to the UK, the crews swapped back, and the *Antic* then stood by during the landings by Royal Marine Commandos on Walcheren Island on 1 November 1944. This proved to be one of the toughest battles of the war as the island, situated in the mouth of the River Scheldt leading to Antwerp, was heavily fortified, for the Germans knew how vital Antwerp – in Allied hands since September – would be as a supply port for the final Allied push into Germany.

The *Antic* ended the war rescuing and salvaging mined or torpedoed ships along the convoy route to Antwerp. *Champion* and *Sea Giant* were also stationed there, notably extinguishing a raging fire aboard the 4702-ton British freighter *Alan-A-Dale*, which had been run aground in the Scheldt after being torpedoed on 23 December 1944.

In January 1945, the *Antic's* master complained bitterly about the conditions under which his crew had to work. He finished by saying: 'At the moment we seem to fall between the Royal Navy and the Merchant Navy on the one hand and between the British and the Dutch on the other,' and though his complaints were brushed aside by the NOIC Antwerp, one can't help suspecting he had a point.[33]

TROUBLES AND TRAGEDY

The Dutch were naturally worried about their families, and worried too that they might never see their country again, so it is not surprising there were difficulties in assimilating them. An early incident, in June 1940, showed there might be trouble to come. Ten of *Witte Zee*'s crew refused to sail to St Nazaire, as the vessel was not armed. Under the circumstances, and the proximity of the advancing Germans, this seems not unreasonable, but the local police imprisoned them, and they were replaced by RN ratings. Later, the Dutch skipper of the *Antic* also refused to conform when he went alongside a naval sloop in Freetown to pump out water the crew had just used to extinguish a fire. He naturally wanted to place the *Antic* as close to the flooded compartments as possible, but a boat's boom, to which the ship's small boats were moored when in harbour, prevented this. The sloop's duty officer refused to move the boom, so the Dutch skipper came alongside anyway, carrying away the boom and anything that was moored to it.

The C-in-C America and West Indies also aired the complaints he had about the *Roode Zee*, which was based in the West Indies, but in April 1942 the Director of the Trade Division wrote urging him to be diplomatic:

> Experience with Dutch tugs in Home Waters has shown
> that crews require tactful handling. Before rescue tugs
> are used for duties other than rescue work the matter
> should be referred to the Admiralty... Request for escort
> is considered reasonable having regard to the intense
> U-boat activity off the American coast. Master cannot
> be ordered to proceed on work of non-rescue nature
> and persuasion is the only course open.[34]

Again, the matter must have been smoothed over, and the *Roode Zee* assisted several merchant ships in trouble during her time in the West Indies. In July 1942, she rescued survivors from the tanker *Beaconlight*, which had been torpedoed off Trinidad, and two days later she towed another tanker, SS *San Gaspar*, into Port of Spain. But by 1943 the crew wanted to be closer to the action and after helping to tow AFD 53 across the Atlantic, the *Roode Zee* left Gibraltar for the UK on 20 November 1943 and was then transferred to the Ministry of War Transport.

The following April, the *Roode Zee* was towing a part of the MULBERRY prefabricated harbours called a PHOENIX, a massive concrete caisson, when disaster overtook her. The caisson had to be taken from Tilbury in Essex to the south coast in preparation for it being towed across the Channel to the assault beaches after the D-Day landings. So large were some of these caissons – affectionately dubbed 'council houses' – that they had to be towed by two rescue tugs. George Corke, commanding officer of the rescue tug towing with the *Roode Zee*, takes up the story:

> We had to pass through the Straits of Dover in
> the dark, to avoid the Germans spotting us. I was
> towing with the Dutch tug *Roode Zee*. We had passed
> the Straits of Dover safely and were approaching
> Dungeness about 2 o'clock in the morning. E-boats
> were attacking a convoy ahead of us and our destroyer
> escort had left us to assist it. Soon after, we were
> attacked by a single E-boat who luckily for me
> attacked from the south [Corke's must have been the
> inshore rescue tug of the two]. He fired only one
> torpedo, which hit the *Roode Zee* in her fuel tanks,
> and she went up in one flash. I gave the order 'hard
> a-starboard' and circled round the Mulberry to keep

it between me and the E-boat. Eventually the E-boat cleared off, leaving me anchored to the sunken *Roode Zee* and the council house. We cleared up this mess and carried on safely.[35]

There were no survivors from the same crew that had left Holland in *Roode Zee* four years previously.[36]

DUTCH SKILLS HIGHLY VALUED

Whatever they lacked in their willingness to conform, the Dutch certainly made up for with their expert knowledge of ocean towage. This the British could not match, although the comments at one TDC meeting in November 1942 showed they would have liked to.[37] When the CCRT announced that the Admiralty 'were of the opinion that greater use should be made of the towing experience of the crews of those Dutch tugs unsuitable for ocean-going operations, and it was proposed to employ them on some of the newly-built Admiralty tugs', the representative for the British tug owners on the committee protested. He said that as British tug owners hoped to embark on ocean towage after the war in competition with the Dutch, he thought it undesirable they should be given the opportunity of requiring detailed knowledge of the country's largest and most modern tugs. But the shortage of both rescue tugs, and those with the necessary expertise to man them, was too severe, and the following year the *Antic* and *Dexterous* were handed over to the Dutch, and performed admirably.

Undoubtedly, the Dutch were highly valued by the Admiralty, and for their work during the Normandy landings in June 1944 the masters of *Thames* and *Amsterdam* were mentioned in despatches, and the masters of *Dexterous* and *Zwarte Zee* were each awarded the DSC.[38] The latter's decoration was also for assisting the 6034-ton American freighter SS *Antinous*, after she was torpedoed near Trinidad on 23 September 1942, and for rescuing her crew after the freighter had been attacked for a second time.

NOTES

1. Letter from Messrs JD McLaren to J Olyslager dated 8 October 1943. Courtesy of Willem Pop.
2. Stewart W. *A Mate in HMRT in Wartime.* Privately published booklet, in DSRTA archive. p.2.
3. ADM 199/1239.
4. ADM 199/1238, memo from CCRT, 9 February 1941.
5. ADM 199/1239. From Commanding Officer's report, 4 June 1941.
6. 13 September 1943.
7. ADM 1/12332.
8. *The London Gazette*, 9 June 1942.
9. *Ibid.*, 10 July 1940. The other commanding officer was Lt. GMM Robinson RNR.
10. ADM 199/2134.
11. Van der Vat D. *Stealth at Sea.* London: Weidenfeld & Nicolson; 1994. pp.202–204.
12. Report of an interview with Captain JC Walker, ADM 199/2134.
13. Strowger was a third generation fisherman from Kessingland on the Suffolk coast, and was *Salvonia*'s skipper in 1941 when she salvaged SS *Royal Crown*. He was awarded £19 salvage money, rather more than the 15/- he had earned as a fisherman for three weeks at sea. From a letter by a relative in an unidentified newspaper in DSRTA archives.
14. This narrative is based on: Lund P, Ludlam H. *The Night of the U-Boats.* London: Foulsham; 1973.
15. Masters D. *In Peril on the Sea: War Exploits of Allied Seamen.* London: Cresset Press; 1960. pp.96–97.
16. When Light returned to civilian life he became an underwriter at Lloyd's, owned a shipyard in Holland, and eventually

retired to his villa on Mallorca to sail a yacht he had designed himself.

17. ADM 199/1238.

18. ADM 199/1237, 7 August 1941.

19. ADM 199/1129.

20. This report, written by Captain Louis (Johnnie) Colmans, is in the DSRTA archives. Courtesy of Mrs Elsie Colmans.

21. ADM 199/1239.

22. OB-318 will be remembered for the capture of U-110 by three of the convoy's escorts. An intact Enigma cipher machine and other material was found on the U-boat, which proved a vital breakthrough for Bletchley Park in deciphering U-boat signals.

23. Thomas D. *The Atlantic Star, 1939–45*. London: WH Allen; 1990. p.83.

24. Morison S. *History of United States Naval Operations in World War II*. Vol. I. Urbana and Chicago: University of Illinois Press; 2001. pp.387–88.

25. From a letter in *Shipping*, July 1991, written by ATM Hawkins, a signalman aboard *Zwarte Zee*. In DSRTA archive.

26. Elphick P. *Liberty: The Ships that Won the War*. Rochester: Chatham Publishing; 2001. pp.212, 299.

27. www.uboat.net has a detailed report on this incident.

28. War Intelligence Report No. 189 22.10.43: 'A Dutch Tug's Record'.

29. ADM 1/11425.

30. There is a description of the *Dexterous'* war record on www.worldnavalships.com/forums

31. 'HMS *Buccaneer*' by Jack Philip-Nicholson, *Towrope*, 2008 (Xmas issue): 20–21. In DSRTA archive.

32. *Ole Wegger* had an interesting wartime history, which can be found on www.warsailors.com

33. ADM 199/1632.

34. ADM 199/2165, 3 April 1942.

35. George Corke memoir. Courtesy of Mrs Joanna Barron.

36. Information from Dutch tugs' logs in red file B marked HMRT in DSRTA archive.
37. TDC meeting held on 19 November 1942, in MT 63/152.
38. ADM 1/30115.

5

THE ASSURANCE CLASS AND THE BATTLE OF THE ATLANTIC

THE FIRST OF the new Assurance class was launched from Cochrane's of Selby, Yorkshire, in May 1940. Rescue tugs were desperately needed and the Admiralty committed itself to an open-ended building programme. There was no time to design from new. Instead, the class was modelled on the Cochrane-built *Salvonia*, which had been launched in 1937 and was the most recent ocean tug for which the shipyard had plans. Twenty-one were built, but were steam-powered as it was impossible at that stage of the war to obtain diesel engines. A serious drawback was that none of them was fitted with towing winches, which decreased their efficiency and quite unnecessarily increased the crew's workload. However, unlike the Saint class, they were equipped with motorboats to take a boarding party to abandoned ships to connect up.

At 156ft 6in overall, the class was slightly longer than the *Salvonia*, had a speed of twelve knots, an endurance of eighteen days and a displacement of 700 tons. Their armament was a three-inch dual-purpose gun, two Oerlikons and two Lewis guns. Their principal defects lay in their inadequate endurance and their lack of power for heavy, protracted towage. As one expert put it, 'they were not man enough for the arduous task of towing large, badly damaged vessels single-handed through the winter weather of the North Atlantic. The fact that this was frequently achieved speaks volumes for the determination and seamanship of the men who manned them.'[1]

Extreme weather proved too much for some of them: *Adherent* foundered while on convoy duty in the North Atlantic in January 1944 with the loss of two officers and ten ratings; and besides *Horsa* (see page 48), two others were wrecked: *Assurance* in Lough Foyle in October 1941 and *Adept* in the Hebrides in March 1942.

Assurance, the first of the class to be commissioned, had a difficult start to her short career when in bad weather she was dispatched to find the 9568-ton freighter *Fishpool*, owned by the Ropner Shipping Company of West Hartlepool. The *Fishpool* was on her maiden voyage when on 14 November 1940 a German bomber deluged her with incendiaries, setting her on fire and killing all those on deck.[2] The survivors abandoned ship, so there was no one aboard to help connect the tow when the *Assurance* arrived. Instead, the mate, Edwin 'Tubby' Turner, used the rescue tug's motorboat and managed to get aboard the freighter and connect up, quite a feat under the circumstances. Later, he was given his first command, aged just twenty-one, almost certainly the youngest commanding officer the Service had. 'Physically he was a large and strong man with a temperament to match when the occasion arose,' a contemporary wrote of Turner,[3] and we shall be meeting him again later.

The *Fishpool* was towed safely into Greenock and repaired. She was the latest addition to what was known as 'Ropner's Navy', so called because of the impressive record of the firm's ships striking back at their attackers. The nickname originated from the First World War when the Ropner freighter *Wandy*, after a fight that lasted three-quarters of an hour, sank a U-boat with her single gun. But it wasn't until the Second World War that the phrase became common currency. In November 1939, the House of Commons was debating how best to operate the country's merchant fleet and one MP rose to say that the government should take total control of it. At once, Colonel Leonard Ropner was on his feet to oppose this suggestion (he didn't succeed, the Merchant Navy came under the Admiralty's orders for the duration of the war). Recording this exchange, *The Times* ended its report:

> He paid a tribute to help given to merchant shipping
> by the Royal Navy. Two of his company's ships had
> been sunk by submarine; two others were attacked
> but gave such a good account of themselves that they
> disabled two German submarines, both of
> which were finally sunk by destroyers within a few
> hours of breaking off with the Mercantile Marine.
> At the Admiralty 'Ropner's Navy' was almost as well
> known as that of his Majesty (Laughter and cheers).[4]

In the First World War, Ropner's lost twenty-one of its fleet of fifty-seven ships; between 1939 and 1945 it lost thirty-four of its fleet of forty-five, with the loss of more than six hundred men. A prime example of the heavy losses suffered by the Merchant Navy during both world wars.

The last of the Assurance class, *Sesame*, was launched in October 1943, by which time the others had been distributed to all parts of the world. Two of them, *Tenacity* and *Frisky*, were stationed at St John's, Newfoundland. They were chosen because of the strength of their bows, essential when rescue work was conducted where pack ice was common, and the Admiralty War Diary[5] for January 1943 shows a glimpse of just how hazardous operating so far north could be.

In November 1942, the American motor tanker *Brilliant*, bound for Belfast in convoy SC-109, was torpedoed but managed to make St John's. She was patched up and was being towed by the *Frisky* to Sydney, Cape Breton, for permanent repairs when a gale – combined with a blinding snowstorm – sprang up, and on 20 January the tanker broke in two. The fore part sank immediately, taking with it eleven of the crew, and that day's War Diary notes that the escort signalled that she was unlikely to be able to keep in touch with the tanker's remains during the night and that *Frisky* was 'not in company'. An Admiralty report duly recorded that the escort had lost touch 'at 2100 and proceeded to St John's short of water and badly iced up. On 1230Z/21 she reported that *Frisky* was ice-bound and unnavigable and had to run before the sea; her main wireless apparatus was iced up.'[5]

The stern section of *Brilliant*, with thirty-three men aboard, was adrift for several days before the *Frisky* found it after the weather moderated. She rescued those aboard the wreck, and managed to get a tow line aboard, but on 25 January she was given permission to sink it with gunfire as it was a hazard to navigation.[5]

SERVICE OFF NEWFOUNDLAND

St John's was Newfoundland's principal harbour. A narrow entrance made it easily defended with boom defence nets, but difficult to enter when towing a large ship. Anchored in the harbour was a captured German tanker, renamed *RFA Empire Salvage*, which was used to refuel the rescue tugs based there. When both rescue tugs were in harbour, one was on twenty minutes' notice, the other at four hours' notice, alternating daily. If one was called out, the other went on to twenty minutes' notice until the first returned, or she was herself called out.

St John's was close to the departure points of the Atlantic convoys, now being attacked by U-boats having a second 'Happy Hour' off the east coast of the United States. When *Tenacity* returned to Campbeltown after her first tour there, her wardroom was decorated with twenty-four small flags representing the two dozen British, American, Danish and Norwegian ships she had towed to safety.

One of the first she assisted, on 30 March 1942, was the tanker *Imperial Transport*, which, it will be remembered, had returned to service with a new bow after being torpedoed in February 1940. This time, while in convoy ON-77, the tanker, which was in ballast, was hit by two torpedoes on the port side. At the time she was about five hundred and thirty miles east of Newfoundland, and she was towed to St John's by one of the convoy's Canadian escorts. She was then handed over to a tender and a small tug to take her through the narrow harbour entrance. The only available tow line was connected to the tanker but this broke, and *Tenacity* was dispatched from the harbour to finish the job.

It was a tricky operation, as the heavy swell that was running made it impossible, until the last minute, to shorten the tow in order to take the tanker safely through the narrow entrance. Doing this took time – remember, it all had to be done by hand – and needed fine judgement to keep the tow under control so that the ship did not end up aground and blocking the entrance. The truth was that *Tenacity* should have been equipped with a modern towing winch, something her commanding officer, Lt AM Leckie RNR, did not fail to point out in his report.[6]

Another British tanker the *Tenacity* towed in was the 10,627-ton *GS Walden*, part of convoy ON-115, attacked by a wolf-pack about three hundred miles from St John's in early August 1942. The convoy's commodore took evasive action by ordering a series of sharp course changes, but one of the convoy's columns could not follow the manoeuvre and 'romped' away from the other ships. The U-boats focused on them, sinking one and damaging two others, one of them *GS Walden*. She was torpedoed in the boiler room, flooding her engine room and disabling her steerage gear.

A sudden deterioration in the visibility saved her from the U-boat's *coup de grâce* and she was taken in tow by two Canadian warships. They towed her for thirty-four hours, but only managed to cover fifty miles before the *Tenacity* arrived on the scene. Lt William McNaughton RNR was now in command, as Leckie had recently been promoted to lieutenant-commander and appointed maintenance officer rescue tugs at the expanded rescue tug base at St John's. McNaughton immediately took over the tow and within seventy-two hours had brought the damaged ship two hundred and fifty miles safely into St John's. It was a good example of how powerful modern rescue tugs were needed on these occasions.[7]

Tenacity's highest profile operation during her time at Newfoundland was to tow in the crippled US Coast Guard cutter *Campbell*. *Campbell* had been transferred to the US Navy as a convoy escort and was one of the first American warships to be fitted with 'huff-duff', which was of such value in the fight against U-boats. In February 1943, she was escorting a westbound convoy, ON-166, when she became a casualty during one of the seminal convoy battles of the war. At the time there was the highest-ever concentration of U-boats in the North Atlantic, one hundred and twenty of them, and two wolf-packs totalling fourteen U-boats attacked the convoy, having been alerted to its position by *B-Dienst*.

On 22 February, *Campbell* spotted a U-boat on her radar, which had been damaged by an earlier depth charge attack and forced to surface. *Campbell* closed the contact and opened fire before ramming it. The U-boat sank, but in doing so ripped the cutter's hull open below the waterline, flooding her engine room and cutting all power. *Campbell* lay helpless, wallowing in the swell, and the *Tenacity* was dispatched from St John's to bring her in, steaming the eight hundred and fifty miles to the cutter without an escort, as none was available.

'Ignoring the signal that there were other U-boats in the vicinity,' one report recorded,[8] 'and that the *Campbell* should be left alone to sink, the *Tenacity* came alongside and made fast a tow line. It put its big modern pumps to work aboard *Campbell*; then, with the cutter in tow, headed to St John's.' The report concluded by saying that while being towed, the cutter was almost continuously awash, and the tow rope developed a layer of ice six inches thick. But *Campbell* was brought in safely. She was repaired and returned to service, and went on to have a long and illustrious career.

Of the forty-nine ships in convoy ON-166, fourteen were sunk and seven damaged. One of those damaged was the Dutch motorship *Madoera*, which was lucky to survive when a torpedo almost tore off her forefoot. She managed to make St John's under her own steam and was eventually repaired and put back into service, but it was one of the worst losses inflicted on a convoy during the Battle of the Atlantic.

However, by the end of May 1943, the mid-Atlantic air gap south of Greenland had been finally closed and the deployment of the long-range Liberator bomber gave convoys air cover across the entire width of the North Atlantic. By then Admiral Dönitz had suffered such heavy losses that he withdrew most of his U-boats to await an improved acoustic torpedo. Once this was available, he proposed to introduce a new tactic: the convoy escorts would be attacked first before the wolf-pack turned on the convoy itself.

Within thirty-six hours of returning to St John's, the *Tenacity* again put to sea, this time to bring in a small sealer, the 684-ton *Neptune*, carrying coal to St John's. It had run into trouble in bad weather some miles off the Newfoundland coast, and in an interview with a local paper McNaughton described what happened: 'We saw her about 150 fathoms off our port bow. She was rolling very heavily. Must have been a 45-degree roll and the sea was breaking over her decks.'[9]

He had manoeuvred to a position under the *Neptune*'s port bow to pass a heavy towing line on board her when *Neptune*'s captain shouted that he had no steam to work his winches to haul the tow line aboard, and McNaughton was forced to back off. 'I had 100 fathoms of 5-inch wire,' he said, 'and I decided to take a chance towing him with it. It was easier to handle than the heavier lines and could be hauled in by hand with [the help of] our windlass.'[9]

He closed again and, despite the high seas that were running, held *Tenacity* to within six feet of the sealer. The wire was passed and secured to her foremast, and the tow to St John's began. McNaughton kept his speed at about two knots, as any greater strain on the tow could have pulled the sealer's mast right out of her. They arrived off the harbour entrance shortly before midnight, and *Neptune* was allowed to drift while the wire tow was shortened for the run-in.

Just as this had been done, shouts were heard from the sealer to come alongside. *Tenacity* closed and it could be seen that *Neptune*'s decks were awash and that she was, in the newspaper's words, 'just about done for'. McNaughton jammed *Tenacity*'s quarter up abreast of *Neptune*'s foredeck and her crew of twenty, plus the master, came sloshing through the water that was running across the sealer's deck, and scrambled aboard. The last few had to jump from the built-up fo'c'sle as the rest of the sealer had become submerged.

'We got away from her then,' McNaughton said, 'and left her astern of us. I made a turn around her, lost her for a while in the darkness and then picked out a light that was still burning in the wireless cabin. Suddenly the light went out. That was the last trace of her. We steamed over the spot but the ship had vanished.'[9]

Tenacity's time at St John's was neatly summed up by a signal she received from the FOIC Newfoundland: 'I congratulate you and your ship's company on your excellent service this year in salving USS *Campbell* and numerous other well-executed assignments under most adverse weather conditions.' On his return to Britain, McNaughton was awarded the MBE.[10]

By 1944, *Tenacity* was back at St John's under a new commanding officer, Lt Ian Taylor RNR. On 24 June 1944, a massive fire broke out at the Imperial Oil premises on the harbour front. This threatened to raze part of the port, and *Tenacity*'s role in getting it under control earned Taylor a well-merited OBE.[11] A local newspaper described the rescue tug's contribution to fighting the fire:

Real heroism was displayed by the men of HMRT *Tenacity*. With the nose of their tug jammed as close as humanly possible to the jetty the sailors stood upon the forepeak, and, wreathed in smoke and blasted by terrific heat, continued to heap streams of water on the flames.[12]

One of *Tenacity*'s last tasks of the war was to tow in the destroyer HMS *Highlander*, which, on 15 April 1945, hit ice while escorting an Atlantic convoy. The ice carried away twenty feet of the destroyer's forward structure below the waterline, disabling her, and *Tenacity* towed her stern first into the Canadian Navy's base at Bay Bulls, Newfoundland, for temporary repairs.[13]

FRISKY IN THE NORTH ATLANTIC

Frisky (Lt Harry Tarbottan RNR) also assisted a US Coast Guard cutter while she was stationed at St John's. On 15 January 1942, *Alexander Hamilton* joined an assorted group of Canadian and US naval warships to escort convoy HX-170 from its Newfoundland rendezvous to the MOMP (Mid-Ocean Meeting Point) south of Iceland. From there, Royal Navy escorts would take over escort duties while the original escorts refuelled at Iceland before picking up their next westbound convoy.

Before the handover, *Yukon*, a store ship in the convoy, broke down and *Alexander Hamilton*, escorted by a destroyer, began towing her towards Reykjavik. *Frisky* was ordered to the scene and took over the tow, but soon after she did so a U-boat that had been shadowing them fired a spread of torpedoes. One hit *Alexander Hamilton* amidships, destroying the engine room and killing twenty-six of the crew. The survivors abandoned ship and were picked up by the destroyer escort, but before doing so they managed to counter-flood her to keep her on an even keel, and she remained afloat.

While *Frisky* was towing the *Yukon* into Reykjavik, another Assurance class rescue tug, the *Restive* (Lt JW Evenden RNR), arrived from Iceland and tried to take the cutter in tow. But it was now dark and the sea very rough as it invariably was off Iceland in winter. This made launching *Restive*'s motorboat problematical, though by now a technique for doing so had been perfected. *Restive*'s second engineer, Stanley Butler, described how it was done:

> The motorboat would be swung out, and the engine started just before it entered the water. While this was going on, the rescue tug would be steaming in a port turn so that the motorboat could be dropped into the calm stretch of water created on the port side of the rescue tug.[14]

Once aboard the abandoned cutter, each member of the party had his job to do: the coxswain would be responsible for getting the towing gear on board, making fast, and ensuring the towing wires would not fray; the engineer officer would check the ingress of water; a pump would be manhandled aboard to dry out any spaces that would increase the ship's buoyancy; and all watertight doors would be closed.

When *Frisky* returned the next morning, she and *Restive* took *Alexander Hamilton* in tow. But by now the cutter's list had increased to nearly twenty degrees, her bows were out of the water and the sea was breaking over her aft. After being towed eighteen miles towards Iceland the cutter turned turtle, and the destroyer escort had to sink her with gunfire.[15]

In July that year, *Frisky* had better luck when she assisted the 8093-ton British motor tanker *British Merit*. The tanker was on her maiden voyage when, some days out from the Clyde, a wolf-pack of ten U-boats attacked the convoy she was in (ON-113). The tanker was struck by two torpedoes, but was in ballast so there was no explosion of high-octane fuel that so often ripped such ships apart, killing their entire crew. It was also lucky that she was streaming anti-torpedo nets as these prevented one of the torpedoes hitting her, but the other struck her on the unprotected port quarter in the engine room, killing one of the crew. 'Engine room flooded immediately,' the master wrote in the ship's log, 'and ship entirely out of control, swung round with wind and sea on port beam.'[16]

As a precaution, the master ordered the lifeboats to be lowered and manned. He gave orders for the port side ones to move to the lee side, but in the strong winds and the heavy seas that were running, this proved difficult, and two of the lifeboats, with thirty-three men aboard, drifted astern. The master reported this to one of the escorting destroyers, which signalled a corvette would be sent to help. 'The wind freshened to moderate gale early morning of 25th inst.,' the master noted, 'with heavy sea and continuous rain. Vessel rolling heavily and continuously. At break of day (about 4am) 2 corvettes arrived.'[16]

The corvettes picked up the men in the lifeboats, and one of the corvettes signalled the master to ask if he intended to abandon ship. 'We replied, "Not if there is any chance of being towed." The corvette replied that there was every chance of someone being sent to our assistance.' On the evening of 27 July *Frisky* arrived from St John's.

'We had some difficulty in connecting up,' the master recorded, 'but at 11.37pm the towing wire was fast to our starboard [anchor] cable.' In the weather conditions, it was a long and laborious task before the ship was properly connected and slowly manoeuvred round, but by 12.45am on 28 July *Frisky* was towing her steadily towards St John's, escorted by one of the corvettes. During the night the weather improved and the tanker only occasionally sheered off course. Even so, it took until the afternoon of 2 August for *Frisky* to bring her safely into harbour.

THE THRICE-ABANDONED TANKER

Prudent was another Assurance class rescue tug that had a spell working out of St John's, and her involvement in trying to salvage the 8106-ton Anglo-Saxon oil tanker *Diala* is an example of the enormous effort that was taken to save every ship possible. The tanker was attacked on 15 January 1942 after her convoy, ON-52, had become dispersed by storm force winds. She was in ballast some three hundred miles south-east of Cape Race, Newfoundland, and proceeding at her maximum speed of twelve knots when two torpedoes hit her simultaneously on the port side, opening three of the port wing tanks to the sea.

Diala immediately took on a list and a distress signal was sent, but was apparently never received by anyone. As the engines had been stopped and the engine room evacuated, the master gave orders to abandon ship. Two of the lifeboats were launched successfully, but a third drifted away almost empty. The release gear of the fourth lifeboat jammed, capsizing it, and its eight occupants were drowned. The chief officer, an apprentice and some of the Chinese crew launched a raft, paddled to the capsized boat, righted it and climbed into it. Despite the master's order that the lifeboats were to stand by the ship, they all became dispersed during the night and were never seen again. The master was now left stranded on the ship with his fifth engineer, a naval gunner and five Chinese members of the crew, and had no means of leaving his ship even if he had wanted to.

In the early evening the tanker was again torpedoed, this time on the starboard side, which had the curious effect of righting her. Four hours later a fourth torpedo hit her where the first two had struck. This blew what remained of her bows off forward of the No. 9 tank, but there was no apparent damage further aft, and the tanker remained floating buoyantly on an even keel. The next day, 16 January, the damage was inspected and the fifth engineer reported that the engine room was intact, but he had not been able to restart the engines. Regular messages continued to be sent on an emergency W/T set, but this only had a short range.

On 17 January, another fierce gale set in, but *Diala* rode it out without difficulty. Two ships passed near her on 18 and 19 January. Their offers to take the men on board were declined, but they were asked to signal for naval assistance. With the gale still raging, the second ship stood by *Diala* overnight before proceeding, and by the next day the gale had abated. That evening, a third ship appeared. This time the master accepted the offer to take him and the remainder of his crew aboard, as there was no sign of help arriving. In doing so he ordered *Diala* to be abandoned for the second time.[17]

Coming up behind ON-52 was another westbound convoy, ON-56, comprising forty-one ships and a close escort of four corvettes and one sloop, and this, too, ran into trouble. 'During the course of the third day,' wrote MT Dodds, an apprentice aboard the 12,000-ton British tanker *Athelcrown*, 'depth charge explosions could be heard intermittently, indicating a submarine under attack.'[18]

A fog did give some relief from the attacking U-boats, but it became impossible to keep station, and those aboard *Athelcrown* could soon only see two other ships from the convoy. The following evening, 22 January, just as everyone had decided any further attacks were unlikely, there was a loud explosion, the lights went out and the engines stopped. The crew was ordered to prepare to abandon ship, and as they assembled by their lifeboats a second torpedo hit aft, destroying one of the lifeboats. The master now ordered the ship to be abandoned and the other three lifeboats managed to get away before the tanker sank. After two days of extreme discomfort, the survivors in two of the boats were picked up by another ship in the convoy.

Aboard the third lifeboat was a senior apprentice, Colin Baptist, the chief engineer, the ship's carpenter and nine others, five of whom were injured. After a week they sighted a derelict tanker, and worked down to leeward towards her. In a sworn statement, Baptist wrote:

> [H]er bows were badly damaged. The foremast was hanging over the starboard bow into the water. The after bulkhead of the forecastle was standing fairly erect but all structure forward of that had disappeared with the exception of odd frames and bits of plating. Light could be seen through the ship's bows from side to side. Passing to the port side it could be seen that the ship's side some 10 feet or more abaft the forecastle had a very large hole, big enough to take a boat through. In view of the condition of the ship the wounded men in the boat refused to board her and the boat drifted away.[19]

At dawn, two days later, the derelict was sighted again and it was decided to board her. Being to leeward, the exhausted survivors had great difficulty reaching the ship. However, about midday they came along the tanker's starboard side, which was low enough in the water for them to board. The carpenter went round the abandoned ship with Baptist and said he thought she would stay afloat. The chief engineer examined the main engine and found it intact and in working condition, but the survivors were too exhausted to raise sufficient steam. About six nights later, a ship's lights were seen and distress rockets were fired. The vessel, a neutral Swedish steamer, stood by until daylight and then took the survivors on board. The derelict ship, now abandoned for a third time, was, of course, *Diala*.

In the meantime, the naval authorities at St John's had dispatched the *Prudent* to search for *Diala*. The weather was excellent and when the abandoned wreck was found a party was put aboard her to connect the tow. But there was no anchor chain to attach it to as it had been blown away with the tanker's bows, so she had to be towed stern first, a tricky undertaking as the after part of the ship was almost awash. However, *Prudent*'s boarding party managed to connect up, and they remained aboard the wreck, but during the middle watch the tow parted, and by the time *Prudent* had retrieved her towing gear, *Diala*, along with the rescue tug's boarding party, had disappeared into the darkness.

The *Prudent* was now joined by *Frisky*, which had been sent from St John's to help, and both rescue tugs began a box search[20] that lasted eight days, but without success. *Frisky* started a second search, but *Prudent*, short of fuel, returned to St John's where, to her crew's relief, *Diala*'s boarding party was on the quay to greet them, having been picked up by the trawler escort.

On her second attempt, *Frisky* found *Diala*, but signalled that she was unable to board because of the weather, and that 'situation almost impossible with 1 tug unaided'. She, too, was now running low on fuel and was forced to return to harbour. So it was that *Diala* was abandoned for the final time, and on 23 March 1942 a fifth U-boat torpedo finally sent what remained of the tanker to the bottom – a fact, of course, that remained unknown until the reports of U-boats were examined after the war.

At a Board of Enquiry held at Cardiff on 31 March 1942 into the abandoning of *Diala*, a surveyor assisting its members had this to say about Baptist's deposition:

> I formed the opinion that Mr Baptist, aged 21, was
> a young man with initiative, good self confidence and
> observation, although quite unassuming. His description
> of the damage was more detailed than I expected it

would be, considering the physical condition of them all in the boat... Mr Baptist's narrative was quietly told and I certainly admired his conduct.[21]

The board found that the master of *Diala* had been justified in ordering his ship to be abandoned, little knowing when it came to this decision what efforts had been made to save her.

GHOSTLY APPARITION

By the end of April 1942, *Prudent* was at Ardrossan, where Stanley Butler joined her as chief engineer, and soon afterwards she became part of a convoy bound for her new base at Gibraltar. Her commanding officer was Lt Guy Quine RNR, who later that year was awarded the MBE.[22] One of his first tasks after reaching Gibraltar was to bring in the 5372-ton freighter *Lavington Court*, which was torpedoed on 19 July 1942 about two hundred miles north of the Azores while part of convoy OS-34. Seven of the crew were killed and the remaining forty-one were taken off by one of the convoy's escorts. Butler had a strange experience with this abandoned vessel, which showed how easy it was for the eyes of even the most experienced seaman to be tricked at night.

The *Prudent* found *Lavington Court* at dusk on the fourth day, having covered one thousand five hundred miles. The weather was fine with a smooth sea, but as it was a bright moonlit night – ideal conditions for an attacking U-boat – it was decided to do nothing until the following morning, but to circle the wreck at a distance of about one and a half miles. 'At about 2130 hours the CO sent down a message for me to come to the bridge,' Butler later wrote.[23] When he reached the bridge Quine asked him if he believed in ghosts, and Butler advised him that he was open-minded about the subject:

The *Lavington Court* had been torpedoed in her stern just forward of the sternpost, so that she had lost her rudder and propeller. Her cruiser type stern containing the crew's quarters was distorted so that it pointed downwards at about 15 to 20 degrees. The after deck house was on this section with a gun mounted on top – the barrel of which was pointing down to the sea. The bows of the vessel were pointing roughly to the north-east and, at the time we were discussing ghosts, the moon was fairly high and to the south.[23]

As the *Prudent* approached the ship's stern, Quine told Butler to look carefully at the port side of the sloping deck house. This was out of the moonlight and under the extended gun platform, which made that area quite dark. 'As we came round he said, "Now watch carefully, Chief, and you'll see a moving whitish glow." Sure enough we did. It was very uncanny indeed.'

After watching the phenomenon several times, they decided to turn in and investigate the next day, and before dawn the rescue tug's motorboat was launched to take the mate and some of the crew to connect up the tow rope. Butler went, too, to have a look at the engine room and the damage aft where the 'ghost' had been seen:

It is very eerie aboard an abandoned ship, particularly when down below. The first hour or so aboard is the worst until one locates and becomes accustomed to all the strange noises. Much depends on the weather. In calm weather there is usually a swell causing some movement to the vessel so that a form of creaking takes place, which is more evident when below in machinery spaces, or a hold. In bad or heavy weather it was the noise of the wind through the various guys and ropes, masts, and derricks, in addition to the sea slamming into the side of the ship, and even breaking across the decks.[23]

After inspecting the engine room, Butler moved aft to look at the damage done by the torpedo and found a motor launch (ML) mounted on chocks secured to the deck with wire tightened by bottle screws. Thinking the launch might be useful as a lifeboat if the ship was torpedoed again, he undid the bottle screws so the launch would float free if the ship did sink. He then came to the entrance door of the crew's accommodation:

> It was still fairly dark and my torch was getting dim. After stepping over the weather step into the passageway, I took a few steps before tripping over an obstruction. I found myself full length on top of a very dead man.

He shone his torch to the accommodation below and could see more bodies lying there. The alleyway where the sailor lay had entrance doors at both port and starboard ends. Both doors were painted white, and Butler realised that the 'ghost' was nothing more than the reflection of the moonlight off the white paint, with the ship's motion causing the movement of the 'ghost', while varying the angles of reflected moonlight.

The mystery solved, Butler and the others began the standard procedure for preparing a ship for towing by ensuring all portholes and doors were closed, and collecting all personal items of any value and locking them in the ship's safe, or in a locked cabin. The eighteen-inch manila tow rope was then connected, always a complicated business that took time and care even in good weather.

In the case of the *Lavington Court*, it was also a waste of effort as on 1 August 'the vessel broke in two with the after end sinking immediately to be shortly followed by the remainder of the ship as the aftermost bulkhead went. The strain on the 18-inch tow rope was immense as the tow sank and it took only two chops of an axe to cut through the rope at the after tow rail.'[24] But thanks to Stanley Butler's caution the motor launch, HMML 1151, floated clear, and was taken in tow and delivered to Milford Haven, so at least something was salvaged.

Butler witnessed the *Lavington Court* sink:

> The whole ship slid down under the waves, surrounded
> by foaming water. Then all was quiet – very deadly
> quiet. It was a sad sight, and I found during discussions
> with other crew members from the CO downwards, that
> pretty well everyone was affected emotionally. I have
> seen a few ships large and small go to their watery
> graves, and always felt it was like attending the funeral
> of a relative or friend. As this one was slipping away
> in the moonlight, I thought of all the skill of design
> and building that had gone into it. A nearly new ship
> with lovely accommodation, that in peacetime would
> have been a great pleasure to work and sail in. What a
> terrible waste.[25]

TOUGH MAIDEN VOYAGE

Prosperous was one of the later Assurance class tugs to be launched and her crew had a particularly tough introduction to the business of rescuing damaged vessels. She left Cochrane's shipyard for Methil (Firth of Forth) on 27 November 1942, under the command of Lt JEL Brice RNR, after commissioning and some preliminary trials. She was then delayed at Leith by engine room defects, brought about by the carelessness of her chief engineer, who was promptly relieved of his duties. It was not an auspicious start, but one the crew soon put behind them. She joined a convoy at Methil and left it at Loch Ewe for Campbeltown, arriving there on 18 December for her final trials and crew training. But on 22 December, before these could take place, she was sent to assist the 5704-ton Dutch freighter *Jan van Goyen*, which had dropped out of the westbound convoy ON-153 (Liverpool–New York) in mid-Atlantic with damaged steering gear.

Prosperous, accompanied by a corvette, which was also on her maiden voyage, found the drifting ship on 26 December. The weather was exceptionally bad, with a full gale blowing, but the tow rope was eventually connected. For the next four days the engine room staff had to work in almost impossible conditions when the storm stove in the engine room skylights, allowing water to pour down into it. The chief engineer, Sub-Lt (E) CH Hall RNVR, was a naval pensioner and had been appointed only ten days previously, making his ability to manage both staff and engine room all the more remarkable. But manage them he did, and *Prosperous* delivered the freighter back to the Clyde on 2 January 1943.

In a memorandum headed 'Meritorious Towing Operation', the CCRT wrote about the commanding officer:

> Notwithstanding the appalling weather conditions the operation was completely successful; the absence of accident or breakage of towing equipment reflecting exceptional ability, care and anticipation. This officer has commanded HM rescue tugs for twenty months and been very well reported on, and this is the first time he has been given an opportunity of demonstrating his ability.[26]

Hall also deserved recognition for the handling of a difficult situation. After serving in the Royal Navy as an engine room artificer from 1924 to 1929, he was promoted chief ERA before becoming a pensioner. He then worked in dockyards before signing a T.124T Agreement in January 1940 and being promoted to chief engineer in August 1940. But as he had not obtained a Board of Trade Certificate, he was not eligible for the rank of Lt (E) RNR T.124T. This did not deter the CCRT from recommending him for promotion to that rank. He had always resisted increasing the numbers of temporary lieutenant-commanders, but he recommended that Brice be promoted with immediate effect.

On 9 May 1943, the crew of *Prosperous* again distinguished themselves by rescuing the crew of a Dutch coaster, SS *Jutland*, which was on the point of foundering near St Ann's Head at the entrance to Milford Haven. When first sighted, she had a 50-degree list to port and was being driven towards the rocks by a gale force wind from the north-west. A rough, confused sea was breaking over her, and her crew could be seen aft clinging to her upper works.

In rescuing the crew, Brice's report describes an outstanding example of ship-handling in exceptionally difficult circumstances:

> Proceeded to pump oil over side and at full speed
> made a complete circle of oil around the wreck to stop
> seas breaking, then approached from the South West at
> half speed under her stern with the wind on my port
> bow. When closing the wreck I went full speed astern
> causing my bow to sheer to starboard and the wind
> to blow *Prosperous* alongside the stern of the wreck
> somewhere about amidships of *Prosperous* but with my
> ship still making headway. I stopped the engines as
> I had reckoned on keeping sufficient headway on to

carry *Prosperous* clear of the wreck before using engines again.

Some of the crew were apparently numbed with cold and exposure and could not move quickly enough to jump the first time of my approach. I had to alter my plans quickly and came astern again as the coaster was even then commencing to turn turtle, so that had I gone out and taken another run in it would have been too late to save their lives. I rang the telegraph for all stern power the engines were capable of giving. This had the effect of bringing the bow to starboard on the low side of the wreck, the wind blowing her down to its stern. The remaining crew then jumped on to the after deck of *Prosperous*.[26]

At that moment, the coaster started to roll over on to the rescue tug and Brice had to react instantly to save his ship:

I rang the telegraph for all possible power ahead and with wheel to port to clear the overhanging mast of the wreck. *Prosperous* came clear. But not before the coaster had practically capsized, and some part of her stern had fouled the stern of *Prosperous*. There was a terrific jar. *Prosperous* heeled heavily and then dragged herself clear.

The entire operation had lasted only fifteen minutes, and moments later the coaster turned turtle. Brice concluded his report:

The behaviour of the ship's company of *Prosperous* was in keeping with the traditions of the Service. I respectfully call attention to the Engine Room staff who remained calmly at their posts giving every possible assistance. The engine's movements were all made very smartly and thus helped greatly towards the successful conclusion of the operation.[26]

All the survivors were landed safely, and by early evening *Prosperous* was anchored in Milford Haven. The speed of the operation, and the skill with which it was handled, was witnessed by a Trinity House Pilot, who immediately wrote to the FOIC Milford Haven:

> I respectfully beg, as an eye witness and purely
> unconcerned party, to write you on an incident
> which took place outside Milford Haven yesterday
> the 9th instant. At this time I was one of a watch
> of pilots on duty in the Examination steamer
> HMS *Merkop* when we were ordered out to assist
> the Dutch Coaster *Jutland*, which was in serious
> trouble. The weather at the time was extremely
> bad, a very heavy sea running, and the *Jutland*
> was lying on her side liable to capsize completely
> at any moment; yet, in spite of this, HMRT *Prosperous*
> was, solely due to the magnificent handling of her
> Commanding Officer, able to go alongside and
> rescue the entire crew. As a pilot for this port and
> the Channel Islands, and a seaman of twenty years'
> experience, I wish to pay tribute to an outstanding act
> of seamanship.[26]

Two other expert witnesses also attested to Brice's skill, and the FOIC Milford Haven was equally impressed. He suggested to the Admiralty that it would make a good propaganda story, and in due course both incidents were released to the newspapers.

What they printed was, of course, for propaganda purposes, but it still rings true:

> Not one man aboard the *Prosperous* took off his clothing for 10 days. Cooking was impossible. The staple diet was corned beef from tins and hard biscuits. 'That was the menu for our Christmas and New Year dinners,' said the first lieutenant, Sub-Lt Alan McLean RNR, of Langside, Glasgow, 'instead of our beautiful turkeys which were left behind at the base.'
>
> Cabins, alleyways and mess-decks were feet deep in water. Huge seas smashed the engine room skylights, and the water, pouring in, fused all the lights, tore away deck fittings and broke all the crockery aboard. Men took turn about at sleeping on the floor of the radio cabin, the only dry spot in the ship.[27]

On returning to base, the crew of the *Prosperous* found a message of congratulations awaiting them from the C-in-C Western Approaches. *The London Gazette* cited Hall, who was mentioned in despatches, for his 'courage and skill'[28] and Brice, cited for 'coolness and courage', was awarded the MBE for saving the lives of the crew of one ship, and towing safely to port a second that had been damaged. Another newspaper[29] reported the reaction of the workers at Cochrane's shipyard at Selby who had built *Prosperous*: they passed the hat round and raised £50 for the crew as a tribute to their seamanship.[30]

UNNECESSARY ABANDONMENT

The gravity and dangers of unnecessary abandonment was highlighted in 1943 when the British 3670-ton freighter SS

Coulmore, carrying general cargo, was torpedoed in mid-Atlantic. At the time she was part of convoy SC-121 bound for Liverpool, which had departed New York on 23 February 1943. By 6 March, when the convoy ran into two U-boat wolf-packs, a north-west gale had dispersed many of the ships and there was a heavy swell.

During the next three days twelve ships were sunk, and on the evening of 9 March *Coulmore* was torpedoed in the forepeak. The concussion was slight, but there had been foreboding among the crew that they were going to be sunk, and they immediately made for the boats. The master raised the alarm with six short blasts on the ship's whistle, and chaos ensued when the lifeboats and rafts were launched. One of the lifeboats overturned and another drifted away empty. Of the crew of forty-seven, only seven survived the night to be picked up by escort ships.

The next afternoon, 10 March 1943, the Bustler class *Samsonia* and a Lend-Lease rescue tug, the *Eminent*, were ordered from Campbeltown to assist the destroyer HMS *Harvester*, damaged after ramming a U-boat. They picked up their corvette escort, HMS *Aubretia*, at Lough Foyle, but *Harvester* was then sunk by another U-boat and they were diverted to search for *Coulmore*, and found her on the evening of 13 March. *Eminent*'s commanding officer, Lt Louis Colmans, wrote in his report:

> Closed vessel. She was abandoned and wallowing in the trough of a rough sea and westerly swell. By first inspection it was noticed she was badly holed forward of her collision bulkhead, No. 1, hatches were nearly all off and water was spouting from her hold at times. State of the weather and the approaching darkness did not permit any connecting operations.[31]

By first light the weather had moderated and a party from the *Aubretia*, under the command of Sub-Lt PC Coyne RNVR, managed to board the abandoned steamer. The reports from the two rescue tugs kept to the bare facts of the operation, but Coyne's report eloquently describes the extreme difficulties of connecting up and towing an abandoned ship in rough Atlantic weather some thirteen hundred miles from land:

> On boarding I immediately went forward to
> ascertain damage caused by the explosion, and
> found that forepeak collision bulkhead and
> forward bulkhead of number one hold had been
> blown away, the weight of water thus being
> taken on the after bulkhead of number one hold.
> The starboard cable and locker had fallen through
> the bottom of the ship, the cable parting on
> the windlass. The port cable had also parted on
> the windlass but was still held by the whelps.
> The hatch covers of number one hold had
> been blown off and hold apparently empty of
> cargo.[31]

As it was impossible to tow the ship from her bows, the towing wires were made fast to her stern. This was not so easily done, as the *Eminent*'s four-and-a-half-inch wire hawser had to be manhandled on to the towing bollards on the port side of the *Coulmore*'s poop. It needed the whole party of fourteen men aboard the *Coulmore*, using two luff tackles, to succeed, but eventually the *Eminent* was connected. *Samsonia* attempted to connect up by passing a four-inch messenger rope through *Coulmore*'s starboard after fairlead, but it promptly broke as it could not bear the weight of the sixty fathoms of wire in the water.

The operation was not going well and the weather was deteriorating, so while *Samsonia* was recovering, her wire *Coulmore*'s boarding party took the precaution of making an emergency raft from the hatch covers of No. 1 hold. After *Samsonia* had again failed to connect, her commanding officer, Lt-Cdr Owen Jones RNR, took her alongside the *Coulmore*. The wire's messenger rope was led back to the rescue tug's after capstan, and this hauled the wire aboard the freighter. The boarding party led it through the after fairlead and secured it to the towing bollards on the starboard side of the *Coulmore*'s poop so that at 14.45 on 14 March, both rescue tugs were ready to commence towing together.

During the afternoon, the wind continued to increase again from the south-west, kicking up a rough sea with a short but heavy swell. The tow rope on both rescue tugs was inspected regularly, but in the early hours of the following morning, 15 March, the *Coulmore* began to sheer violently, and at 07.30 the *Eminent*'s wire parted. 'Commenced to heave wire aboard,' Colmans wrote laconically. Coyne's description was more graphic: 'The port wire jumped the fairlead and parted, carrying away the guardrails and one support to the gun platform. The wind was blowing about force 6 and the ship was rolling heavily.'

Samsonia was also in trouble, as at about the same time as the *Eminent*'s tow rope parted, *Samsonia*'s wire suddenly wrenched its fairlead out of the *Coulmore*'s deck, and carried away the freighter's starboard guardrails. The wire was now across the beading on the starboard quarter and chafing badly, but before this could be prevented with packing, the starboard bollard, to which the wire was attached, cracked across the middle. The inboard half began to lift out of the deck, but Coyne considered it too dangerous for the boarding party to do anything in case the bollard gave way altogether.

Samsonia continued to tow until around midday on 16 March, when the wire suddenly broke. By now it was far too rough for her to try to reconnect; and that evening the *Eminent*'s towing wire 'snapped', as Coyne described it, 'throwing the broken bollard twelve yards away'.

The *Coulmore* was now adrift again. The weather made reconnecting impossible, so Coyne decided to use the ship's main engines, which were still in working order. The ship was steered stern first, taking a course that protected her damaged bows from the worst of the weather. But she had barely any way on and steering her, as may be imagined, was very difficult, and, anyway, in the early hours of 17 March both engines seized up. But the rescue tugs had been standing by and reconnected when the weather moderated, although it took the *Eminent* more than three hours to do so.

The weather continued to improve and early in the afternoon of 19 March *Aubretia* departed for Londonderry, and the two rescue tugs headed for Rothesay, leaving the *Coulmore* at Kames Bay the following evening.

In due course the abandonment of the *Coulmore* was referred to the Leggett Committee, which investigated such cases. The committee's findings were unequivocal and severe, but as 'unhappily none of the principals concerned survived', the Board refrained from censoring any individual.

Another report called it 'a very sad story of panic and premature abandonment, which resulted in unnecessary loss of life',[31] and added that if the damage had been examined it would have shown 'that the only safe and sane course was to remain on board'. The only good note this report struck was that it concluded by saying that the ultimate salvaging of the ship by the two rescue tugs and their corvette escort 'was a very fine piece of work'.

The sole dissident voice among this barrage of recrimination was that of the second radio officer, the only officer to have survived. After describing the bravery of a sixteen-year-old deck boy who could not swim, but who had let go the seaman who was supporting him when he found he was dragging the man under, he ended his report with the following words:

> Captain Ashford was an extremely fine type of ship's master, and I am deeply sorry he was not amongst the survivors. I feel sure that he placed the safety of his crew before any other consideration, including his own life.

DANGER OF COLLISION

If premature abandonment was one of the many dangers for those manning the Atlantic convoys, collision was another that often had fatal consequences. One particularly horrendous incident occurred when the eastbound convoy HX-252 of fifty-two ships was off Newfoundland on the night of 18 August 1943. In the thick fog that blanketed the convoy, the Liberty ship *J Pinckney Henderson* and the tanker *JH Senior* collided. The former was carrying a particularly combustible cargo, which included magnesium, glycerine, resin and wax; the tanker was loaded with aviation fuel. The force of the collision was such that the aviation fuel was sprayed over both ships, and within seconds both were ablaze. Three of the Liberty ship's crew of seventy-two survived the inferno by jumping into the sea, as did six of the tanker's crew before she sank. The Liberty ship stayed afloat and in the thick fog drifted off into the Atlantic where she was found nearly two weeks later, still ablaze, by the Assurance class *Griper*, which had arrived with a westbound convoy at St John's the previous week.

'In a brilliant display of seamanship,' wrote the historian of the Liberty ships,[32] 'Charles Stanford [*Griper*'s commanding officer] managed to place six of his men on board the Liberty ship to secure the towing wire. The deck plating on the ship was so hot that men of the boarding party had to wrap sacking around their boots. It had been planned to use the ship's anchor chain as one end of the towing line but the chain was too hot to handle. In consequence the end of the tug's 120-fathom long wire was manhandled aboard and secured', and the funeral pyre was brought back to Sydney, Nova Scotia, where hundreds of onlookers gathered to watch.

The horrific scene that met those who went aboard the smouldering wreck was described by one of the rescue tug's crew, seventeen-year-old Tom Gay:

> The crew of the *Griper* were to age at the sight
> before them. The fire had been so instantaneous that
> bodies lay on the deck where they fell, all over the
> place. On the after deck only an arm remained
> visible of a victim still clutching a bucket.
> The victims in effect were simply 'kippered' in the
> inferno. The Canadian search party were supplied
> with bins into which the remains were placed.[33]

NOTES

1. Sanders RE. *The Practice of Ocean Rescue*. Glasgow: Brown, Son & Ferguson; 1947. p.10. The author was a member of the Rescue Tug Service. The US Coast Guard continues to use it as basic reference material on the subject.
2. Dear I. *The Ropner Story*. London: Hutchinson Benham; 1986. p.96.
3. Williams J, Gray J. *HM Rescue Tugs in World War II*. Privately printed. pp.122–23.
4. Dear I. *The Ropner Story, op. cit.* pp.82–83.

5. Williams J, Gray J. *HM Rescue Tugs*, *op. cit.* pp.54–55, although another source says forty-four men were rescued. The Admiralty War Diary for January 1943 is in fold3.com

6. ADM 1/17265.

7. Booklet on HMRT *Tenacity* in DSRTA archive and ADM 1/17266.

8. Davidson B. 'Warships in Dungarees' *Yank* (6 February 1944):8.

9. *Evening Telegram*, St John's, Newfoundland, 8 March 1943.

10. *London Gazette*, supplement 36033, 28 May 1943.

11. *Ibid.*, supplement 36866, 1 January 1945.

12. *Daily News*, St John's, Newfoundland, 26 June 1944.

13. Booklet on HMRT *Tenacity* in DSRTA archive and naval-history. net

14. Butler S. *Not For Davy Jones*. Bound manuscript, p.23. Courtesy of Peter Butler.

15. There are different versions of this incident. This one is based on the account written by Dr Robert M Browning Jr, which is on the United States Coast Guard website. Also Butler S, *Not For Davy Jones*, *op. cit.*, pp.22–24.

16. ADM 199/1271.

17. ADM 1/2139 and ADM 1/12028.

18. *Ships Monthly*, July 1992.

19. ADM 1/12028.

20. Butler S, *Not For Davy Jones*, *op. cit.*, p.7, describes a box search as 'searching the area around where the ship in distress is believed to be. It is marked out on a chart as a large square divided into smaller squares. Allowances are made for the direction the ship could be drifting in. The rescue tug would then proceed back and forth until the complete area had been covered.'

21. ADM 1/12028.

22. *London Gazette*, issue 35586, 5 June 1942.

23. Butler S, *Not For Davy Jones*, *op. cit.* pp.30–32.

24. Williams J, Gray J. *HM Rescue Tugs*, *op. cit.* pp.67–69.

25. Butler S, *Not For Davy Jones, op. cit.* p.33.
26. ADM 1/15549.
27. *Hull Daily Mail*, 19 January 1943.
28. *London Gazette*, second supplement, no 36062, 18 June 1943.
29. *Yorkshire Post Leeds Intelligencer*, 23 June 1943.
30. £50 in 1943 is roughly worth £1,900 today: see www. measuringworth.com.
31. ADM 1/15521.
32. Elphick P. *Liberty: the Ships that Won the War*. Chatham Publishing, Rochester 2001, p.301.
33. *Ibid.*, p.302.

6

LEND-LEASE TO
THE RESCUE

THE ENTRY OF the United States into the war in December 1941 tilted eventual victory in favour of the Allies, but as in the First World War, it took time for the Americans to gather their resources. While they did so the Lend-Lease Act, enacted by Congress in March 1941, was an essential aid to help underpin the Allied war effort. It authorised the president to lend or lease – or sell – war supplies of all kinds, including food, to the country's allies, on terms agreed by the parties concerned. This agreement was of crucial benefit to the Rescue Tug Service, which otherwise would never have been able to expand in the way it did.

However, the Admiralty did not rely entirely on Lend-Lease for its rescue tugs, and throughout the war British ones continued to be constructed, adapted from designs of commercial tugs already afloat. As we have seen, the new Assurance class was based on the very successful *Salvonia*, and in the late 1930s the London firm of Overseas Towage & Salvage Company had decided they must find a new design to compete with the large ocean-going tugs that the Dutch and Germans were constructing. The one they chose was essentially an improved *Zwarte Zee*, although with modifications suggested by the

Thames, Smit's most modern tug. The firm concluded that the most economical method of powering the new design was with two diesel engines coupled to a single screw. Without a tow, or with a very light one, only one engine was necessary; when a high speed was needed, or when towing a very large ship, both engines were employed.

With this new design still at an early stage, in September 1939 the company's technical staff began to work with the Admiralty's Naval Construction Department. The result was the Bustler class, named after the first one to be commissioned in 1942. Compared with the 792-ton, 208 ft *Zwarte Zee*, the Bustlers were 1100 tons and 205 ft long, the same length as the Flower class corvettes that did such sterling work as convoy escorts. But the Bustlers were far more powerful than any corvette, being equipped with two British Polar-Atlas diesel engines, giving them a pulling power and speed comparable with *Zwarte Zee*.

The Bustlers had a complement of forty-two and were well armed with a three-inch dual-purpose gun, an A-A two-pounder 'pom-pom', two Oerlikons and four Lewis A-A machine guns, and were constructed at the Leith shipyard of Henry Robb. *Bustler* and *Samsonia* were commissioned in 1942, followed by *Growler* and *Hesperia* in 1943, *Mediator* in 1944, and *Reward*, *Turmoil* and *Warden* in 1945. Not before time, they were equipped with electric, automatic, self-rendering towing winches.

In December 1944, *Lloyd's Shipping Gazette* published a long article about rescue tugs, which included details of three of these powerful vessels:

> The *Bustler* has assisted five ships, totalling 38,894 tons gross, disabled by enemy action or weather, including the *Empire Treasure*, which was towed 110 miles in gales

of up to force 10 in strength. For this fine piece of work the commanding officer of the tug [Lt RE Sanders RNR] was appointed MBE. The *Bustler* also towed the steamship *Durham*[1] from Gibraltar to Falmouth and assisted and towed five naval craft. For 12 months she was employed on convoy escort work in the North Atlantic.

Another tug, the *Samsonia*, assisted four ships of about 24,000 tons gross which had been disabled by enemy action or weather; she made 14 North Atlantic voyages in 11 months on convoy escort work.[2]

The third rescue tug to be mentioned was *Growler*, 'which has assisted one ship of 5,000 tons with weather damage, and she was engaged in Atlantic convoy escort work for nine months, making eight voyages'.[2]

The best known of the class, *Turmoil*, made her name after the war when she attempted to salvage the 6711-ton freighter *Flying Enterprise*. The ship was en route for the United States when she encountered a storm off south-west England on 28 December 1951. Her cargo shifted and she began to list, and the ten passengers and most of the crew had to be taken off. *Turmoil* reached her on 3 January, but the storm was still so bad that, with *Flying Enterprise* some three hundred nautical miles from Falmouth, the *Turmoil* could not connect up with the freighter for two days. The *Turmoil* managed to tow her within forty nautical miles of Falmouth, but the freighter had suffered structural damage to her hull, and on 10 January 1952 she sank.

In 1955 the writer Ewart Brookes published a book about the incident. An ex-naval officer, he had seen rescue tugs at work, and thought highly of them and the men who manned them. In his Author's Note, he wrote that the *Turmoil* was 'the representative of a type of ship sailed by a type of seaman who conceded nothing in quality of seamanship to any other branch in the seagoing world, even of any other generation. They go unsung, often unhonoured, never glamorized.'[3] However, he had never seen a rescue tug close to, until his ship lay alongside one late in the war:

> She was, to within a few feet, as long as the fighting ship I commanded. But her engines were more than four times as powerful. Whereas we had scarcely enough room to swing a very short cat (the nine-thonged variety, not the milk-drinking species) on our decks, she had enough room on her towing deck to hold a dance with a fair-sized band to accompany it.[3]

In 1944, an American armed forces magazine gave the Bustlers an enthusiastic review:

> [These] huge well-equipped heavy-duty escort tugs that shuttle back and forth across the North Atlantic today as easily as if they were going from San Francisco to Oakland... Their new-type pumps can remove water from flooded holds at the rate of 800 tons an hour; their fire-fighting chemical jets can extinguish flames from a distance of 60 feet. They are death to an attacking aircraft. And they can take in tow a battleship as easily as a jeep can tow a 20-mm gun. All the equipment on the Bustlers – windlasses, winches, capstans – is electrically operated. So modern and complicated is the machinery that each ship carries a special electrical officer. The Bustler is to the ordinary harbor tug what a Packard is to a baby carriage.[4]

Two other classes of rescue tug were also built in Britain during the war. The Nimble class was very similar to the Bustler class and was also powered by two diesel engines, but had twin screws. They were the same length, and had the same speed as the Bustlers, but were not quite as heavily armed. *Nimble*, the first to be commissioned in 1942, was built at the Paisley shipyard of Fleming and Ferguson, as was *Expert*, commissioned in November 1945. The other two, *Capable* and *Careful*, were built by the Aberdeen firm of Hall, Russell & Co. These were not commissioned until 1946, so only *Nimble* saw any wartime action. She was based at Gibraltar but also stationed at various ports in the western Mediterranean.

The Envoy class was developed after the responsibility for the design and construction of rescue tugs had been moved to the Admiralty's Department of Merchant Shipbuilding and Repairs in January 1943. The following month its director, Sir Amos Ayre, received a brief from the CCRT for a new class of rescue tug. In it he remarked that the diesel-type rescue tug was not popular as its maintenance was beyond the normal capacity of the crew, while the Assurance type tug had insufficient endurance to take the place of the diesel. What he wanted was a new type of 'A' class tug (see Appendix), similar to the Assurance class but with greater endurance, a minimum of twenty days, and this probably meant a two-boiler ship.[5]

The same month Ayre wrote to Cochrane's about building a new class along the lines recommended by the CCRT. Cochrane's replied by warning that 'we may be starting a vicious circle. The Assurance tugs have been recently so altered and added to that it is nearly time they were entirely re-designed.' On 9 February, Ayre replied that as Cochrane's were obviously ready for a new design a new prototype could be constructed, from which Cochrane's could then build as many as possible, as fast as possible. But he warned that 'we have to introduce a greater degree of austerity in all we are doing', and added in a later letter, that 'provided we can supply everything of a highly seaworthy and dependable nature, there are no longer to be extravagances or frills'. One wonders what frills and extravagances he had in mind.

Commercial opinion favoured a similar design to the *Neptunia*, which Cochrane's had designed and built, and this received the backing of the Assistant Chief of Naval Staff (U-boat Warfare and Trade). The principal small ship designer in the Admiralty's Department of Merchant Shipbuilding and Repairs, Mr A Caldwell, re-examined the design of the *Neptunia* and an order was subsequently placed with Cochrane's for a vessel, which was in effect a modified version of her, with twin boilers and a single screw. During 1944, six of these Envoy class rescue tugs were commissioned. They have been described as an intermediary class between the Assurance and Bustler classes, but they hardly figure in operational documents.

By January 1943 the number of operational rescue tugs at the disposal of the Rescue Tug Service had risen to fifty-one, and to seventy-seven by January 1944. By the end of 1943 they had towed to safety one hundred and eighty-five British and Allied warships, and merchant ships totalling 2¼ million tons. But this was not achieved without casualties, and fourteen rescue tugs, and a number of personnel, were lost.[6]

LEND-LEASE AND SHORTAGE OF CREWS

The planned programme could not possibly provide the solution to the acute shortage of rescue tugs, and in numbers they hardly replaced those that had already been lost. What was urgently needed, particularly in the Atlantic, was a large injection of powerful rescue tugs capable of working in the open ocean.

It was here that the Lend-Lease Act was of critical help to the Rescue Tug Service. In June 1941, the first of several requests was made under it, and between 1942 and 1944 the Americans provided the Royal Navy and the Royal Australian Navy with twenty-seven rescue tugs.

Twenty-three of these were called the Favorite class, and were powered by twin General Motors diesel-electric engines. Like the Bustler class, they had an electric-powered towing winch, but with the added luxuries of electric water pumps – these were hand-operated on British ships – and even an ice-water fountain on the mess deck, which were perhaps the frills and extravagances Sir Amos Ayre was referring to. They were 143 ft in length with a tonnage of 835. They had an armament of one three-inch dual-purpose gun and two Oerlikons, and had a top speed of fourteen knots.

Most of these vessels were built by the Levingston Shipbuilding Company at Orange, Texas, but three – *Oriana*, *Tancred* and *Weazel* – were constructed by a sister company, Gulfport Boiler & Welding Works, Port Arthur, Texas, and four – *Aimwell*, *Bold*, *Destiny* and *Eminent* – were built by the Defoe Shipbuilding Company, Bay City, Michigan. Three of the class, *Reserve*, *Sprightly* and *Tancred*, were transferred to the Royal Australian Navy.

Four larger, wooden-hulled ATRs (Auxiliary Tug – Rescue) – *Director*, *Emulous*, *Freedom* and *Justice* – were also handed over to the British under the Lend-Lease Act. Built at the Camden shipbuilding yard, Camden, New Jersey, they were 165 ft long, had a tonnage of 850, and were powered by a single triple-expansion steam reciprocating engine, which gave a speed of twelve knots.

Thanks to Lend-Lease, the scarcity of rescue tugs began to ease by 1943, but more of them brought another problem: insufficient T.124T personnel to man them. The recruitment by EG Martin of Sea Cadets would have been prompted by this shortage, and it also led to several rescue tugs being manned by civilian crews. Such was the need to increase recruitment that in September 1942 an advertisement, 'Men Wanted for Rescue Tug Service', had been placed in a Hull newspaper,[7] and in June 1943 the Director of the Trade Division signalled the C-in-C Western Approaches:

> It is to be regretted that after full consideration the manning situation does not permit of an additional watch-keeping officer being appointed to Rescue Tugs. Owing to the great shortage of deck officers, two new tugs will have to be manned by Overseas Towage and Salvage Co. The matter is constantly in mind and additional officers will be appointed as soon as the manning situation permits.[8]

The two new rescue tugs to which the Director of the Trade Division was referring were *Assiduous*, one of the last Assurance class to be launched (June 1943), and the Bustler class *Hesperia*. Initially, *Assiduous* flew the Red Ensign until she was commissioned into the Royal Navy after the Normandy landings the following year.[9] *Hesperia* was based at Campbeltown, and was employed as an Atlantic escort tug in 1943, and in 1944 was stationed with the Eastern Fleet at Trincomalee where she was due to stay until 1945.[10] However, there was some unspecified disagreement with the crew about this, and she returned earlier, but was wrecked in a storm off the Libyan coast in February 1945, along with the American Lend-Lease AFD 24 she was towing with *Empire Sandy*.[11]

The rescue tugs and their tow were routed to pass six miles off Ras Aamer, Libya, the standard eastbound route that enabled ships to make a good landfall after the four-hundred-mile stretch from Malta. The available weather reports to the naval authorities in the Eastern Mediterranean on the evening of 6 February forecast westerly winds force 4–5 for the passage between Benghazi and Port Said, but during the next morning the barometer fell eleven millibars and by evening the wind was blowing force 8–9.

The weather deteriorated rapidly and the wind then veered to the north, giving the tugs no chance to make an offing. Soon they were forced to head into the gale but could make no headway and were slowly driven to leeward. At about 17.00 *Empire Sandy* had to slip her tow as she was unable to hold her position and was in danger of capsizing. Half an hour later, *Hesperia*'s tow rope parted and five minutes after that she and the AFD were driven ashore, and although there was no loss of life both became a total loss.[12]

TRANSATLANTIC CONVOY ESCORTS

The greater power and endurance of the Bustler class and the Lend-Lease rescue tugs allowed a new method of employing them, which was heralded by an Admiralty signal dated 4 January 1943:

> It is intended to attach HM Rescue Tugs to the
> [Escort] groups of Trans-Atlantic convoys and
> to establish Tug Pool Base at Campbeltown in
> UK with Western Base in Newfoundland where
> administration, rest and recreation can be provided for
> 2 or 3 rescue tugs.[13]

Then, in early March, the Admiralty informed the C-in-C Western Approaches, whose headquarters at Liverpool led the fight against the U-boats, that as 'there may be occasions when rescue tugs can keep up with the convoy while towing, it has been decided that they may sail in Atlantic convoys without special escort'.[14]

These signals were followed in June by the remarks of the Director of the Trade Division, who wrote in a progress report that it had not been until the spring that enough rescue tugs had become available to sail one in each trans-Atlantic convoy. Doing so provided:

> the great advantage that, if a ship became a casualty,
> she could be taken in tow at once instead of a tug
> having to be sent out to search for the casualty which,
> without air cooperation, frequently proved to be a
> fruitless task.[15]

However, the C-in-C Western Approaches, while doubtless happy with this new arrangement, was not satisfied with how it was to be operated. He now had two of the new and powerful Bustler class rescue tugs, *Samsonia* and *Growler*, allotted to his command, and he suggested that they 'should now be allocated to me by name and that I should assume complete operational and administrative control of these vessels'.[16] This may have caused the CCRT some consternation. If every command made the same demand, there would be precious little left for him to control, and the comments the FOIC Greenock added on 22 April would not have reassured him:

> As a result of considerable experience of rescue tugs in
> the Greenock Sub-Command, and after full discussion
> with Naval Officer in Charge, Campbeltown, I consider
> that the present arrangements for the administration and
> maintenance of rescue tugs in this area are not entirely
> satisfactory.[16]

In his opinion, the general organisation of the Rescue Tug Service, as originally laid down, had envisaged a large measure of centralisation:

> [But it was] indefinite in regard to local responsibility. The result of this in practice has been that the Rescue Tug personnel are to some extent left in the air and do not know to what extent they are being administered by the Admiralty, the local Rescue Tug organisation, or the local Naval authority. Frequent complaints have been made recently by Rescue Tug Commanding Officers that they are now 'nobody's children'. Within the last few days a Dutch Captain volunteered the information that he was 'nobody's darling'. **The large majority of these vessels fly the White Ensign and are Naval vessels and should be treated as such** [author's emphasis]. In the past, every effort was made to impress on the officers and men that they were an integral part of the Royal Navy, but this effort has been largely nullified recently.[17]

He suggested this was at least partly due to an Admiralty Fleet Order (AFO) that had been issued on 28 January 1943.[18] This stated that all engineering matters concerning the Rescue Tug Service would be divided into four geographical areas under marine superintendents – a term only used in the Merchant Navy – who would report to the chief marine superintendent at the Admiralty:

> Morale has deteriorated in recent months and the attitude of some of the more experienced Captains towards their administration is definitely critical.
> I would strongly urge that the administration of these

tugs should be decentralized to a greater extent than at present, and that any tendency to organize or administer them as a separate service should be severely repressed.

When tugs are allocated to a Command, the local Naval authority should be responsible for their efficiency and welfare, assisted by the Rescue Tug maintenance personnel, whose specialist knowledge is invaluable. Similarly, emergency repairs to these very important ships should be dealt with by the local Naval authority in just the same ways as any other Naval vessel, and should not be delayed for authority from London before being taken in hand.

It is fully appreciated that many matters such as the allocation of tugs, appointment and drafting of personnel, and technical questions peculiar to Rescue Tugs, must be centralized in the Captain in Charge of Rescue Tugs, Admiralty, but as far as possible, the operational efficiency of tugs and the welfare of their personnel should be left in the hands of the local Naval authorities concerned.[19]

The C-in-C Western Approaches forwarded this memorandum to the Admiralty with the attached note:

I concur that the existing arrangements are not entirely satisfactory. Since the policy of sailing rescue tugs with Trans-Atlantic convoys has been implemented, these vessels become virtually a part of the Escort Group and work in the closest cooperation with their own attendant escort trawlers. **This, in my opinion, emphasizes the importance of stressing the fact that these vessels arc an important integral part of the Royal Navy** [author's emphasis].[20]

As the C-in-C Western Approaches was no less a person than Admiral Sir Max Horton, the principal guiding hand in winning the Battle of the Atlantic, this showed unequivocally the commitment the Royal Navy had to the Rescue Tug Service. It was one of its own and should be treated as such.

THE NEW GNAT TORPEDO

The policy of allowing the more powerful rescue tugs to accompany Atlantic convoys worked well if the salvage of a torpedoed frigate by a Lend-Lease rescue tug is a typical example.

At the end of August 1943, Admiral Dönitz returned to the North Atlantic with a wolf-pack of twenty-eight U-boats. Some were armed with the latest version of the GNAT acoustic torpedo (T5), and with this Dönitz employed the new tactic of attacking the escorts before the wolf-pack turned on the unprotected convoy. The westbound convoy ON-202 departed Liverpool on 15 September and was intercepted by the wolf-pack five days later, shortly before ON-202 combined with another convoy, ONS-18, some six hundred and fifty miles out into the Atlantic. The battle lasted several days. It cost Dönitz three U-boats; six merchant ships and three escorts were also sunk. As the escorts were the primary targets, it was a poor return for Dönitz, but the score was slightly improved when one of the escorts, the frigate HMS *Lagan*, had her stern blown off by one of the new acoustic torpedoes, which resulted in her never seeing action again.

The *Lagan* was torpedoed in the early hours of 20 September 1943, and such was the force of the explosion that her commanding officer later reported:

> A large quantity of debris was thrown high into the
> air and began to rain down upon the ship. A large

tangled mass of steel, 12 feet by 6 feet (which was probably a part of the deck of the after provision room passage) dropped onto the fo'c's'le head, cutting the starboard cable and causing other minor damage. Three depth charges landed on the boat deck, damaging the motor-boat, and the Carley floats. Pieces of metal of various sizes, and quantities of tinned food, fell on the upper deck, including a moderate amount of the compass platform.[21]

The torpedo also caused heavy casualties amongst the crew and threw their bodies all over the ship:

Shortly after the torpedoing, the body of a rating, whose action station was on the quarter deck, was found on the port side of the fo'c's'le immediately abaft the breakwater. Another was found in the dinghy on the starboard side of the boat-deck. A further two bodies were found, one hanging over the guardrail on the port side of the quarter-deck and one at the forward end of the quarter-deck. The following day another body was recovered from amid the wreckage of the quarter-deck... Subsequent searching revealed a further body wedged amid the wreckage in an inaccessible position of vertical portion of the quarter-deck overhanging the starboard quarter.[21]

Altogether, one officer and twenty-eight ratings were killed.

The following morning, the Lend-Lease rescue tug *Destiny*, commanded by Lt RE Sanders RNR, which was part of ON-202's ocean escort group C2, arrived with her trawler escort and, the frigate's commanding officer wrote, 'was skilfully manoeuvred close to the stem' so that two hundred and ten fathoms of

5-inch wire could be connected. Towing commenced and good progress was made until the following evening when the tow line parted. The towing gear was recovered by the escort and Sanders suggested that connecting up again should be left until the morning:

> But as the weather appeared threatening, he was
> persuaded to try again in the dark. With further
> skilful manoeuvring a new tow was passed; at 0055 on
> 22 September towing was again commenced, satisfactory
> progress being maintained during the remainder of
> the day.[21]

Inishtrahull Light was sighted abeam to starboard the following evening, and at 20.00 on 24 September the *Destiny* and her tow and escort arrived off the entrance of the swept channel to the River Mersey, having covered six hundred and eighty miles in eighty-five hours at an average speed of eight knots. If she'd had to sail from Campbeltown, where she was based, to bring in the *Lagan*, the operation would have taken twice as long. The C-in-C Western Approaches ended his report on the battle to the Admiralty with the remark that the *Destiny* 'performed her duties very well in the face of numerous difficulties'.[22]

Although not particularly successful, Dönitz persisted with his tactics of attacking a convoy's escorts first. In the battle for convoy ONS-224 the following February, two of the convoy's escorts, part of Captain Walker's famous Second Escort Group, were attacked five hundred miles west of Cork when a U-boat fired its bow and stern GNAT torpedoes at them simultaneously. One missed Walker's sloop, HMS *Starling*, but the other destroyed the stern of the sloop HMS *Woodpecker*, which had been credited with helping to destroy six U-boats and was an invaluable member of the escort group. The Assurance class rescue tug *Storm King* was dispatched and for a week nursed the stricken sloop towards Devonport. However, the rescue tug was eventually foiled by the weather – as they so often were – when *Woodpecker* capsized and sank in a gale near the Scillies, though the skeleton crew was saved.

NOTES

1. This 10,393-ton cargo ship was one of the cripples discussed in Chapter 8 after she hit a mine off Pantellaria in the Mediterranean in August 1941. She was taken to Gibraltar where she was torpedoed by an Italian one-man submarine, and had to be beached. She was refloated and drydocked for temporary repairs before being towed to Falmouth the following September.
2. *Lloyd's Shipping Gazette*, 18 December, 1944.
3. Brookes E. *Turmoil.* London: Jarrolds; 1956. pp.10–11.
4. Davidson B. 'Warships in Dungarees', *Yank* (6 February 1944): 10.
5. Letter from Captain Bateson, 3 February 1943, in ADM 1/15352, as is all the other relevant correspondence quoted. The Lend-Lease diesel tugs did seem to have a propensity to break down, and *Eminent* caught fire twice.
6. Signal in 'Trade Division History' in DRSTA red folder.
7. *Hull Daily Mail*, 28 September 1942. Because so many volunteers for the Rescue Tug Service came from the city it was nicknamed 'Hull's Navy'.
8. ADM 199/2165, 17 June 1943.
9. From information supplied to Len Reed by Tom Osborne, who served as a galley boy, aged fifteen, in the *Assiduous* during the Normandy landings. Also *Towrope* 1999 (October)1:10. Courtesy of Len Reed.
10. ADM 1/16284.
11. See www.empiresandy.com for her wartime – and post-war – career.
12. Letter from secretary, Rescue Tug Section, to Paymaster Rear Admiral Manisty, 4 April 1944, in ADM 199/2165.

13. ADM 199/186 Loss and damage HM ships, 1944–45.

14. ADM 199/2165, 2 March 1943.

15. ADM 199/2165, 1 June 1943.

16. ADM 1/15548, 17 March 1943.

17. *Ibid.*, 22 April 1943.

18. AFO 331 in ADM 162/113.

19. ADM 1/15548, 22 April 1943.

20. *Ibid.*, 2 May 1943.

21. ADM 199/2069.

22. See www.warsailors.com/convoys/on202.html

7

THE MEDITERRANEAN AND BEYOND

O N 10 JUNE 1940 Italy's dictator, Benito Mussolini, declared war on France and Britain, having waited to make sure Germany had the upper hand over both of them. He invaded eastern France immediately and in September launched an attack into Egypt from the Italian colony of Libya to capture the Suez Canal.

Opposing him at sea in the Mediterranean were powerful British naval forces, based at Gibraltar in the west and Alexandria in the east, with Malta – roughly equidistant between them – being a vital staging post. The island was of critical importance to the Allies, as it was from there that submarines and aircraft were able to intercept the convoys that supplied Axis forces intent on capturing the Suez Canal.[1]

So intense were the Axis air attacks on Malta, and on the ships that supplied the island, it seemed that the island would be starved into surrender. Once North Africa fell to the Allies in May 1943 and Sicily was captured in August, Axis aircraft became less of a threat – though, as will be seen, they caused one of the worst tragedies of the war at sea in November 1943 – but in the early years of the conflict they closed the central Mediterranean supply route, forcing convoys to be diverted around the Cape of Good Hope. As a consequence, rescue tugs were based at Freetown, Sierra Leone, and elsewhere on the Sub-Saharan coastline.

From the start, Mussolini's vainglorious attempts to build a new Roman Empire went badly awry, and Hitler was soon obliged to support his ally by dispatching aircraft to the Mediterranean and by underpinning Italian forces in Libya with Rommel's *Afrika Korps*. Also, much to the displeasure of Dönitz, Hitler ordered some U-boats to be withdrawn from the Atlantic and redeployed in the Mediterranean. But while German bombers were ideally positioned to attack Allied Mediterranean convoys from Axis-held territory, and did so very effectively, U-boat operations were never as lethal as they were in the Atlantic – but lethal they were, as will be seen.

The Italian Navy had between sixty and eighty operational U-boats, some of which patrolled outside the Mediterranean, but nothing like that number were active simultaneously and their tactical expertise, compared with the Germans, was low. German U-boats only entered the Mediterranean after September 1941, and rarely exceeded twenty at any one time. The tactics of both sides varied from those employed in the Atlantic: The confined waters of the Mediterranean precluded diversionary moves by convoys and the use of wolf-packs by U-boats, which relied instead on patrolling Allied convoy routes individually. At the end of 1943, the Allies began to employ 'Swamp' tactics where, if enough Allied A/S aircraft and escorts were close enough to make it economically worthwhile, a U-boat was hunted to exhaustion, a technique that by September 1944 put an end to U-boat activities in the Mediterranean.[2]

Unlike the Battle of the Atlantic, the war at sea in the Mediterranean did not entirely revolve around convoys, as it was where the Allies first mounted large-scale amphibious landings. First, on 8 November 1942, they invaded the French North

African Vichy-controlled (pro-Nazi) colonies of Algeria and Morocco. From there, the Anglo-US armies moved eastwards, and by May 1943 the whole of the North African coastline, including Libya, was under Allied control. An amphibious assault on Sicily followed in July 1943; and when the island had been liberated, the Allies moved on to mainland Italy, with one pincer crossing the Strait of Messina (3 September 1943), while the other landed at Salerno, south of Naples (9 September 1943). When these operations failed to achieve a swift advance northward, a third major landing was launched at Anzio (22 January 1944), south of Rome. Lastly, as part of the attack on Hitler's northern European citadel, the Allies landed on the French Riviera on 15 August 1944.

All these operations involved the Rescue Tug Service. Working with American rescue tugs, it escorted the convoys that supplied the men ashore, towed off stranded ships and landing craft, and removed to safety warships that had been damaged during the pre-landing bombardments and in the gunnery support they subsequently gave the troops ashore.

GIBRALTAR'S RESCUE TUGS

One of the earliest U-boat successes in the Mediterranean was sinking the aircraft carrier HMS *Ark Royal*, which was torpedoed thirty miles from Gibraltar on 13 November 1941. She took on an immediate list of ten degrees, which quickly increased to eighteen degrees, and the captain ordered an accompanying destroyer to take off most of the crew, including the animals aboard. The canaries were let out of their cages and made their way to land, and an enormous ginger tomcat was taken aboard the destroyer in the arms of a marine. Counter-flooding reduced the list, and gradually steam was raised. The Dutch rescue tug *Thames* arrived from Gibraltar in the evening, after returning from a vain attempt to tow in the destroyer HMS *Cossack*, which had been torpedoed west of Gibraltar.

The *Thames* connected to the carrier, and soon the '*Ark*' was making two knots towards Gibraltar, though unfortunately there was a one-knot current running against her. The arrival of the Saint class rescue tug *St Day* from Gibraltar soon afterwards raised hopes that Gibraltar could be reached, but in the early hours of the following morning a fire broke out in the port boiler room, bringing all salvage work to a standstill. The carrier's list increased again, and soon reached twenty-seven degrees, and the fire continued to rage. When all hope had gone of saving the ship, every available rope was taken forward and secured inboard, abreast of the *St Day*, so that the two hundred and fifty men on board could leave quickly and cross the rescue tug to reach a destroyer, which was also helping with the tow. This was safely accomplished and shortly afterwards the '*Ark*' turned turtle. She remained bottom up for some minutes and then sank from sight.[3]

The *St Day* spent most of the war at Gibraltar, and her time there was clearly recalled by a member of the crew, Charlie Ghent, one of the 215 Newfoundlanders who volunteered for the Rescue Tug Service:

> I joined *St Day* in Gibraltar in April 1942. We 'dodged' behind the Malta convoys, and also patrolled the Straits of Gibraltar checking what cargoes ships had. The shipping was mostly Spanish.[4]

After the North African landings, Charlie remembered:

> [*St Day*] spent some time towing landing craft off the beaches after troops had been landed ashore. Xmas day was spent in Algiers. On to Philippeville docking ships

in the harbour. On New Year's Eve we towed a tanker that had beached trying to get into Bougie harbour. After securing the tanker to the docks, it was bombed that night. We spent the next day pouring water on to her to put out the fires.

We spent some time docking ships in Bougie and then Bône. Where we were docked in Bône the Captain decided to move the *St Day* to the next dock round the corner to make it easier for sailing the next day. We were having dinner when an air raid started. A German plane was shot down by a Spitfire and crashed into the water where the *St Day* had been berthed before we moved her!

While at Bône we had a 'near miss' when a bomb exploded alongside us. It caused a crack in the bunker tank so we kept the pumps going as we returned to Gibraltar in convoy. On the way a torpedo crossed our bows and hit a merchant ship. We picked up all 30 crew who were later transferred to a destroyer and taken to Gibraltar.[4]

The *St Day* was part of the naval forces supporting the North African landings on 8 November 1942. One of the ships she assisted was the American attack transport USS *Thomas Stone*, which had been hit aft by an aerial torpedo on 7 November while bound for the Algiers' beaches with tanks and fourteen hundred troops. Rudderless, but in no danger of sinking, the *Thomas Stone* launched her landing craft and sent all but two of them, loaded with troops, to the Algiers' landing beaches one hundred and forty miles away. The convoy corvette assigned to protect her went with them, leaving the two remaining landing craft to circle round the damaged transport ship as an anti-submarine screen.

The weather, calm at first, deteriorated, and one by one the landing craft had to be abandoned long before they reached their destination. The troops aboard them transferred to the corvette, which landed them at Algiers, but too late for them to take part in its capture. Meanwhile, two British destroyers hooked up with the *Thomas Stone*, but found they were unable to tow her as she could not be steered; and it wasn't until the *St Day* arrived at dawn the next morning to take over that the *Thomas Stone* at last reached the comparative safety of Algiers on 11 November.

The Assurance class rescue tugs *Hengist* and *Restive* were also deployed for the North African landings and later took part in the Sicilian landings, as did the Lend-Lease *Oriana* and the Saint class *St Monance*. *Hengist* and the Lend-Lease *Favorite* were both at Salerno, and the Assurance class *Prosperous* did some good work at Anzio. On 24 January 1944, she went to the assistance of the destroyer USS *Mayo*, which had struck a mine while supporting the landings. The mine blew a hole in the destroyer's side about twelve feet by twenty feet, killing several men, and the *Prosperous* towed her to Naples to be patched up. She also took the 7176-ton American store ship *Hilary A Herbert*, to Naples for repairs, after an aircraft crashed on to the store ship's decks on 26 January. On 21 February, she worked with the American salvage tug USS *Hopi* to tow off an American landing craft, tank (LCT) from Green Beach, but they were heavily shelled and had to withdraw. They succeeded the next day and also assisted in refloating an American tug, USS *Edenshaw*, which had gone aground earlier.[5]

One magazine reported:

> For D-Day and 41 days afterwards, the *Prosperous*
> never left the bombed and shelled anchorage.
> Throughout the beachhead's hottest spells of

bombardment the tug was hard at work towing landing-craft off the beaches, laying booms, and handling a dozen other jobs close inshore. Back in Naples [where she was based] and in a howling gale the *Prosperous* achieved one of her outstanding rescue jobs. Despite high seas she hauled a large merchant ship to the harbour entrance but found it impossible to shorten the tow, so the vessel was skilfully jockeyed into the port on a tow nearly a quarter-of-a-mile long...
First Lieutenant of the *Prosperous*, Sub-Lt CA Turner of Dovercourt, has been with the ship since her commissioning. He checks the tug's rescues on a score-board of national flags, each denoting a ship towed to safety. [Her Commanding Officer] Lt Lloyd has had long experience with rescue-tugs. He played a prominent part when the Dutch tug, *Hudson*, assisted in pulling a blazing ammunition ship out of Algiers nearly two years ago [see Chapter 8]. He served in HMS *Superman*, and took HMS *Empire Denis* into the beaches of Salerno.[6]

Other rescue tugs involved in operations in the Mediterranean were the Lend-Lease vessels *Mindful*, *Aspirant* and *Athlete*, and the Assurance class *Charon*. All of them participated in the French Riviera landings, the last three being part of Delta Force's 'combat and firefighting group'.[7]

TROOPSHIP CASUALTIES

Another casualty of the North African landings was the 23,722-ton British troopship *Strathallan*. She was part of convoy KMF-5 from the Clyde to Oran when she was torpedoed in the early hours of 21 December 1942; aboard her were two hundred and ninety-six military officers, two hundred and forty-eight nurses, four thousand one hundred and twelve American and British army personnel and four hundred and sixty-five members of the crew. The torpedo struck the ship in the engine room on the port side. The master later wrote in his report:

> All lights failed and the ship listed 15 degrees to port
> at once. The explosion was very violent, throwing a
> huge column of water over the ship, and blowing
> No. 8 boat over the head of the davits, from where it
> could not be dislodged.[8]

Fearing another torpedo, the master ordered the boats to be lowered, but after the damage had been inspected it was thought the ship would remain afloat, and he ordered them to return. As the pumps were holding their own, one of the escort destroyers started to tow the troopship towards land, while two other destroyers took off the troops and all but a skeleton crew. At 1pm, when it appeared very probable that the ship would reach Oran, the Assurance class rescue tug *Restive* (Lt DM Richards RNR) arrived from Gibraltar to help pump out the water in the engine room. But soon afterwards oil reached the troopship's red-hot boilers. Flames shot high out of the funnel and continued to burn fiercely, stripping the paint from the funnel and ventilators.

Fire hoses were passed from the *Restive*, and ammunition from a magazine on *Strathallan*'s 'A' Deck was jettisoned. The fire had broken out in several places, and the centre of the ship was soon ablaze. The master ordered the skeleton crew to abandon ship, and the *Restive* took over the tow from the destroyer, but at 4am the next morning, just twelve miles from Oran, *Strathallan* rolled over on to her side and sank. With more than five thousand men and women aboard her, it is amazing the casualties were so light: six members of the crew, five nurses and five soldiers died.

The *Strathallan* was lucky to suffer such few casualties; the *Rohna* was not so fortunate. By the end of 1943, air attacks on convoys were becoming a more serious threat than U-boats, and on the afternoon of 26 November 1943 thirty German bombers, some of them armed with a new aerial weapon, the Henschel Hs 293 radio-guided glide bomb, attacked convoy KMF-26 some fifteen miles from Jijelli, Algeria. About sixty of the glider bombs were released, but because they were too difficult for the aircraft to handle, or could not be guided in properly because of the convoy's intense A-A fire, the attack largely failed.

One bomb did find its target. Released by a Heinkel 177 flying at about ten thousand feet, it homed in on the *Rohna*, a 8602-ton British troopship with almost two thousand people aboard, most of them US Army personnel. The bomb exploded on the port side aft of the funnel just above the waterline. Such was its power that it blew a seventy-five square foot hole on the other side of the ship, by the waterline, and an eyewitness from a nearby ship said he could see right through *Rohna*'s hull.

The explosion rocked the ship and flooded her engine room, and started a fire in one of the holds. The fire quickly spread aft, causing heavy casualties among those on the troop decks below. It also destroyed six of the ship's twenty-two lifeboats, and only eight were lowered safely into the water, but these became overloaded and quickly filled with water or turned over. However, most of the ship's liferafts were launched, and hatch covers were also thrown overboard.

Survivors later told horrific stories of the wounded and dying in the water. Several ships converged on the scene to pick up survivors, and as darkness fell, the new Lend-Lease rescue tug *Mindful* arrived just as the *Rohna* slipped beneath the waves. A heavy swell prevented the rescue ships launching any boats, and although eight hundred and nineteen survivors were picked from the water, one thousand one hundred and forty-nine men were killed or drowned, including one thousand and fifteen US Army personnel and one hundred and thirty four British and Australian officers, and Indian members of the crew. It was the largest single loss of life the US Army suffered at sea during the war, and the number of fatalities was kept secret for some years.

Among the survivors the *Mindful* picked up that night were two Americans, Lt Robert Brewer and Dr Wilmot Boone, one of the ship's doctors; their recollections were later included in a book about the disaster.[9] After commenting that the manoeuverability of the *Mindful* made her more useful for rescue work than the larger ships, the author wrote:

> [Brewer] could see men waiting on deck, ready to throw lines and other equipment to them. Brewer grabbed a doughnut life preserver, put it around his neck, and headed for the stern of the ship, where the deck was closer to the water than the bow. But there he found dozens of men struggling, so he backed away from them. He rode in against the side of the *Mindful*, bracing his arms against the hull, and waited for a big wave. 'Pretty soon one came along raising me a good ten feet up to the rail.' He reached out and felt strong arms grasp him. He was thrilled to hear someone with a 'distinct British accent' tell him, 'Easy as you go there, lad.' They were the sweetest words Brewer had ever heard.
>
> But Brewer's legs would not work; the *Mindful* crew had to take him below, where they cut off his clothing and wrapped him in a warm blanket. They gave him a huge cup of hot tea, but he could not keep it down. The best thing he could do, he thought, was to pass out.[9]

Which is exactly what he did.

The author also describes how Boone and some other survivors were rescued from a raft by *Mindful*:

> After floating an interminable time, Dr Boone
> heard 'a voice from the Gods' speaking to him in a
> "wonderful" British accent'. Lines were lowered to the
> raft and its occupants hauled on board where they
> were treated to mugs of warm rum, followed by hot
> tea, 'though all we asked for,' said Boone, 'was a cup
> of coffee!'[9]

The part that *Mindful* played in rescuing survivors from the *Rohna*, and also for rescuing one hundred and thirty-five men from the French tanker *Nivose* earlier the same month, earned her crew a Mediterranean Fleet Order of the Day, signed by the C-in-C Mediterranean, Admiral John Cunningham. It read:

> I wish to record my appreciation of the gallantry, skill
> and devotion to duty which has been shown
> by Lieutenant ER Waller RNR and the Officers and
> Crew of HM Rescue tug *Mindful* in a series of
> rescue operations in which this ship has
> taken part.
>   On the night of 11/12 November 1943, when
> KMS31 was attacked by enemy aircraft off Oran, the
> French tanker *Nivose* was hit and sank. HMRT *Mindful*
> proceeded to pick up survivors and the actions of
> S/Lieut. IP Crawford RNVR, the First Lieutenant,
> and Petty Officer R Baxter who went over the side
> to the assistance of those in difficulty are particularly
> noteworthy.
>   At dusk on 26 November 1943 SS *Rohna* carrying
> troops was bombed and sunk off Bougie. HMRT

Mindful arrived on the scene as the ship sank and spent the night picking up survivors of which 250 were taken on board. Again S/Lieut. Crawford was conspicuous in leading rescue operations during which the majority of the crew, despite heavy seas, jumped on to rafts and into boats to assist survivors on board.

On both these occasions the care and attention which was given to survivors was outstanding. HMRT *Mindful* was also responsible for the successful towing of HMS *Cuckmere* into Algiers after she had been torpedoed on 14th December. A few days later she towed SS *John S. Copley* into Oran, after this ship had been torpedoed by a U-Boat.

In all these operations the high standard of courage, perseverance and seamanship shown by all the Officers and Ships Company is worthy of commendation.[10]

Lt Waller and Sub-Lt Crawford, and five others aboard the *Mindful*, were subsequently awarded the French Life Saving Medal, though it seems they never received it. Crawford later wrote a novel, *The Burning Sea*, which vividly described both episodes and sold three hundred thousand copies.[11] Aged seventeen, Crawford was too young to join the Royal Navy in 1939. Instead, he entered the Merchant Navy and served in three ships, all of which were torpedoed under him. On the last occasion, he and a handful of others spent ten days in an open boat in the Atlantic, and rowed more than five hundred miles to reach Trinidad. He then joined the Rescue Tug Service and took part in the invasions of Sicily, Italy and southern France, and in operations in the Adriatic. After the war, he helped clear mines in Venice and acted as a liaison officer for both the French and Italians. For his wartime exploits he was twice mentioned in despatches.[12]

AFRICAN OPERATIONS

Another rescue tug to receive a letter of commendation was HMRT *Masterful*. Launched in August 1942, she was one of the first Lend-Lease rescue tugs to be handed over. She spent a couple of months working with the US Navy around New Orleans and Charleston, and then escorted some American-built landing craft across the Atlantic. After her arrival in Freetown, her first lieutenant, Sub-Lt WV Mackay RNVR, was unexpectedly pitched into a tow of epic length when on 8 November 1942 the 5161-ton British freighter SS *Benalder* was torpedoed off the coast of Ghana. Her propeller and rudder were blown away and she had to be towed by a local tug to Takoradi where her cargo was unloaded and she was temporarily repaired. On 14 March, the *Masterful* left Freetown with orders to tow the *Benalder* to Saldanha Bay sixty-five miles north of Cape Town, where she could be repaired properly. *Masterful*'s commanding officer fell ill on the way, and was transferred to another ship, which had a doctor on board, and Mackay took command.

On 19 March, Mackay received a signal that one of the trawler escorts astern of the convoy he was part of had broken down. He towed her to Takoradi, and then berthed alongside the *Benalder* to prepare her for towing. The commanding officer returned, but two days later was sent to hospital and Mackay resumed command. The *Masterful* was now one watch-keeping officer short, but *Benalder*'s second officer volunteered to assist and help with the navigation, and the rescue tug and tow left Takoradi on 26 March. Forty-eight hours later, she encountered a tropical storm that washed away the freighter's jury rudder, and rigging wires and rope had to be trailed astern of her to prevent her yawing so wildly.

Most days the *Masterful* covered between one hundred and twenty-five and one hundred and fifty miles. She reached Walvis Bay, nearly eight hundred miles north of Cape Town, on 10 April, where she refuelled and took on water and other supplies. Tug and tow left on 15 April and after weathering a fresh southerly gale that brought *Masterful* almost to a standstill, both vessels arrived at Saldanha Bay on 22 April. The rescue tug had steamed two thousand seven hundred and thirty-four miles in twenty-three days, excluding the stopover at Walvis Bay.[13]

In his report, Sub-Lt Mackay wrote that he would be pleased to know if towing a ship 'in light trim, with no rudder, propeller, etc. over the above distance, and by only one tug of this class, represents a record tow for rescue tugs'.[14] If it did, the letter of commendation from the C-in-C South Atlantic did not mention it. He did remark that great credit was due to Mackay 'for the able and seamanlike manner' in which the voyage was handled; and for a second time Mackay, after his handling of *Superman* during an air attack in March 1942, was mentioned in despatches.

Masterful's next tow was the 20,000-ton tanker *Edward F Johnson*, loaded with aviation fuel. Her crankshaft had broken near Mombasa and *Masterful* towed her to Durban, the nearest port to have suitable repair facilities and be able to handle such a large cargo. In October 1943 she towed another tanker, *British Loyalty*, to Addu Atoll, the southernmost atoll of the Maldives, which was to be used as a refuelling base for what was to become the British Pacific Fleet the following November. In 1942, *British Loyalty* had been sunk by a Japanese midget submarine but had been salvaged, and would now act as a storage hulk in the atoll. The problem was getting her into the atoll, a circular coral reef with one narrow entrance, so one of the smaller Empire tugs accompanied the *Masterful* to help. To conserve her fuel, she was towed behind the tanker:

> After an unscheduled stop at the Seychelles, the tow continued with the Empire tug still behind. Every other day she slipped her wire and came up to us to collect

some fresh food, etc., and then hooked herself back on again. On arrival at Addu Atoll the tanker acted as if she knew the place and went straight through the narrows without the aid of the Empire tug, pulling herself up on her anchor in exactly the right position.[15]

However, her luck did not hold, as on 9 March 1944 a U-boat fired a torpedo through the gap in the reef and sank her.

Once the American Lend-Lease rescue tugs started to arrive, several were based in the southern half of Africa. The *Masterful* was one of them, the *Aimwell* was another. Both were based at Freetown, but in January 1943 the *Aimwell* moved to Bathurst [now Banjul], the capital of the Gambia, to await the arrival of a very important visitor. Before and after his meeting with Winston Churchill at Casablanca, President Franklin D Roosevelt flew to and from Bathurst in a seaplane, and each time spent two days aboard the light cruiser USS *Memphis*. His secretary, Grace Tully, wrote a detailed log of the entire trip, and an extract from the entry for 26 January 1943 describes a small piece of history so far as the Rescue Tug Service is concerned:

Lord Swinton, the Resident Minister of British West Africa, came on board [USS *Memphis*] at 4:00 P.M. and chatted with the President until 4:30. Thereupon the President invited him to come along for a short trip up the Gambia River on the seagoing tug, HMS *Aimwell*, standing by to receive the President. The President and Lord Swinton went on board the *Aimwell* at 4:40, accompanied by Mr Harry Hopkins; Captain H. Y. McCown, U.S.N., Commanding Officer, USS *Memphis*; Admiral McIntire; and Captain McCrea. On board, the President was met by Commander E. F. Lawder, Royal Navy, Naval Officer in Charge at Bathurst. A British armed motor launch took station on each quarter and at 5:00 P.M., Lt Commander H. Vaughan commanding HMS *Aimwell* had the ship underway and standing up river.

This 560-ton seagoing tug was the first to be completed under the terms of the Lend-Lease agreement for British account. Built at Bay City, Michigan, she was placed in commission on 6 June 1942, her officers and men having been sent from Scotland to America for this purpose. She is Diesel-electric driven and mounts one three-inch gun on the forecastle and two 20mm rapid fire guns on the bridge deck. Her trip from Bay City, Michigan, to Freetown, Africa (the latter port being the one out of which she normally operates), was marked by stops at Detroit, Cleveland, Toronto, Quebec, New York, Norfolk, and St. Thomas, Virgin Islands.

For the trip across the Atlantic the *Aimwell* had taken a large, floating, wooden dry dock in tow, capable of accommodating vessels as large as a cruiser. An escort was assigned consisting of two coastal minesweepers and two corvettes. Five days out of Freetown, the dry dock broke her back, although the weather had not been rough, and the dock became unmanageable and started to lose buoyancy. After a survey it was decided that it would be impossible to tow her any farther. She was set on fire, and shortly thereafter the dock sank. This tug, normally good for 14 knots with a clean bottom, can now make a bare 12 knots. Manned by a complement of 10 officers and 23 men, she was a compact, powerful little vessel that had been putting herself to good use in towing into port various vessels that had become victims of enemy submarine attack.

After watching the President as he sat chatting on the fantail with the various members of his party, one of the British seamen described the President's free and easy manner of making himself at home everywhere, with the remark to Chief Ship's Clerk Terry that, 'The President certainly sits "proper natural" back there, doesn't he?'

After proceeding upriver for an hour, course was reversed at 6:00 P.M. for it was desired to return to the anchorage before dark. On the run back Mr Hopkins and Admiral McIntire trolled a couple of lines with feather lures, but had no luck. Anchor was dropped at 6:45 P.M. and upon thanking Commander Lawder and Lt Commander Vaughan for a pleasant trip, and after saying goodbye to Lord Swinton, the President left the *Aimwell* for the *Memphis*, going aboard at 7:00 P.M.[16]

President Roosevelt gave the *Aimwell* a photograph of himself inscribed 'to the officers and crew of HM rescue tug *Aimwell* from their friend F.D. Roosevelt', which was hung in the wardroom and copies of it distributed among the crew. He also talked to one of the rescue tug's officers, Lt A Craig, who told him about the rather unusual circumstances of his marriage, a conversation which was later recorded in a British newspaper:[17]

'While in the United States commissioning the *Aimwell* I met by pure chance a girl I had known when we were both children,' said Lt Craig. 'Within 24 hours we were married. The President asked if he could take a letter to her, which he did. He was also interested in the rum ration and asked for a sip. It made him cough and he was surprised at its strength.'

The President followed Lt Craig's letter with one of his own, congratulating Lt Craig's wife on the birth of her son.[17]

NOTES

1. The Allies sank more than 800,000 tons of Axis shipping in the Mediterranean, yet 2.8 million tons of supplies (84.6 per cent of the total), and just over 206,000 men (91.7 per cent of the total) reached their destination, remarkable statistics. See Ceva L. 'Italy: Navy' in Dear I, editor. *Oxford Companion to World War II*. Oxford: Oxford University Press; 2005. p.469.
2. Grove E, editor. *The Defeat of the Enemy Attack on Shipping, 1939–45*. London: Navy Records Society; 1997. pp.132,143.
3. From MOI leaflet 'The Spirit of the Ark' in ADM 1/12121.
4. *Towrope*, 2001; 3(7):11.
5. From: Winser J. de S *British Invasion Fleets: the Mediterranean and Beyond, 1942–45*. Gravesend: World Ship Society; 2002.
6. RNVR notes in *Yachting Monthly* (April 1945): 362–63.
7. Tomblin BB. *With Utmost Spirit: Allied Naval Operations in the Mediterranean, 1942–45*. Lexington: University Press of Kentucky; 2004. p.410.
8. ADM 199/1274.
9. Jackson C. *Forgotten Tragedy: The Sinking of HMT Rohna*. Annapolis: Naval Institute Press; 1997. pp.116–18. This is one of the few books that makes any mention of a rescue tug, so the author can be forgiven for remarking that *Mindful* 'frequently had been used as a tugboat'! See www.rohnasurvivors.org/ bibliography for other books about the sinking.
10. In DSRTA archives. Courtesy of Len Reed. Admiral John Cunningham should not be confused with Admiral Andrew Cunningham whom John Cunningham succeeded as C-in-C Mediterranean in 1943 and as First Sea Lord in 1946.
11. Odhams, 1958.

When convoy ON-166 was attacked by two U-boat wolf-packs, February 1943, one of the casualties was the 9382-ton Dutch motorship *Madoera*, but she managed to reach St John's a week later. *Inset*: The hole in *Madoera's* forefoot was used as a short cut by local boats while she awaited repairs at St John's (courtesy *Downhome* magazine, St John's, Newfoundland)

The hole blown in the 10,627-ton British tanker, G.S. *Walden*, after a U-boat wolf pack attacked convoy ON-115 about 300 miles from St John's, August 1942. Despite the extent of her damage, *Tenacity* brought her safely into harbour

Growler, one of the eight British built Bustler Class rescue tugs. From 1943 some of them were part of the escort groups that guarded Atlantic convoys (IWM)

Petty Officer Harry Bonser (right) and Leading Stoker Mick O'Hara with *Growler*'s mascot, Pluto, which had been found injured on the Normandy beaches (IWM)

Frisky was towing the torpedoed SS *Brilliant*, to Sydney, Cape Breton, when the US tanker broke up in a bad storm, January 1943. The stern half, and 33 men, was adrift for some days before *Frisky* found it. Seen here are the men abandoning the wreck, which *Frisky* then sank with gunfire

Tenacity approaching the US Coast Guard cutter, *Campbell*, badly damaged after ramming a U-boat, February 1943.
Photo from Leonard Martin, navigator *Tenacity*

The last hours of SS *Neptune* before she sank near St John's, Newfoundland, March 1943. This photograph was taken by Adolph Wiseman, a crew member of *Tenacity*, which was trying to tow her to safety

Tenacity fighting an oil fire in St. John's, Newfoundland, June 1944, which was threatening to raze part of the port

The 7022-ton Liberty Ship *Empire Treasure* dropped out of Convoy ON-219 when her stern frame fractured in heavy Atlantic weather, January 1944. She lost her propeller and it took HMRT *Bustler* a week to tow her to the safety of Barry Docks, South Wales (courtesy Peter Sanders)

Empire Treasure sheering badly while under tow in storm force 10 winds (courtesy Peter Sanders)

Destiny at St John's, Newfoundland, November 1942 (courtesy Peter Sanders)

'Tug' Wilson manning one of *Destiny*'s Oerlikons (courtesy John Wilson)

Despite darkness and high seas *Mindful's* First Lieutenant, Sub-Lt Ian Crawford RNVR (right) and Sub-Lt (E) G MacDonald RNVR, dived overboard repeatedly to rescue US servicemen after the troopship *Rohna* sank with heavy loss of life in the Mediterranean, November 1943 (IWM)

Left: This photograph of Able Seaman Len Reed was taken in Perth, Western Australia, January 1945, while serving aboard the rescue tug *Integrity* (courtesy Len Reed)
Below left: Lt-Cdr RE Sanders MBE RNR, one of the Service's most outstanding officers. Among his commands were *St Mellons*, *Destiny*, and *Bustler* (Courtesy Peter Sanders)
Below right: Sub-Lt Stanley Butler RNVR, was a Rescue Tug Service engineer officer throughout the war (courtesy Peter Butler)

A rescue tug, probably *Bustler*, towing a conundrum used to lay the fuel pipeline PLUTO (Pipe Line Under The Ocean) to Cherbourg after the Normandy Landings, June 1944. Another member of the team was *Marauder* and, seen here on the right, the smaller *Danube V* (courtesy Peter Sanders)

An aerial view of the assembly area off Lee-on-Solent for tugs towing parts of the MULBERRY harbours to the Normandy beaches. By the plane's wing tip is the tugs' depot ship, *Aorangi* (IWM)

12. Obituary, *Scotsman*, 22 July 2011.

13. ADM 199/534.

14. Copy of letter of commendation in *Towrope*, 2009 (Spring): 12 and *Towrope*, 2009 (Summer): 8.

15. Anon. *Towrope* 2000 (Spring): 20.

16. Extract from log of the trip of the President to the Casablanca Conference, 9–31 January 1943. It is part of the Grace Tully Archive in the Franklin D Roosevelt Presidential Library and Museum, and is online at www.fdrlibrary.marist.edu/resources

17. *Western Morning News*, 7 February 1944.

8

JAUNTY, THE CRIPPLES, AND THE FEISTY EMPIRE CLASS

T HE ASSURANCE CLASS *Jaunty* was another rescue tug that had a busy war, mostly in the Mediterranean.[1] But after her launch in June 1941, she started her operational life by taking part that December in a raid on the Lofoten Islands (Operation ANKLET), which lie off the Norwegian coast about a hundred miles north of the Arctic Circle. Led by the cruiser HMS *Arethusa*, a force of British commandos and Norwegian troops were landed on the islands on 26 December as a diversion from the much larger Vaagso raid three hundred miles to the south. Sub-Lt (E) TL Mosley RNVR, who was aboard *Jaunty* for the raid, later explained:

> Our job was to take the force into the narrow approach
> to the islands. While towing a supply ship in the fjord
> we were attacked by aircraft. But, though we towed
> in the *Arethusa* and other ships through repeated air
> attacks, we brought them all out again when the raid
> was completed.[2]

On her return *Jaunty* was stationed at Stornoway from where, in January 1942, she went to the assistance of the 1088-ton steamship *Thyra II*, which had been bombed off Barra Head, the southernmost part of the Outer Hebrides, and she later towed two other damaged ships to Reykjavik.

In August 1942, she and the *Salvonia* sailed with Operation PEDESTAL, the famous convoy mounted to relieve the besieged island of Malta. They were attached to Force R, the refuelling tankers and their escorts, which sailed from Gibraltar on 9 August at the rear of the convoy. At 0855 on 11 August, *Jaunty* and the two cruisers, *Sirius* and *Phoebe*, joined Force F, the convoy's escort force, but at 13.00 those aboard the rescue tug witnessed the sinking of the British aircraft carrier HMS *Eagle*. She was torpedoed some seventy nautical miles south of Cape Salinas, the southernmost point of Mallorca, and *Jaunty* immediately went to the carrier's assistance.

'On approaching the position she was observed to be listing heavily,' *Jaunty*'s commanding officer, Lt-Commander Harold Osburn OBE RNR, later reported, 'eventually sinking in about fifteen minutes from the time of the explosion.'[3] By then his crew had prepared every possible means for rescuing the survivors. One boat was lowered and floating nets and lines were hung overboard. 'I could see many men in the water and we started to pick them up as quickly as possible, there being at the time a heavy covering of fuel oil on the water.'

Jaunty's first officer took command of the lowered lifeboat, and had soon picked up several exhausted survivors, while Osburn manoeuvred *Jaunty* to pick up those struggling in the water further away. Two members of his crew in particular distinguished themselves during the rescue operation by repeatedly diving overboard with lines they then attached to survivors so that they could be hauled aboard. Osburn estimated that *Jaunty* rescued about two hundred and fifty men. The injured were transferred to one destroyer and the rest to another, with one dead man being left for *Jaunty* to bury at sea.

At dusk, the main convoy was attacked by Ju 88 dive bombers and Force R to the southward also came 'in for attention', the official despatch recorded:

> [O]ne Ju 88 dropping two bombs, one of which fell between the oilers and the escort, another diving on *Jaunty* which was about seven miles to the westward and endeavouring to join Force F [after picking up *Eagle* survivors]. She claims to have damaged it with Oerlikon fire. No damage was done to any ship in these attacks.[4]

Osburn was more detailed about this encounter, writing in his report:

> The hostile aircraft flew in to attack us from the port side, but no bombs were dropped by it as we immediately opened fire with our two Oerlikon guns, and observed two direct hits on the body of the aircraft just behind the wings on its starboard side. Being now rather dark we could not see its definite end, but was sure of it being damaged.[3]

Jaunty was then ordered to return to Force R, as she was too far behind Force F to catch up. Once she had rejoined, she screened the oiler *Brown Ranger*, eventually arriving back in Gibraltar on 16 August, 'but all on board,' Osburn concluded his report, 'were disappointed in not having been able to continue the operations to Malta'. Meanwhile, the *Salvonia* stood by as a rescue ship for Operation BARITONE, which involved flying off thirty-two Malta-bound Spitfires from HMS *Furious* before she, too, returned to Gibraltar on 18 August.

Following the North African landings in November 1942, *Jaunty* assisted the 6736-ton US Army attack cargo ship USS *Almaack*. Having delivered her cargo to the beaches, *Almaack* was returning to Britain in convoy MKF-1Y when she was torpedoed one hundred and twenty miles north-west of Gibraltar, and *Jaunty* reached her the next day and towed her back to Gibraltar.[5]

Another important tow for *Jaunty* came in March 1943, when she and the *Restive* brought in the *Seminole*, a 10,389-ton British tanker. She was in convoy TE-16 some twenty miles west of Oran when a U-boat hit her with two torpedoes, which, luckily, did not ignite her load of high-octane fuel. Her crew abandoned her, but she remained afloat, and *Jaunty* and *Restive* towed her to Oran, where the fuel was transferred to another ship. The following month she was taken to Gibraltar and was later returned to Britain to be repaired, one of a series of cripples, as they were called, to make the twelve-hundred-mile passage under tow.

Jaunty had a remarkable record in the Mediterranean. On her return home, a local newspaper interviewed her commanding officer, who claimed, with understandable exaggeration, that it was *Jaunty* and *Restive* that had really taken the surrender of the Italian fleet at Malta on 10 September 1943, as it had been their responsibility to transfer armed guards from British warships onto the Italian ones.[6] Both rescue tugs also played their part in helping to tow HMS *Warspite*, a First World War battleship of 33,410 tons displacement, from Malta to Gibraltar, after she had been badly damaged during the Salerno landings.

EMPIRE CLASS

By 1943, Empire tugs of different sizes were stationed in the Mediterranean, but the *Empire Wold*, just 114 ft overall, was sent to work in the atrocious weather around Iceland where in January 1944 she distinguished herself by going to the aid of a trawler that had run aground. The weather was just about as bad as it could be, with an eighty-mile-an-hour gale and blinding snowstorms, and several times the *Empire Wold* was forced to abandon her search and return to harbour, her crew exhausted. Eventually, the weather moderated, the *Empire Wold* located the trawler's crew, and they were eventually all rescued. For displaying 'courage and leadership of a high order, and also great skill and determination', her master, Captain William Russell, was awarded the MBE,[7] but sadly the weather eventually got the better of her and in November 1944 she disappeared without trace while searching for an abandoned tanker.

The majority of Empire tugs in the Mediterranean assisted in ports handling the huge amount of shipping created by the fighting in North Africa, but some – and not necessarily the largest – acted as rescue tugs, accompanying the numerous convoys destined for different parts of the Mediterranean. For instance, in November 1943 the *Empire Larch* – now armed with a three-inch gun and two machine guns, far in excess of the armaments the class had been originally allotted – helped escort convoy KMS-31 from Liverpool to Gibraltar.

As an article in *Lloyd's List and Shipping Gazette* pointed out, the smaller Empire class tugs, like those already mentioned, showed they were capable of performing tasks for which they had not been designed:

> The 'Coastwise' tugs were originally coal burners,
> but a certain number were fitted to burn oil fuel and
> excepting a few of the earlier vessels, they also had
> fire and salvage pumps fitted. Some of these were also
> used for rescue work. Of this class the following extract

from the Master's letter of one on passage gives some indication of their adaptability:

Leaving Milford Haven we towed two Free French submarine chasers on separate lines; we towed them to Gibraltar at a speed of 6.7 knots, and consideration must be given to the fact that bad weather was experienced in the last 36 hours. The chasers then escorted us to Gibraltar. Leaving this port, we again took them in tow and towed them to Bathurst in the Gambia, maintaining a speed of seven knots. We remained in Bathurst three weeks doing all sorts of jobs, and on arrival at Freetown we were kept back, with another tug, to tow a crane barge, taking her to Takoradi at an average speed of 5.7 knots.

After calling at Pointe Noire [Congo Republic] and Walvis Bay [Namibia] we went into Luderitz Bay [Namibia], picked up a barge, and towed it to Saldanha Bay [near Cape Town] at 6.5 knots. It was on this passage that we met the Cape rollers, but the little ship rode them like a duck. From Cape Town onwards we did no more towing, but called in at Durban, Laurenço Marques [Maputo], Beira, Mombasa, and Aden just in case we were required, the final distance being 13,525 miles, steaming time 74.4 days, average speed 7.6 knots. She behaved splendidly throughout: she was a sturdy little tug, and made the 13,525 miles by which she was routed without one stop for engine trouble.[8]

The crew of one of these smaller type of Empire tugs, *Empire Fred*, behaved with exceptional courage when, on 16 July 1943, fire broke out aboard a Liberty ship, SS *Fort Confidence*, while she was unloading ammunition on to the Norwegian freighter *Bjørkhaug* in the port of Algiers. The resulting explosion blew the stern of *Bjørkhaug* on to the quay and set the area alight. *Fort Confidence* also had several thousands of tons of petrol on board, which if it had exploded could have flattened large parts of the port. The firefighting services eventually brought the blaze under control on most of the quay, and in the forward part of the ship, but it could not be contained elsewhere and ammunition continued to explode.

Holland's most modern tug, the *Hudson*, commanded by Captain Benjamin Weltevreden,[9] now proved her worth in this dangerous situation. She had already towed a troopship and a hospital ship clear of the disaster, and the Dutchman now backed his ship's stern to the bows of the burning vessel, intending to tow her clear. A line was passed through the eyes of the bow moorings to pull them free, but they were too taut and could not be moved. Securing a tow rope to the bows of the burning ship, the Dutchman pulled her forwards just enough to allow the slackened mooring ropes to be cast off.

Rear Admiral JAV Morse RN, the senior naval officer at Algiers, had witnessed the explosion from his office window. He hurried to the scene and went aboard the *Hudson* to witness the unfolding drama, and he later wrote in his report:

> HM Rescue Tug *Hudson* commenced towing at once
> and was able to get *Fort Confidence* clear of the jetty.
> By this time all shipping in the vicinity of Quai Lorient
> had been shifted and there was a clear run towards the
> South Entrance. The wind at North East was slightly
> on the port bow, but to tow the ship through the
> entrance a turn of nearly 90 degrees was necessary and
> the Boom Defence extended half way from the northern
> Breakwater...

HM Rescue Tug *Hudson* is an ocean-going
tug driven by diesel engines and has not the
manoeuvrability of a harbour tug. Although the Master
handled her with great skill it was necessary to bring
the tow across the stem [of the ship] to turn the
ship into the entrance, but the hemp mooring ropes,
which had taken the straight pull, parted before the
Fort Confidence could be brought round, and the ship,
carrying a fair amount of way, ran into the northern
half of the net defence. She was nearly head to wind
and the flames from her after hold started to envelop
the after platform with its ready-use ammunition
lockers and shell stowage.[10]

The situation was now critical, and may well have ended in
complete disaster if the *Hudson* had not received the assistance
of the *Empire Fred* and the French harbour tug *Furet II*. *Empire
Fred*, commanded by Lt A Craig, whom we last met aboard
the *Aimwell* with President Roosevelt, was one of the smaller
type of Empire tug, but this had not deterred the Admiralty
from commissioning her in January 1943 as a rescue tug. After
two crewmen from the *Hudson* had boarded the burning ship to
secure the tugs' tow lines – 'a very gallant action', wrote Admiral
Morse, 'as ammunition was continuing to explode' – each of
the tugs in turn tried to take the burning ship in tow, but each
time the tow parted. However, through their efforts, or maybe
because of the wind, *Fort Confidence* eventually floated free of
the Boom Defence nets.

A destroyer waiting just outside the harbour now tried her
luck at taking the burning ship in tow. She managed to secure
a wire hawser to *Fort Confidence*'s anchor, and began pulling her
out of the harbour by going astern. But the wind and swell
foiled her, and in a further attempt the *Empire Fred* came so

close to *Fort Confidence* that she nearly caught fire. The *Hudson* did manage to get another rope aboard her, but by then *Fort Confidence*, still ablaze, had run aground, and there was nothing the *Hudson* could do to shift her. The plan to tow her right away from the port had to be abandoned, although other reports say she was eventually taken out of the harbour and beached. Admiral Morse concluded his report:

> I cannot speak too highly of the behaviour of the
> Masters, Officers and Crews of the tugs. Ammunition
> was going off continuously and the sides of the ship
> were red hot, yet all went about their work with the
> phlegm for which these fine Dutch seamen are famous.[10]

The Honours and Awards Committee noted that the *Empire Fred* and the *Hudson* towed SS *Fort Confidence* 'from a position at Algiers where she was a menace to the security of the whole port. They were handled with great courage and skill'. In due course, Lt Craig was awarded the OBE and one of his crew, Able Seaman Harry Haxell, was mentioned in despatches for his 'courage and skill'.[11] An honorary MBE was awarded to Captain Weltevreden, and honorary BEMs to two of his crew, RH Hansen and L Fillekes.

Later the same month, the *Empire Samson*, another of the smaller type of Empire class which had been commissioned as a rescue tug, was part of the escort for convoy OS-52/KMS-21 heading for Gibraltar when, on the afternoon of 26 July 1943, it was attacked by high-flying bombers. One of the freighters in the convoy was hit, and sank so quickly that the *Empire Samson* was able to pick up only eight survivors. The rescue tug's commanding officer, Lt AS Pike RNR, then noticed that another ship in the convoy, *Empire Brutus*, had stopped and went to investigate. As he approached, he saw two of the convoy's escorts returning the crew to her, as they had apparently abandoned ship when the bombing started. Pike wrote in his report:

> I was informed by her Master that the engine room, stokehold, cross bunker and No. 3 hold were flooded from a hole in the port side caused by a near miss, but as there seemed no immediate danger of [her] sinking I informed him of my intention to attempt to tow her into Lisbon, a distance of 230 miles. He agreed and requested me to take twenty of his crew for safety. We received his permission to take provisions for these men and whilst they were being put on board we took about 3 tons of coal from his starboard side bunker to mix with our own which was of poor quality.[12]

The eight survivors from the sunken freighter were transferred to one of the convoy escorts, and *Empire Brutus* – which was without any power for her pumps or steering gear – was taken in tow. As the *Empire Samson* only had an ihp of 1100, and was just 114 ft overall, the tow to Lisbon was no easy task, particularly as the weather soon began to deteriorate. Accompanied by one of the corvettes, tug and tow headed for Lisbon in a moderate wind and a swell that made both roll heavily.

'At approximately 0300 on 27 July,' Pike wrote, 'I received a signal from the Master of *Empire Brutus* informing me that he doubted her ability to make Lisbon as she was making water and listing to starboard.'[12] The master requested this information be passed to the escort by R/T (radio telephone), but as Pike thought there might be U-boats in the area, which could home in on the transmission, he did not do so; and as he could not see any difference in the trim of the *Empire Brutus*, he continued to tow, although by the next day she was well down by the stern.

Early the next morning they were attacked by a Focke-Wulf Condor, but it was soon driven off. As the *Empire Samson* had had difficulty in maintaining steam during the night, Pike asked the nine Arab firemen he had taken aboard from *Empire Brutus* to assist his own firemen. When they refused:

> I produced a revolver (unloaded) and promised to introduce them to their ancestors if they persisted in their refusal. Within two minutes they had organized Watches and were singing at their work in the stokehold. They worked cheerfully and well from then on and I think they deserve a good deal of credit for the success of the tow.[12]

In the afternoon, the master of *Empire Brutus* reported that the engine room bulkhead was buckling and was likely to give way, which would have quickly sent the ship to the bottom. The remainder of the ship's crew were therefore transferred to the corvette escort. When the corvette's commanding officer asked Pike what he intended to do, he replied that he was going to go on towing until the ship sank.

During the night, the weather deteriorated further and the tow became almost unmanageable – towing a ship that could not be steered was always problematical – and the next morning Pike informed the escort that he did not have enough coal to reach Lisbon. He asked, and was granted, permission to go alongside the damaged ship and take some coal from her bunkers, and by early afternoon the rescue tug was alongside, bumping badly in the ten foot swell.

A whip that could lift about half a hundredweight at a time was rigged and two gangs with buckets were formed. The escort transferred the master, chief officer and cook of the *Empire Brutus*, and everyone began shovelling, heaving and tipping coal from 'tween decks, which was six inches deep in water. By early evening, about eighteen tons had been taken aboard, enough for forty hours' steaming. Good progress was made and at dawn the next morning, the escort put the rest of the crew aboard *Empire Brutus*, and left soon afterwards to avoid entering territorial waters. At 09.00 a local pilot came aboard and the *Empire Brutus* was handed over to local tugs.

When Lisbon was reached, Pike wrote that 'we were greeted with enthusiasm by the Portuguese who made Pro-British demonstrations at the sight of the White Ensign, [and] I was conducted on a good-will tour of several Portuguese Government Offices by the British Naval Attaché'. It may, or may not have been a coincidence that when a British base opened on one of the Portuguese islands in the Azores later that year, *Empire Samson* was one of two British rescue tugs to be stationed there.

On 5 September 1943, the C-in-C Mediterranean, Admiral of the Fleet Sir Andrew Cunningham, issued an Order of the Day, No. 1. This began: 'I wish to record my appreciation of the devotion to duty and resourcefulness of Lieutenant Alfred Sidney Pike RNR and the officers and crew of HM Rescue Tug *Empire Samson*' and ended: 'The perseverance and good seamanship of Lieutenant Pike and his crew in difficult and trying circumstances are worthy of commendation.' As the rescue tug's second mate, Sub-Lt TW Thornley RNVR, later commented: 'We were, I think, justifiably proud that a White Ensign tug, crewed by 19 ex-MN T.124T officers and ratings should be chosen for Order of the Day No.1.'[13]

Another of the smaller Empire tugs that distinguished herself in the Mediterranean was the *Empire Ann*, and her story was written up in *Lloyd's List and Shipping Gazette*.[14] In her first six months in the Mediterranean, under the command of Lt CII Burgess RNR, she handled 1.5 million tons of shipping before being given a 'roving commission' during the invasion of Sicily and one night, when operating from Syracuse, she was sent to the rescue of a stranded 8000-ton merchant ship.

'It was in very dirty weather,' explained her first lieutenant, Sub-Lieutenant I Sturrock RNVR of Hull. 'We had everything that night – lightning, thunder, squalls, hail, high wind, heavy seas and little visibility. We spent 16 hours getting the grounded ship afloat. Luckily, she was then able to proceed under her own steam, and we took nine hours getting into Syracuse, about ten miles away.' When they eventually arrived, they found the storm had caused chaos among the ships in the harbour; and although they had just spent thirty-eight hours at sea, *Empire Ann*'s crew turned out and struggled for another four hours with other tugs to sort out the mess. The *Lloyd's List* article ended:

> There are about a dozen 'Empire' tugs on duty in the Mediterranean, each of them having gone out from England under her own steam. The story of the *Empire Ann* is typical of them all. They have all tackled jobs they were never built to handle, and have done invaluable work in the invasion harbours in North Africa, Sicily and Italy.[14]

GIBRALTAR PATROLS AND THE AZORES

Permission to base a rescue tug at the Azores had first been sought from the Portuguese in 1941, and the *Salvonia* had been chosen. However, Portugal – Britain's oldest ally, sealed by a treaty ratified in the fourteenth century – prevaricated as she was understandably fearful of how the Germans would react. Instead, the *Salvonia* had been based at Campbeltown and Iceland before being sent to Gibraltar from where, as we've seen, she took part in the PEDESTAL convoy to Malta. She was at Mers-el-Kébir for part of December 1942,[15] before returning to Gibraltar, and it was from there she was called to assist the 7100-ton British freighter *Empire Mordred*, whose engine had broken down about forty miles east of Gibraltar's Europa Point.

It was a routine task for the rescue tug, but one that brought unexpected complications when *Mordred*'s master declined to take the tow, saying that he expected to have made the necessary repairs by early the next morning. The freighter's escort was informed, and the master was advised to take the tow as he was an easy target for U-boats, which were probably in the vicinity. Perhaps reluctantly, the master agreed and the next morning the *Salvonia* brought the freighter into Gibraltar's commercial anchorage.

Salvonia's commanding officer duly submitted a claim for salvage, but the freighter's owners must have queried the claim, for the Treasury Solicitor became involved. Such an incident had never happened before and memoranda flew to and fro within the Admiralty. The Director of the Trade Division remarked it was deplorable that the freighter's master allowed the fear of salvage expenses to endanger his ship, and two questions arose from his refusal: Could an escort order a merchant ship to accept a tow, if in the opinion of the commanding officer, the operational situation demanded it? And if such an order was given to a merchant ship, was the merchant ship liable for salvage charges? The short answer – though it seemed to take an inordinate amount of time to come to it – was yes and yes, and in due course an Admiralty Merchant Shipping Instruction (AMSI) was issued, which explained what had happened, and gave the Admiralty's verdict on it:

> It should be clearly understood that the risk of a
> valuable ship being lost through remaining stopped in

dangerous waters cannot be accepted for considerations
of this nature, and there must therefore be no hesitation
on the part of a Master in accepting towage from tug
or other vessel which has been sent to his assistance.[16]

While the *Salvonia* was based at Gibraltar, Jack Close joined
her as second wireless operator, and he later described her main
task there:

The *Salvonia* left harbour at dusk, patrolling in Gibraltar
Bay all night and returning alongside at early light,
her job being to counter the piloted torpedoes and the
swimmers with limpet mines who came out under cover
of darkness from Algeciras on the Spanish side of the
bay. Spain, although ostensibly neutral, was Axis-friendly
and turned a blind eye to activities along her coastline
opposite Gibraltar. There was known to be an Italian
tanker alongside Algeciras harbour, the *Olterra*, which
had been adapted for the use and concealment of
underwater craft and swimmers, from which attacks were
carried out against Allied shipping...

We left harbour at dusk, patrolling between the
anchored merchant ships, trying to spot anything
suspicious in the water, dropping anti-personnel charges
or light depth charges overboard if suspicions were
aroused. The area covered during these patrols was
often considerable, particularly when a convoy had just
arrived in the Bay, or one was assembling before sailing.
At such times the ships at anchor could cover an area
up to three miles long and a mile across.[17]

Sometimes the *Salvonia* was called out to ships in trouble in
the Atlantic or in the Mediterranean. In March 1943, when a

U-boat attacked convoy MKS-10 west of Gibraltar, she and another rescue tug were sent to assist two torpedoed freighters, *Fort Battle River* and *Fort Paskoyac*. The former sank, but the *Salvonia* towed the 7134-ton *Fort Paskoyac* back to Gibraltar where the freighter was made watertight, before being towed to Britain by the *Empire Harry* and *Empire Larch* in convoy XK-6. The convoy also included the two Dutch rescue tugs *Hudson* and *Schelde*, towing the British tanker *Seminole* mentioned earlier.

By November 1943, the *Salvonia* was back in Britain, undergoing an extensive refit at Liverpool, prior to being sent – at long last – to the Azores after successful negotiations for British and Americans' air and naval bases had been concluded. The first British base was opened at Horta in October 1943, and both the *Salvonia* and *Empire Samson* were stationed there. They remained at Horta for the rest of the war, and helped a number of ships, including the British cruiser, HMS *Glasgow*, which ran aground while leaving the harbour.

On 19 September 1944, the *Salvonia* brought in the disabled US Liberty ship *Edward P Alexander*; and on 21 December she was dispatched to assist the Buckley class destroyer USS *Fogg*, which had been torpedoed by a U-boat north-east of the Azores. The *Salvonia* reached her the next afternoon, but that evening the destroyer's stern section, about a third the length of the ship, sheered off. Nevertheless, the *Salvonia* managed to bring what remained of her into Terceira safely, where she was temporarily repaired. She was then towed back to the United States, given a new stern section and returned to service.[18]

RETURN OF DAMAGED SHIPS

Returning badly damaged vessels to Britain for repair was one of the tasks rescue tugs performed regularly. Vulgarly known as 'cripples', most were part of XK convoys from Gibraltar. To go to this length shows how valuable each vessel, both merchantman and warship, was to the war effort, and rescue tugs were the only vessels capable of performing this task.

One of the warships returned to Britain was the 'I' class destroyer HMS *Ithuriel*, which was badly damaged by two near misses in Bône harbour in November 1942. She was beached and temporary repairs were carried out, and in February 1943 *Jaunty* towed her to Gibraltar in convoy ET-12. She remained there as an accommodation and training ship until August 1944, when the *Prosperous* towed her to Plymouth. She was judged to be beyond economic repair, but scrap metal was a valuable commodity in wartime so it was not entirely a wasted effort.

Sometimes, a cripple had to be towed back in two halves if a torpedo had broken it in two, though the 'P' class destroyer HMS *Porcupine* was deliberately cut in half at an Oran shipyard after being torpedoed off the port on 8 December 1942. The torpedo had caused such extensive damage amidships that the destroyer was declared a total loss, but it was then decided to strip her of all her armaments, and to send the two halves back to Britain. Perhaps some far-sighted naval bureaucrat had already earmarked them for future use, as after the two sections had been towed to Portsmouth – the forward half by the Assurance class *Charon*, the after half by the *Aimwell* – they were turned into accommodation hulks at Stokes Bay for landing craft crews. The front half was commissioned as HMS *Pork* and the rear half as HMS *Pine*.[19] Waste not, want not.

Another cripple that had a successful outcome was the 'W' class destroyer HMS *Wivern*. In February 1943, she went to the aid of the Canadian corvette HMCS *Weyburn*, badly damaged after hitting a mine off Cape Spartel, on the Moroccan coast. The *Wivern* took off the survivors, but was herself then severely damaged when two of *Weyburn*'s depth charges – whose primers could not be removed because of wreckage – exploded as the *Weyburn* sank.[20]

The next month, the *Wivern* was towed to Britain by the Lend-Lease rescue tug *Destiny*, whose commanding officer, Lt RE Sanders RNR, was to be awarded the MBE the following year.[21] He was one of the Rescue Tug Service's most experienced officers, and in his book *The Practice of Ocean Rescue* (see note 1 in Chapter 5) he describes how, while towing the *Wivern* back to Britain in convoy XK-3, he rigged a large lug sail in her bows to prevent her yawing, that alarming tendency common in all towed vessels, especially in bad weather. The *Wivern* was under repair for over a year. During this time she had a twin six-pounder army gun installed for use against E-boats, and did useful work with the Harwich Escort Force for the rest of the war.

Not so fruitful were the efforts to return the Hunt class destroyer HMS *Derwent* to service after she was badly damaged in Tripoli harbour. In January 1943, British and Commonwealth troops captured Tripoli while chasing Rommel into Tunisia, and its harbour became an important supply base for them. It also became a prime target for German bombers and on one occasion a medium-calibre bomb narrowly missed the rescue tug *Brigand*, which was anchored there. It exploded fifteen feet from the port side just forward of the engine room. Blast and shrapnel caused considerable damage to the superstructure and peppered the hull plating with small holes, but on 17 March the NOIC Tripoli was able to report to the Rear Admiral, Alexandria that the *Brigand* was again seaworthy.[22]

This was just as well, because two days later a dozen Ju 88 bombers again attacked shipping in the harbour. Surprise was total as the telephones in the area were not working, and no warning could be given. Bombs hit two of the merchant ships,

Ocean Voyager and *Varvara*, and the *Derwent* was hit by a circling torpedo.[23] Both the *Derwent*'s boiler rooms and the engine room were flooded, leaving her in a sinking condition and an obvious candidate, if she survived, to become a cripple.

The *Brigand* was quickly on the scene and her commanding officer, Lt David Gall RNR, was later mentioned in despatches for the promptness with which the rescue tug responded to this crisis. He later reported:

> Engines were brought to immediate notice and when shrapnel ceased to fall crew were set to rig extra fire hoses in case we could help some of the ships. A motor boat with KHM [King's Harbour Master] on board closed and we were ordered to the assistance of destroyer *Derwent*. We slipped buoy and proceeded. The vessel was hit amidships on the port side and as she was reported to be very unstable it was decided to lash up to her and proceed into shallow water [at the southern end of the harbour]. This was done and she was made fast to a buoy close inshore. Salvage hoses were rigged and assistance offered but this was declined as the ship seemed about to sink. We cast off while she slipped from the buoy and stood by while she drove on shore.[24]

However, the *Derwent*'s troubles were far from over. Just after midnight, the first of the two damaged merchantmen, *Ocean Voyager*, blew up with a tremendous explosion. The resultant waves shook the beached destroyer so severely that her stern was lifted bodily inshore about thirty feet; and the bows were swung back into the harbour, and refloated. Some three hours later, the Greek cargo ship *Varvara* also exploded in 'a terrific spurt of flame'. Her entire cargo of petrol caught fire, sending a blazing mass of debris towards the beached destroyer. The destroyer's action damage report recorded:

> All hands were called, and preparations were made
> to abandon ship, in case this mass of burning petrol
> floated down on *Derwent*, as it showed every sign of
> doing. Quarter of an hour later, when the inferno had
> got dangerously close, all hands, with the exception of
> sixteen, were landed at a small jetty abreast the ship by
> motor boat, whaler and skiff. Magazines were flooded,
> and all remaining ready-use ammunition was jettisoned,
> with the exception of a small amount for the pom-pom
> and Oerlikons in case of a further attack.
>   When the fire was about a hundred yards from
> the ship all the remaining hands were ordered into
> the boats. A similar order was given to the officers.
> By this time, however, the fire had lost some of its
> intensity, and an unspoken decision was reached to
> hold off the burning cases and attempt to save the
> ship from catching fire. Invaluable work was performed
> by the very shattered remains of the whaler, which
> was lowered, and formed a physical obstruction to the
> burning petrol at the most dangerous area where the
> ship was holed.[25]

Eventually the fire petered out, allowing the crew to reboard the ship and begin the long task of making her seaworthy again. Meanwhile, a general signal had been received to weigh anchor and leave the harbour to avoid the blazing oil on the water's surface. 'The east end of the harbour was then almost completely covered with oil,' Gall reported, and when ships from that end had left the harbour, 'we proceeded to the west end but apparently the vessels there being on the weather side, and unwilling to risk the passage through the burning oil, had decided to remain.'[24]

One ship was still anchored in mid-harbour. Her master refused assistance, but as it was not in a very safe berth, the *Brigand* decided to remain nearby, and when burning wreckage began to drift down on both ships, *Brigand* took up position ahead of her 'and by means of jets and sprays succeeded in breaking up the larger patches and extinguishing the smaller ones. The merchant ship was then able to keep her sides clear with her own hoses.'[24]

As all the remaining ships in the harbour were clear of the burning oil, Gall decided to moor up for the night, but found the rescue tug was unable to move as the engine's inlets were choked with debris. His report ended:

> The anchor was dropped, engines rung off and fire hoses placed round the sides. Signal was made then to NOIC reporting defect and requesting services of diver. Nothing could be done for the two bombed merchantmen.[24]

Temporary repairs on the *Derwent* were completed on 21 April. She was towed to Malta where, after further repairs, the *St Day* took her in tow for Gibraltar in convoy MKS-15. The convoy ran into bad weather, which was too much for the *St Day*. She was forced into Bône and then had to hand over the *Derwent* to the more powerful *Restive*, which took her to Gibraltar. The destroyer was strengthened for the passage to Britain, and on 23 July she was taken in tow by the rescue tug *Allegiance*, as part of convoy MKS-18.

Focke-Wulf Condors attacked the convoy west of Cape Finisterre, but *Derwent*'s commanding officer said the worst enemy was the weather. It deteriorated steadily as the convoy moved north, reaching a climax around midnight on 31 July when two hundred miles west of southern Ireland. The destroyer's commanding officer wrote in his report:

> A very unpleasant night was spent with the Tug hove-to in a North-westerly heading, with *Derwent* lying helpless and yawing forty degrees either side of the tow…
> So great was the force of the wind and sea, that the centre-line bollards, round which the tow was secured with two complete round turns, were buckled and wrenched together.[26]

The bollards held, but the *Allegiance* made little progress and it was not until the morning of 2 August that the *Derwent* could be turned on to her correct course, and speed slowly increased. By now the convoy was out of sight, though one of its corvette escorts had been detached and was standing by, and on the evening of 4 August the rescue tug entered Devonport with her tow. However, despite the effort involved in getting her to Britain, the destroyer was past repairing, although again the effort had not been totally in vain, as after the war her machinery was sent to the Royal Naval Engineering College, Manadon, for training Royal Navy engineer officers.

More successful was the outcome of returning the destroyer HMS *Marne* to Britain after she was torpedoed on 12 November 1942, one hundred and eighty miles west of Gibraltar, and had most of her stern blown off. At the time, she was escorting the destroyer depot ship HMS *Hecla* and the cruiser HMS *Vindictive* when a U-boat torpedoed *Hecla*. The *Marne* went alongside to assist, but she, too, was torpedoed, causing extensive damage to her stern. She was initially towed by another of the destroyer escorts before the *Salvonia*, with *Jaunty*'s help, took her to Gibraltar where temporary repairs were carried out. She was then towed to Britain by the newly commissioned Lend-Lease rescue tug *Eminent*, a story later covered by *Lloyd's List and Shipping Gazette*:

> The weather was bad during most of the voyage, with high seas running, and there were times when the *Eminent* lost sight of the *Marne* wallowing in the trough of huge waves. After a week the weather became worse and as the towing wire was chafing badly, the *Eminent*'s Commanding Officer, Lt W.A. Phillips RNR of Liverpool, decided to heave to. They lost touch with the convoy but a few days later the *Eminent* and the *Marne* reached harbour safely, and *Marne*'s Commanding Officer signalled: 'Many thanks *Eminent* for a very good tow in.'[27]

Permanent repairs to the *Marne*, undertaken at the Swan Hunter shipyard on the Tyne, took nearly a year. A new stern was fitted, her turbine machinery was overhauled, a Type 272 radar installed, and other improvements made, and on 23 March 1944, after the usual sea trials, she joined the Third Destroyer Flotilla for operational service, and was then employed escorting Arctic convoys. After the war, she was sold to Turkey and remained in service with the Turkish Navy until 1971.

As for the *Eminent*, in her first year of service she steamed nearly a hundred thousand miles and never lost a ship, and her commanding officer was one of several officers in the Rescue Tug Service who was mentioned in despatches for his work during the Normandy landings in June 1944.

Another damaged Royal Navy warship that survived to have a lengthy career with the help of the Rescue Tug Service was the minelayer HMS *Manxman*. On 1 December 1942, she was en route for Gibraltar when a U-boat torpedoed her off Algiers.

The torpedo struck her on the port side, causing flooding in the engine room and elsewhere, and she immediately took on a twelve-degree list. Initially, she was taken in tow by one of the escort destroyers before being handed over to the *Restive*, which towed her to Oran. Temporary repairs were made and she was then taken to Gibraltar, arriving there on 18 December. During the next six months, work was carried out to strengthen her sufficiently to return to the UK, and on 23 June 1943 *Bustler* took her in tow and joined convoy SL-131/MKS-15 to Liverpool. The minelayer spent the next year being repaired, before being sent to join the British Pacific Fleet, but was too late to see any action. She remained in commission as a minelayer, a support ship and a training ship until she was paid off in September 1970.

On one occasion, rescue tugs and their tows almost outnumbered other ships in a convoy. When XK-11 departed Gibraltar on 5 September 1943, it comprised seven merchant ships, four rescue tugs and three cripples: the minesweeper HMS *Fantome*, mined off Bizerta the previous May, was towed by the Dutch rescue tug *Hudson*; the L-class destroyer HMS *Lance*, badly damaged in a German air raid on Malta the previous April, was towed by the Lend-Lease rescue tug *Lariat*; and the 7135-ton Ministry of War Transport freighter *Fort Babine*, which had been damaged by an aerial torpedo, was towed by the *Prosperous*. The Dutch rescue tug *Schelde* also sailed with the convoy in case the others needed assistance. It was as well she did so, as the weather was bad, and she had to help tow both *Lance* and *Fort Babine*.

The convoy was routed up the meridian of sixteen degrees west, and given a provisional speed of five and a half knots. This proved optimistic, as for the first five days, in a rising wind and sea, only four and a half knots was achieved. The wind soon reached gale force, and heavy seas began breaking over *Fantome*'s quarterdeck. This caused an unwelcome crisis, as the dockyard at Gibraltar had secured on *Fantome*'s quarterdeck two armour plates belonging to the aircraft carrier *Indomitable*, which had been damaged earlier in the year. The plates had been put there as ballast, and as a convenient means to get them to the UK. They weighed about fifteen tons each, and had been firmly lashed down and secured with wooden chocks, but the breaking seas washed the chocks away and the plates had begun to slide from side to side. Despite all efforts to keep them in place, the top plate broke away and slid over the side, luckily without doing any damage, and only then could the bottom plate be secured. *Fantome*'s commanding officer recorded:

> At dawn on 12 September, the convoy was not in sight and course was altered to 000 degrees. The wind was now slowly moderating and the convoy was rejoined at 1800. It was noticed that the SS *Fort Babine* and tugs *Prosperous* and *Schelde* were not in company.[28]

The next morning, while two hundred and fifty miles south-west of Cape Finisterre, a four-engined Focke-Wulf Condor was sighted, and shortly afterwards a Heinkel He 111 bomber appeared. Those aboard *Fantome* only saw one stick of bombs being dropped, these falling between two of the escorts on the starboard wing of the convoy. But they soon heard that the Condor had bombed *Fort Babine*, out of sight astern with the two rescue tugs. Two near misses had caused such damage to her hull that her crew were taken off, and she was later sunk by one of the escorts. It was the last successful attack of the war by a Condor.[29]

Fantome's commanding officer concluded his report:

> It is considered that the Master of *Hudson* handled his ship in a seamanlike manner and showed sound

judgment throughout the trip, often under difficult conditions. *Hudson* is an excellent seaboat.[28]

You'd expect nothing less from the Dutch.

In November 1943, two other Dutch tugs, *Zwarte Zee* and *Roode Zee*, towed back cripples, as part of convoy XK-12 from Gibraltar. This divided on 25 November, probably because the rescue tugs and their tows were too slow to keep up. This part of the convoy now became XK-12S, and consisted of *Zwarte Zee*, towing the 11,065-ton British freighter *Essex*; *Empire Larch* towing the 1365-ton British freighter *Pinzon*; and *Roode Zee* towing the 5094-ton American freighter *Cape Mohican*, which had had the bad luck to be torpedoed by an Allied submarine, and each rescue tug had her own trawler escort.

The Plymouth Command War Diary of 5 December listed convoy XK-12S as being 'disabled', which it certainly was, as on 3 December it had been scattered by a north-westerly gale. *Zwarte Zee* still had the *Essex* in tow, although she was hardly making any headway. But *Roode Zee*'s line had parted and her tow was drifting south-west by south; and the *Pinzon*, too, had parted from *Empire Larch*, and hadn't been seen for two days.

The C-in-C Western Approaches requested the C-in-C Plymouth to deal with the situation, and an air search was arranged for the next day to assist *Empire Larch* in locating the *Pinzon*. *Zwarte Zee* and her escort were ordered to proceed independently, and *Roode Zee* and her escort were told to do the same once she had reconnected with *Cape Mohican*. *Zwarte Zee* and her tow arrived at Falmouth on the morning of 11 December, and the same evening *Roode Zee*'s escort arrived there too, perhaps having had to seek shelter after being damaged by the storm. Then on the evening of 13 December *Roode Zee*, accompanied by a different escort, towed *Cape Mohican* into Milford Haven, but it wasn't until 14 December that the *Pinzon* was brought into port by *Empire*

Larch, assisted by *Dexterous*, which had been sent from Falmouth to assist.[30]

The XK convoys continued until May 1945, but the last ones to include cripples were XK-17 and XK-18. The former, which sailed from Gibraltar on 13 June 1944, included *Empire Harry* and *Antic*, which were towing the fighter direction ship HMS *Palomares*, damaged at Anzio. The latter included the 8398-ton RFA tanker *Derwentdale*, which had been damaged by a bomb during the Salerno landings in September 1943. She was one of those hybrid vessels in which the Royal Navy seemed to specialise, as she had been converted to a landing ship gantry (LSG). She could carry and launch fifteen landing craft, medium (LCM), but could still refuel other ships taking part in the landings. She had been bombed soon after some of her landing craft had delivered US troops to the beaches,[31] and had to be towed to Malta by the rescue tug *Hengist* and then on to Gibraltar. XK-18 left there on 7 August 1944, with *Derwentdale* in tow by *Hesperia*, and after arriving at Liverpool, the *Hesperia* took her to the Tyne for repairs. Later she was given engines from another RFA tanker, and returned to service in 1946.

Not all cripples were taken to the UK. On 12 January 1942, the K-class destroyer HMS *Kimberley* was torpedoed and badly damaged aft while operating in support of the Tobruk garrison in Libya. The *Brigand* towed her into Alexandria, and she then went by stages to Bombay for repairs, and eventually returned to service in 1944.

AEGEAN THEATRE

By the autumn of 1943, the focus of the war in the Mediterranean an had shifted to the Aegean, where the Germans defeated British attempts to occupy the Dodecanese islands previously held by the Italians. Six destroyers were lost, and several other warships were damaged. This strained the resources of the nearest major British naval base, Alexandria, where the area's rescue tug, *Captive*, was based, as were the *Brigand* and two First World War Resolve-class rescue tugs, *Respond* and *Roysterer*.

In February 1944, the *Respond* was moved to Malta, but in May the FOIC Levant and Eastern Mediterranean complained to the C-in-C Mediterranean that the shortage of rescue tugs at Alexandria was now acute, remarking that the remaining tugs 'are so heavily employed that it has been necessary to allow them to exceed their boiler hours to twice the normal and it had been impracticable to take in hand any but very minor defects'. The C-in-C, who had already described the situation as deplorable, strongly concurred with this complaint. He added that *Captive* – a German tug that had been scuttled at the start of the war and later salvaged – had, perhaps not surprisingly, 'proved herself unreliable and unhandy', and concluded that, 'I am very apprehensive of conditions here during the forthcoming winter unless relief be obtained.'[32]

THE TREASURE SHIP

It was against this background that the *Brigand* brought off another notable rescue operation alone. On the night of 4 August 1944, the Liberty ship *Samsylarna* was in convoy from New York to India, when, some thirty miles north of Benghazi, she was hit, so her cabin boy related many years later,[33] by an aerial torpedo launched from a lone Italian bomber, which killed one of the ship's gunners asleep in his hammock slung under the gun platform aft.

The citation in *The London Gazette* for the award of the OBE to *Samsylarna*'s captain for saving his ship, recorded:

> [The] torpedo struck the after-peak tank and the
> steering gear was put out of action. The engine-room

flooded and the ship settled rapidly by the stern. Orders were given to abandon ship, the crew being picked up later by an escort vessel. The following morning the Master reboarded with a skeleton crew... By his skill and determination he succeeded in saving his badly damaged ship and a valuable cargo.[34]

What the citation didn't mention was that the ship carried several tons of silver valued at £1 million, destined for an Indian bank. The story is taken up by the author David Masters:

The wireless signals drew a quick response from the naval authorities at Alexandria. The tug *Brigand* put to sea at once to go to the aid of the *Samsylarna* and arrived three days later at the given position. She found the torpedoed ship was still afloat. Her stern and gun platform were completely submerged, but her forward compartments held her up.[35]

Brigand's commanding officer, Lt David Gall, studied the derelict as he circled round it. She had already remained afloat for three days, and seemed safe enough for another hour or two, as there was still plenty of buoyancy forward to support her, though as Masters wrote:

There was, of course, always the chance that a bulkhead would collapse under the pressure and take her to the bottom with a rush. This was the risk that anyone boarding her would have to run.[35]

The commanding officer called for volunteers to board the vessel, and Gunner JH Baldwin, Leading Seaman JC Little and Able Seaman CE Case all agreed to go. The *Brigand* was brought alongside the wreck, and the three men leapt aboard. 'Their strong arms and willing hands,' wrote Masters, 'soon hauled a towing wire over and fixed it without much difficulty.' Subsequently, all three received double shares when salvage money was distributed after the war.[36]

But where was the *Brigand* to take her? Benghazi harbour, thirty-one miles to the south, was too small to accommodate the ship and was, anyway, littered with obstructions. The SNO for Cyrenaica, Commander Evans RN, was stationed at Benghazi and anticipated the rescue tug would choose to take her to Tobruk, but Gall was certain that if he attempted to tow her there, she would sink before Tobruk could be reached. The only chance was to make straight for Benghazi and, despite the rocky coastline, find a place to beach her, and those ashore began a search for a suitable spot. Eventually one was found, which had a sandy bottom that sloped at about the same angle as the ship's keel. Just as importantly, there was enough room for the *Brigand* to manoeuvre the wreck on to the beach. Of course, this had to be done in daylight, but the *Samsylarna* was too far gone for the rescue tug to make more than three knots and they did not arrive until after midnight.

As the *Brigand* approached the coast, Commander Evans boarded her and guided the wreck on to the chosen beach. 'To find that spot and place her there,' David Masters wrote, 'was a fine feat for Commander Evans and the captain of the *Brigand* to perform. She sat there like a bird in her nest.'

The ship was pumped out, temporary repairs made her watertight, and the silver was taken ashore under armed guard; and on 24 August the *Brigand* took her off the beach and started towing her to Alexandria. A storm sprang up – the Gulf of

Sirte is a treacherous place for shipping – and the *Samsylarna* developed a leak. The rescue tug towed her into Tobruk harbour and sheltered there until more emergency repairs had been carried out. She then took her to Alexandria, arriving on 24 September, where, with the help of *Roysterer*, a place was found for her in the old harbour. She was beached well out of harm's way, and stayed there for some years, too badly damaged to be worth repairing.

NOTES

1. www.historicalrfa.org has historical notes on the rescue tugs the Royal Fleet Auxiliary acquired after the war, of which *Jaunty* was one.

2. *Lloyd's List and Shipping Gazette*, 10 February 1944. Clipping in ADM 199/2165.

3. ADM 199/1242. The Navy List first shows Osburn as having been awarded the OBE in, or just before, January 1941. *The London Gazette* has no record of it.

4. Vice-Admiral Syfret's despatch on Operation PEDESTAL. See *The London Gazette* supplement, 11 August 1948, p.4508.

5. War Diary USS *Almaack*, 1–30 November 1942 in www.fold3.com

6. *Hull Daily Mail*, 1 February 1944, p.3.

7. T335/87.

8. 29 May 1945. Clipping in ADM 199/2165.

9. 'Towing the ammunition ship Fort Confidence' (http://alger-roi.fr/Alger/port/hudson/images/50_willem_pop_traduction. pdf) tells the story from Captain Weltevreden's point of view. Admiral Morse made the mistake of telling the veteran captain what to do. Weltevreden put the ship's engines in neutral, pointed out who the helmsman was, and retired to the chart room. The admiral had the good grace to apologise.

10. The admiral's report is in ADM 1/14512, as are the recommendations for decorations.

11. The full citation in *The London Gazette* (supplement 36240, 5 November 1943) read: 'For courage and skill in securing a line from H.M. Rescue Tug *Empire Fred*, to a hawser on a blazing ship in harbour to enable her to be towed out of the entrance.'

12. ADM 1/14767.

13. Harvey WJ, Turrell K. *Empire Tugs*. Kendal: World Ship Society; 1988. pp.37–38. This also includes a copy of the Order of the Day.

14. 17 January 1944. Clipping in ADM 199/2165.

15. Pink List ADM 187/22.

16. ADM 1/15550.

17. Close J. *Beyond the Horizon*. Hull: Riverhead; 2010. pp.102–103.

18. World War II US Navy War Diaries, for September 1944 and 12/21/44 –1/20/45 in www.fold3.com

19. There is a good description of this incident, and photographs of each half of *Porcupine*, on Wikipedia: https://en.wikipedia.org/wiki/HMS_Porcupine

20. From: Cafferkey S. 'The Royal Canadian Navy and Operation Torch' in *The Northern Mariner* Vol. 3, No. 4.

21. Supplement to *The London Gazette*, 8 June 1944, p.2572. The award was for bringing in a merchant ship, *Empire Treasure*, in storm force winds after she was disabled in the Atlantic.

22. ADM 199/2069.

23. A pattern running torpedo, called a *motobomba*, was developed by the Italians. It was dropped by parachute and moved in concentric spirals, varying between four hundred and five hundred metres, until it found a target.

24. ADM 1/14387.

25. HMS *Derwent* damage report, 25 March 1943, in ADM 199/2068.

26. ADM 199/20626.

27. 4 March 1944. Clipping in ADM 199/2165.

28. From report by commanding officer of HMS *Fantome* in ADM 199/1039.

29. Forczyk R. *Fw 200 Condor vs. Atlantic Convoy, 1941–43*. Oxford: Osprey Publishing; 2010. p.69.

30. Plymouth/Portsmouth Command War Diary, December 1943, in ADM 199/633.
31. *Derwentdale*'s war record is in www.historicalrfa.org
32. ADM 1/16007.
33. From a review by Kenneth Hadley of *Epics of Salvage* on www.stonebooks.com
34. *The London Gazette* supplement, 11 December 1945, p.6022.
35. Masters D. *Epics of Salvage*. London: Cassell; 1953. pp.228–34.
36. *Edinburgh Gazette*, 19 December 1950, p.622.

9

THE FAR SHORE

THE ALLIED INVASION of north-west Europe was a long time in the making. The Dieppe Raid of August 1942 had shown that a frontal attack on a port – and a port was essential – would be too costly and unlikely to succeed. Instead, it was decided – and it seems to have been at least partly Churchill's idea – to build two MULBERRIES (prefabricated harbours) off the invasion beaches, a plan approved by the Allied High Command at the Quebec Conference in August 1943.

The harbours were a truly astonishing undertaking, the bedrock on which the whole invasion plan rested, and was one in which the Rescue Tug Service played a vital role, providing some thirty rescue tugs from its force of eighty or so scattered around the world. The chosen landing area for the assault phase (Operation NEPTUNE) was Normandy's Baie de la Seine. The landing beaches extended from the Cotentin Peninsula in the west to the Orne River in the east. The two most westerly ones were American, codenamed UTAH and OMAHA, with MULBERRY A being built at the latter, offshore from the village of Saint-Laurent-sur-Mer. The British and Canadian beaches, from west to east, were codenamed GOLD, JUNO and SWORD, and MULBERRY B was constructed at Arromanches to the east of SWORD.

The harbours' principal parts were steel roadways (WHALES), which floated on anchored pontoons (BEETLES) and connected at the seaward end to pier heads with adjustable legs (SPUDS). There were also more than two hundred hollow concrete caissons (PHOENIXES) of various sizes, which were to be sunk as a sea wall to protect the WHALES and the ships unloading at their pier heads. There were four different sizes: the largest were as tall as a six-storey apartment block (18m/60 ft high, 61m/200 ft long), and they displaced nearly 5500 tons. They had a crew of two, to work the sea valves that allowed the unit to be sunk into place, and a four-man gun crew for the anti-aircraft gun on top.

To give extra protection to the MULBERRIES, and to provide a sheltered deepwater anchorage, sixty-one-metre-long floating tanks (BOMBARDONS) were moored together on the 10-fathom line. Initially, five smaller harbours (GOOSEBERRIES) were to be formed from sinking fifty-five superannuated merchant ships (CORNCOBS), twenty-three of them American, and four obsolete warships. The GOOSEBERRIES were designed to shelter small craft before the PHOENIXES were in place, then two of them became part of the MULBERRIES, while the other three provided separate shelter closer inshore.

The vastness of the enterprise can be judged by the fact that both MULBERRIES totalled four hundred separate units weighing 1.5 million tons, nearly all of which were constructed in Britain, and each unit had to be towed across the Channel. To ensure there were enough of them, all rescue tugs escorting the North Atlantic convoys were withdrawn, and on 28 March 1944, the Admiralty signalled that the only ones available would be single vessels based at Campbeltown, Ponta Delgada (Azores), St John's, and Reykjavik.[1] If a ship was disabled when no rescue tug was available, the crews were to be disembarked and the ship sunk. However, if the Senior Officer (SO) of the convoy's escort force decided there was a reasonable prospect of salvage, the ship was to be left abandoned and the matter reported to the authorities ashore.

'To assist SO of Escorts in making a decision,' the Admiralty signal concluded, 'a daily signal commencing on 1st April will be made by the Admiralty to ships in Atlantic north of 35 degrees North, giving the position and employment of all rescue tugs in that area.'

Another signal from the Admiralty to the C-in-C Mediterranean in March 1945 showed that this policy was still in place.[2] It asked if any of the Assurance class then in the Mediterranean could be spared, as there were not enough rescue tugs available if a mid-ocean U-boat threat did develop. Luckily, none did, though U-boats were still sinking merchant ships up to the last days of the war.

The design, construction and operation of MULBERRY B was mostly an Army responsibility, and the planning staff from Combined Operations, who had originally been handed the task, were moved to the War Office. The Admiralty was responsible for the design and placing of the BOMBARDONS, and for transporting the MULBERRY units, and it was consulted on the MULBERRY design and how they were to be moored.

Once the landings had taken place, on 6 June 1944, the parts of the MULBERRIES were towed to the Far Shore – as the assault beaches were rather romantically called in contemporary documents – and assembled. All vessels had to proceed to the assault beaches along predesignated marked channels, which started from an assembly point eight miles south-east of the Isle of Wight, later nicknamed 'Piccadilly'. Three of these channels were reserved for the MULBERRY tows.[3]

Assembling the MULBERRIES involved ten thousand men and one hundred and fifty tugs. Those tugs suitable to cross the Channel with tows had 'M' for MULBERRY painted on their funnels. They numbered sixty-seven on D-Day, and fluctuated thereafter, rising to a maximum of one hundred and nineteen on 12 July.[4] The British and Dutch provided most of the ninety or so larger tugs in the 1000/1500 hp range; the smaller tugs, of about 750 hp, were provided by the Americans.[5]

COTUG

The command structure for organising the tugs was an Allied one. In overall command was a British naval officer, Rear Admiral William Tennant, designated RAM/P (Rear Admiral Commanding MULBERRY and PLUTO). Under him was Captain CH Petrie DSO RN, in charge of MULBERRY B, and Captain AD Clark USN, in charge of MULBERRY A. Another key player was Captain Ed Moran USNR, who in peacetime owned and ran a well-known New York tug business. Moran's organisation, known as COTUG (Combined Operations Tug Organisation), was based at Lee-on-Solent, where a local cinema became its headquarters. A signal tower, which had been built on top of the cinema, overlooked the tugs' assembly area, and made an ideal control centre, and from early May 1944, the 17,491-ton tug depot ship *Aorangi* was anchored nearby. This converted troopship provided spares and minor engine repairs, as well as hospital facilities and accommodation for a pool of replacement crews. However, by the end of May, the Solent became so overcrowded that *Aorangi* was moved to Southampton, and in mid-July was replaced by the 16,810-ton destroyer depot ship *Empress of India*.[6]

COTUG's responsibilities were wide-ranging. They included organising the sailings and administration of the vessels involved, making arrangements for fuelling and provisioning, executing minor repairs, delivering mail, collecting reports, and distributing orders and instructions. Because it involved so many vessels, the COTUG organisation operated separately from the C-in-C Portsmouth's Movements Staff, but at Plymouth, the Nore and Dover, tugs were sailed by the Staff Officer, Movements, in the normal way.

COTUG's key to success was the close contact it maintained with the tugs and tug masters, and its equally close liaison with CCRT staff for White Ensign tugs, and the managers and agents for Red Ensign tugs. American representatives maintained similar contact with US Naval, War Shipping Administration and Transportation Corps tugs. The future politician Sir Walter Monckton wrote in his report on the part played by COTUG in administering the vessels under its command:

> The selection of Captain Moran USNR as
> Tug Controller was extremely fortunate. It was
> realised that success depended as much on the
> efficiency and willingness of the tug masters
> and crews as on anything else; it was to be
> a long job from which there would be little
> respite. Particular attention was paid to their
> comfort by ensuring that they received their mail
> regularly, that they did not go short of rations
> and water, and that spare towing gear was readily
> available and that refuelling and minor repairs
> were prompt and efficient; having in mind that
> the tugs were operating all along the coast, this
> was not so easy.[7]

The Admiralty's rescue tugs were mostly based at Lee-on-Solent for towing duties under Senior Naval Officer Selsey. They were:

Allegiance	*Eminent*	*Mammouth*
Emphatic	*Assiduous*	*Emulous*
Sabine	*Bandit*	*Flaunt*
Saucy	*Buccaneer*	*Freedom*
Sea Giant	*Cheerly*	*Griper*
Seaman	*Destiny*	*Sesame*
Dexterous	*Lariat*	*Storm King*
Superman	*Antic**	*Krooman*
Resolve		

Note: *Delayed. Due to arrive in the UK on 22 June, but unavailable until a refit had been completed.

Two other Admiralty rescue tugs, *Bustler* and *Marauder*, aided by the smaller *Danube V*, were adapted for what the Supreme Allied Commander, General Dwight D Eisenhower, rated 'second in daring only to the MULBERRY Harbours'. The operation, known as PLUTO (Pipe Line Under The Ocean), was certainly as ingenious. It involved towing 250-ton drums, called conundrums, to Cherbourg, once the port had been captured. These huge drums, thirty feet in diameter, were used to lay flexible steel pipelines on the seabed so that fuel could be pumped to France, and then distributed to the advancing Allied armies. It has been calculated that more than 172 million gallons of petrol were delivered by this method between August 1944 and May 1945. The first four lines were laid from the Isle of Wight to Cherbourg, captured on 26 June, but as the Allies advanced northwards, seventeen more lines were laid to shorten the supply route, from Dungeness in Kent to Ambleteuse in the Pas de Calais.

Five more rescue tugs – *Attentif, Champion, Goliath, St Martin* and *St Mellons* – were based at Portland for duties under SNO BOMBARDON, and *Growler* and *Samsonia* were also based there. They, too, were employed to tow parts of the MULBERRIES after they had towed the old French battleship *Courbet*, engineless and filled with concrete, across to the Far Shore for use as a CORNCOB.

Once scuttled, the *Courbet* proved an irresistible lure for the enemy's fire. Torpedoes were launched at her, and she was constantly shelled and bombed. This, of course, had no effect whatsoever on her efficiency as a blockship. To encourage this waste of effort and ammunition, the *Courbet* was decorated with a huge tricolour and Cross of Lorraine, and from then on she was attacked even more frequently.[8]

Some rescue tugs were also employed towing into position the largest warships bombarding the shore. The biggest danger for these battle wagons were the German pressure mines, which could not be swept, so the largest warships were forbidden to turn their screws in case they detonated one.[9]

COLLECTING THE CORNCOBS

The Red Ensign tugs controlled by the Ministry of War Transport were assembled as follows: twenty-six in the Solent for duties under SNO Selsey; seven at Portland for duties under SNO BOMBARDON, and another five for duties under SNO CORNCOB; and five at Oban for duties under SNO CORNCOB. One of these was *Empire Larch* and aboard her was Jim Radford, almost certainly the youngest person to take part in the Normandy landings. He later wrote:

> I left school at Easter 1944, with no plan except to go
> to sea as soon as possible. My brother Fred was already
> a PO in T.124T and our oldest brother, Jack, had been

lost when the SS *Cree* was torpedoed in 1940. That should have deterred me – but we were a seafaring family, and Monday morning saw me at the Shipping Federation in Posterngate [Hull], asking for a ship. They explained to me that I couldn't join the Merchant Navy until I was 16 and turfed me out. My next call was the offices of the United Towing Company. I was in luck – they needed a deck hand on the docking tug *Bureaucrat* and seemingly didn't care about my age. I started work that day and for the next two or three weeks learnt the rudiments of seamanship in and around Hull docks. One morning the ship's husband [an agent appointed by a ship's owner to manage a ship] called me from the jetty. 'Hey, Jim, we need a galley boy on the *Empire Larch*, do you want the job?'

Did I? I knew the *Larch* was a deep-sea tug and that was where I wanted to be. I signed on that afternoon, collected my MN identity card from the Pool Office – no question about age this time – and joined her at Albert Dock. I never worked so hard before or since. The cook was a Scouse called Paddy Walsh, whose system was to show me once how to do everything, including the cooking, and then leave me to it. We sailed a few days later. No one told us where we were going and being at the bottom of the pecking order I didn't ask. For the first week I was so sick I didn't care.

Eventually it became clear that we were going round Britain collecting a convoy. At each port we stopped – Blyth, Sunderland, Methil, Scapa, Oban – more ships joined us, all rusty old merchantmen with skeleton crews on board.[10]

Empire Aid was another Red Ensign tug assigned to CORNCOB, and her mate, Lewis Dohn, takes up the story when the convoy of blockships left Oban under their own steam six days before the landings were to take place:

> The convoy formed in two columns of three groups.
> Tugs were allocated to each group. Orders were to
> render assistance when necessary. It was anticipated there
> would be a fair number of breakdowns of one kind or
> another, and our job was to take them in tow until the
> problem was repaired. Strangely enough, we had no work
> to do and, as far as I know, only one tug had to put
> out a tow. From time to time, one of the ships would
> raise two black balls signifying 'not under command',
> and the whole group would scatter like scared rabbits to
> reform later when the signal was lowered.[11]

The voyage was otherwise uneventful and after being joined by air cover and six destroyers as escorts, the convoy made its way to Poole harbour and anchored there. The passage across to the Far Shore, Dohn wrote, was equally uneventful:

> Not a single enemy ship, plane or E-boat had been
> sighted. Occasionally a shell from shore batteries passed
> harmlessly overhead. Far more was coming in the
> opposition direction from our own warships some miles
> astern. The sky was filled with Allied planes. A few
> hours later we were at anchor and our assignment
> finished. Harbour tugs took over, and we watched as
> the CORNCOBS were scuttled bow to stern.[11]

After completing her mission to deliver the CORNCOBS 'in the cold grey light of 6th June' as Jim Radford described it (see his song at the end of this chapter), *Empire Larch* towed a PHOENIX from Dungeness to MULBERRY A, and took a small 550-ton

British coaster, empty of her cargo and with a smashed rudder post and propeller, back across the Channel. Later that month, she was one of the rescue tugs caught in the great storm of 19 June while towing the linked railroads (WHALES). Like all the others being towed that day, it broke up and sank.

Empire Larch was also employed as a rescue tug. On the afternoon of 24 September, she left Lee-on-Solent to tow in LCT 651 but failed to find it. Instead, she found the stern half of another LCT (883), whose commanding officer requested he and his crew be taken off as the weather was so bad he felt the LCT was in danger of foundering. The crew of fourteen was taken aboard, and as one of them was injured, *Empire Larch* returned to Portsmouth. She arrived there in the early hours of 25 September, the injured man was transferred to an ambulance boat, and the rest of the crew was landed.

Empire Larch sailed again immediately to bring in the bow of LCT 883, which had been found by *Empire Aid*, but she had fouled her propeller while connecting to the LCT, so *Empire Larch* took both in tow. After anchoring *Empire Aid* off the Isle of Wight, *Empire Larch* took the bows of LCT 883 to Stokes Bay. She then returned to pick up *Empire Aid*, but found she had already been towed away, so *Empire Larch* returned again to the mainland, and at 10.00 on 26 September anchored off Lee.[12] A busy forty-three hours or so, but probably not untypical.

Jim Hardie, a signalman aboard *Attentif*, gave a vivid account of her passage to the Far Shore:

> During the Dog-Watch on the evening of June 5th, orders were received to proceed to Portland, arriving there around eight or nine o'clock we found the harbour almost literally full of LCI (Landing Craft, Infantry) and LST (Landing Ship, Tank), and heaven knows what else. *Attentif*, a requisitioned French tug,

headed straight for the coaling quay to bunker ship, an all-hands job which found us still at it well into the wee small hours. After a brief period of rest we came on deck to find a vast empty expanse of water. Of the multitude of craft that had crowded the place only an hour or two before there was not a sign.

Much later in the morning a large US Army truck drove up, carrying a small contingent of GIs under the command of an extremely tall middle-aged, middle-ranking officer. This group, part of the team responsible for the overall construction of the harbour, were to be delivered to their base off St Laurent (OMAHA). We then cast off, picked up our two BOMBARDONS and sailed for the rendezvous area, known as 'Piccadilly'...

Ships and landing craft from the first assault groups which had gone hours before were already filling the north-bound sea lane, passing to starboard of us as they headed back to the UK. I cannot remember precisely when we arrived off the beaches, only that it was some time around the middle of the next day. On reaching the end of our 'corridor' we made a sweep to starboard, which brought us round and sailing parallel to the Normandy coast. The battleships and cruisers stationed off shore, which we had passed earlier on, were still maintaining their deafening barrage, salvo after salvo, augmented by several large, rocket-firing landing craft closer to shore. Destroyers were constantly on the move, patrolling at speed all along the coastline, and all around us the sea was full of small craft and troopships. A truly incredible and memorable sight.

On our arrival at our delivery point off St Laurent, and with our American passengers safely transferred to their new berth, we handed over our tow and headed

back to Portland at full speed. There we collected
another pair of BOMBARDONS and, with hardly a
pause, were under way again late that same evening.
This was the beginning of a non-stop shuttle service
which continued relentlessly until our final units were
delivered on 16 June.[16]

PROBLEMS WITH *GOLIATH*

Nothing went as smoothly for the Dutch-manned *Goliath* when
she was ordered to recoal at Portland after she arrived there on
30 May. Curiously, she was flying a Red Ensign, though there
was no explanation of this in the SNO BOMBARDON's report on
the incident that soon unfolded.

The SNO briefed *Goliath*'s master that an officer would board
the rescue tug to help him practise handling the BOMBARDONS, but
the master then reported his dynamo had broken down, so the
exercise was cancelled and the dynamo sent for repair. The master
also particularly requested, and strongly stressed, the urgency for
removing a small water tank from inside his coal bunker, but it
was not possible to complete this because other work had higher
priority, so on 3 June SNO BOMBARDON cancelled the work and
told *Goliath* to recoal regardless. The SNO later reported:

The *Goliath* took no notice of this signal at all. At 1945
the vessel had not moved in compliance with my order.
I sent another hand message which read: 'You are to
move immediately to the inner end of outer coaling
pier and do what you are told or you will be relieved
of your Command in the morning.' This message
was acknowledged and signed by the Master, but the
ship did not move. During this time I was continually
getting messages from SNO Naval Store Department,

Portland, about *Goliath* not being ready for coaling and SNO said that unless she did come she would miss her turn, and would throw the coaling programme of the port out of gear.[14]

At 22.30, as *Goliath* had still not moved, *Champion*, the BOMBARDON duty tug, was ordered to move *Goliath* to her coaling berth, and she was then recoaled:

> The next day I reported the matter to the FOIC
> Portland personally, stating the trouble I had had
> with this tug, the action I had taken, and proposed
> to him that the Master and the whole of the Dutch
> crew should be relieved forthwith. With this the FOIC
> concurred. The Master reported to my office the next
> morning and I then told him that in view of his direct
> disobedience of orders and general slackness of his ship,
> he would be relieved from Command, and asked him
> if his Mate was a suitable person to take Command.
> His reply was, 'If I leave, My Mate and crew leave.' I
> therefore ordered the Master and crew to pack up and
> be ready to proceed to Lee-on-Solent pm that day.[14]

The upshot of all this was the entire crew was sent by road under armed guard. As D-Day was so close, they would have had restrictions placed on their movements, but on 29 June a signal was sent authorising *Goliath*'s crew to be released for further employment in tugs. The SNO concluded his report:

> I regret that this drastic action was necessary, as in
> my opinion the Master is a good seaman and the
> Dutch members of his crew appear to know their work
> and to have a good spirit. I explained to the Mate and

the rest of the crew that the action I had taken was no reflection whatsoever on them and that the reason why they were leaving their ship was that the Master had told me that if he left, they all left.[14]

Goliath's log recorded a different version:

Water tank ordered to be removed from engine room in order to increase bunker capacity. Work left unfinished by shipyard workers. Captain refused to sail as ship was not in a seaworthy condition. Navy commander, Portland, ordered to imprison crew of *Goliath*. Later Captain and crew rehabilitated.[15]

STORMY WEATHER

A contemporary report on COTUG's operations records that the tugs came from a variety of sources and each had to be treated differently.[16] Generally speakings, it remarked, there was very little trouble, but the Red Ensign and Dutch tugs were, especially later in the operation, often held up for lack of key members of the crew. This would have been avoided if an adequate pool had been kept in being. It would have been better if tug personnel in Operation OVERLORD had all come under the Naval Discipline Act for the whole period of the operation.

The report also pointed out that tug crews were exempt from the Merchant Navy pool, so there was no official source from which tug hands could be obtained, although the Ministry of War Transport had established a small pool on *Aorangi*:

This was inadequate and did not last long, and after a few weeks it was left to the various tug managers or their agents to fill the gaps. As a consequence working days were lost. This shortage did not apply to White Ensign tugs.[16]

Another contemporary report by Sir Walter Monckton describes the difficulties encountered by the weather:

From D-Day onwards [the weather] was almost continuously worse than that to be expected for the time of year. It not only determined what could be dispatched each day – some tows, particularly the floating roadway [WHALES] were very susceptible to weather – but it also affected the progress of erection and thus varied the daily requirements. These day-to-day variations complicated the economical allocation of the different types of tugs. In preparing the towing programme certain assumptions had to be made. The average speed of towing was estimated at 3 knots; in practice, however, 4½ knots was achieved with the result that the allowance of 72 hours for the round-trip time of the tugs was reduced. On the other hand, it had been assumed that the weather would only prevent towing on one day in four and this guess proved optimistic. Losses to tugs were estimated at 10 per cent but actually only 2 were lost; one US [*Partridge*] and one British [*Sesame*].[17]

He then added that only two PHOENIXES were lost, one by mining and one by torpedo, and that they both sank in thirty seconds, 'which was far quicker than the designers had ever dreamed', but he did not include the one lost through stress of weather in the Bristol Channel in October, which, thankfully, took a lot longer (see below):

But losses to the other equipment were heavier and nearly 40 per cent of the roadway spans (WHALES) failed to survive the crossing. Up to D+10 [ten days after D-Day] the progress of erection had been satisfactory with the exception of the piers and roadway, the dispatch of which had been held up by the weather; the arrival of this equipment now became urgent as it was most desirable to commence the discharge of vehicles from LST in each harbour. Consequently the officer responsible for dispatch from the UK was a continual customer of the weather prophets to ascertain when he could safely send over the equipment and he was delighted to be told on the morning of D+12 (Sunday 18 June) that there was an almost perfect weather forecast. The crystal-gazers were enthusiastic; everything pointed to a 48-hour spell of fine weather; on their charts there were no ominous areas of low pressure, the pressure wedges were all as they should be and even the signs of the Zodiac seemed propitious.

So arrangements were put actively in hand; all possible tugs were mobilized and set out with a record number of units, including 22 tows of roadway each 480 feet long making a total of nearly 2 miles. But not one yard of roadway reached the far shore, because at 0300 hours on the Monday morning (D+13) it commenced to blow. It blew a full gale for three days, such as had not been known in the Channel in summer for 80 years. It has been described as second only in portent to the gale which scattered the Spanish Armada in 1588; and it would have scattered and smashed the Allied Armada of small craft, with disastrous results to the forces already ashore in Normandy, had it not been for the GOOSEBERRIES provided by the 60 blockships. They had already rendered yeoman service during the rough weather in the days immediately following D-Day but during the storm they, as the Eastern Naval Task Force Commander signalled, literally saved the day.[17]

Up to the start of the great storm it could be said that everything was proceeding more or less to plan, except that the original completion date for the two harbours was never going to be met. MULBERRY A was closer to completion than its English counterpart and questions began to be asked as to why this was so. In an effort to make up time an extra PHOENIX was towed over to MULBERRY B in failing light and a falling tide, and was poorly planted near its main entrance, a case, Monckton suggested, of more haste made less speed. But he added that the care with which the units of the British MULBERRY were usually planted might well have been a contributory factor in it surviving the great storm, which its American counterpart did not.[18]

The problems the rescue tugs encountered because of the weather were endless. Before the storm had even reached its height, *Superman* reported that a rating on the unit she was towing had died of seasickness, and what *Saucy*'s commanding officer, Lt JW Evenden, and his crew had to deal with shows just how bad the weather was. She was towing roadways (WHALES) with a number of other tugs when the great storm hit her in the early hours of 19 June, after she had left the Solent the night before in a light north-easterly breeze and a slight sea. The wind began to increase just before dawn, and by 09.30 the sea was becoming rough. The wind had veered and was coming from *Saucy*'s port quarter. She was being steered thirty degrees to port of her correct course to allow for the ebb tide. The tow then started to make a corkscrew motion. Evenden reduced speed to prevent this, and altered course to put the wind and sea dead aft. 'I intended to carry on like this,' he wrote in his report, 'and make Route No. 12 [one of the dedicated channels from 'Piccadilly'] as long as the tow behaved.'[19]

The trouble was that it didn't and in the rising wind and sea each of the six sections began yawing wildly from side to side, as well as pitching. Speed was reduced still further, but this did not improve matters. By now all the other tugs had left *Saucy* behind. A steel cylindrical tank at each end of the WHALE seemed to be affecting how it followed (towed), and during the morning the tank of its first section came adrift and floated away. The section then sank, buckling the decking of the second section, which prevented *Saucy* from stemming the ebb tide. The unit's crew of soldiers aboard *Saucy* tried to save the other five sections, but one by one each section sank. The towing hawser could not be saved either, and had to be cut adrift, and all the towing gear was lost.

'I have towed many craft, and of varied types,' Evenden wrote, 'and this is my first loss, and I feel it very much.' He concluded: 'I would add that the weather was too bad to be happy about the job. I did what I could for the best, in the circumstances.'[19]

As we know, Evenden – who had been awarded the MBE in 1942 and was mentioned in despatches for his work during the Normandy landings – was not the only one to lose his tow in the storm, but unfortunately he lost another on 27 June, and in October he was caught in a gale near Lundy island while towing a PHOENIX from Milford Haven with *Hesperia*. A second PHOENIX was also being towed, and the Canadian Flower-class corvette HMCS *Trentonian* was escorting this small convoy.[20]

Evenden had already received a letter of commendation for towing AFD 17 from Iceland to Gibraltar, but it must have been a first for a commanding officer to receive one following an unsuccessful tow. But Evenden did, and after reading the report of *Trentonian*'s commanding officer, there is no doubt that it was no more than he and his crew deserved:

15 October, 1730: *Trentonian* sailed from Milford with the two Rescue Tugs towing PHOENIX 194.

16 October, 1030: wind southerly, force 5–6, sea and swell rapidly increasing. Both PHOENIXES taken into Barnstaple Bay for shelter.

1705: Wind veering to west-north-west and increasing. Heavy swell entering Barnstaple Bay. *Saucy* [with tow and *Hesperia*] turned and headed for Lundy Island. *Trentonian* followed. PHOENIX 195 remained in the Bay as one of the tugs towing it reported her steering gear defective, but would sail for Lundy as soon as repaired.

17 October, 0015: Arrived Lundy Roads, wind west-north-west, force 6. *Hesperia* anchored with tow and *Saucy* cast off as she had no means of shortening towline. Wind variable during night, conditions improving.

0925: Tugs towing PHOENIX 195 left Barnstaple Bay but turned back on account of wind backing to south-south-west and increasing.

1500: PHOENIX 195 and tugs anchored off Clovelly [on western end of Barnstaple Bay]. Wind south-west, force 6. Very little shelter off Lundy Island for PHOENIX 194 and the two rescue tugs as they had to remain clear of anchored shipping. Tides very strong, and tow swung right around *Hesperia* on turn of tide. *Saucy* connected up to PHOENIX and cleared *Hesperia*, but carried away all her small towing gear in doing so.

PM: Wind south-west to west-south-west, very gusty, force 6–7. During the night weather deteriorated rapidly, wind south-west to west-south-west, shifting and gusty, force 7–8. Tide turned after midnight. *Hesperia* and tow again fouled. *Saucy* could not assist owing to lack of gear. *Hesperia* weighed anchor to clear tow and in doing so was blown clear of lee of island. During the middle watch she held tow against wind, about two and a half miles east of island, but as the flood tide gained in strength and wind increased, she was forced eastwards. *Saucy* could not connect owing to seas breaking over PHOENIX platforms. *Hesperia* was unable to make headway but it was expected she would be able to return to lee of land on ebb tide.

18 October, 0800: Tide turned. Wind increased force 9–10. *Hesperia* hove to 12 miles east of Lundy. *Saucy* standing by unable to connect as seas washing half way up the fore side of PHOENIX. This was the position until *Hesperia*'s towline parted.

1207: *Hesperia*'s towline parted close to her, leaving about 200 fathoms attached to PHOENIX. *Saucy* closed and crew of PHOENIX instructed to stand by to attempt to get second towline connected. Unit now beam on to wind and sea. Just possible for the men to keep footing on lee platform.

1305: *Saucy* successful in passing a line to the crew of the unit and the five men on the platform commenced what appeared to be an extremely difficult and dangerous operation, the hauling on board and connecting up of *Saucy*'s heavy towline. Fleeting it in with a tackle, they got it on board foot by foot.

1420: messenger parted and end of towline was lost. *Saucy* stood clear of PHOENIX, hauled in her line, and waited to enable the crew of the unit to rest.

1700: *Saucy* again closed PHOENIX and got heaving line on board. This time the operation was successful.

1827: *Saucy* connected to one corner of the unit. Reported she would endeavour to hold it up to the gale, but had not sufficient power to tow it under prevailing conditions. Wind west-south-west, force 8–9, very rough sea.

1929: *Saucy*'s towline parted...

2113: Crew taken off PHOENIX by Appledore lifeboat. *Trentonian* and tugs standing by PHOENIX to warn shipping as unit unlighted and visibility bad. Wind during the night westerly, force 9–10, with intermittent rain squalls.

19 October, 0800: wind moderating. Unit 000 degrees, Hurtstone Point 3 miles. During the morning *Hesperia* grappled for the 200 fathoms of line trailing from PHOENIX but could not lift it with gear available, grapnels not strong enough.

0952: wind force 6–7. Sea and swell subsiding but still not suitable for boarding unit. *Trentonian* steamed west to search for Rescue Tug *Hudson* reported to be joining with spare towlines and party of ten naval ratings to man PHOENIX.

1100: *Hudson* sighted and directed to PHOENIX.

1225: *Hudson* arrived and lay off PHOENIX. Instructed to put ten ratings aboard as soon as practicable.

1250: *Hesperia* closed unit and succeeded in putting one officer aboard. *Hudson* then closed and put three of her crew on board, but none of the special boarding party. *Hudson* then got a small line on board and appeared to be commencing to tow. This simply had the effect of hampering the two more powerful tugs in their efforts to connect, so *Hudson* was ordered to cast off and to put the ten naval ratings on board. The object was to connect up the largest Rescue Tug *Hesperia* first, and the men were needed to get her heavy line on board. *Hudson* finally put these ratings on board and *Saucy* and *Hesperia* were both connected.

1455: towing resumed to westward. Wind and sea still subsiding. If the unit had been seaworthy it could probably have been towed wherever ordered. Proceeded towards Barry.

1555: HM minesweeper *Inverforth* joined.

1600: *Hudson* closed tow and took off one of her crew who had been left on board for some reason, also *Hesperia*'s officer.

1633: Closed *Hudson*, lowered whaler and transferred *Hesperia*'s officer to *Trentonian*.

1710: Unit took a list of about fifteen degrees and commenced to settle in water. Towing was stopped as PHOENIX was obviously filling up rapidly and appeared to be on the point of sinking. List increased slowly.

1720: closed PHOENIX to take off crew. *Inverforth* proceeding alongside and *Trentonian*'s whaler standing by.

1725: *Inverforth* alongside, took off eight men but was obliged to go ahead as unit was still listing away from her.

1726: *Inverforth* fouled both tow lines and appeared to be in a very precarious position as unit was still listing and settling in water.

1727: Both towlines slipped and *Inverforth* cleared.

1728: Remaining two men taken off unit by *Trentonian*'s whaler and brought on board. Senior rating reported large hole about six feet in diameter in unit. Nothing could be seen of hole above water.

1745: Unit stopped listing, lying at an angle of about sixty degrees with portion of underside visible. It appeared that with displacement being increased by the leak, the unit would founder when it sank low enough to bring the apertures on the lower side of the top deck under water.

2020: One aperture on top deck below water. *Trentonian* proceeded towards Barry in accordance with orders, leaving *Inverforth* to mark wreck with Dan buoys when sunk.

2105: *Saucy* reported by R/T that PHOENIX had sunk.[21]

OPERATIONS ON THE FAR SHORE

Reports by the rescue tugs during Operation NEPTUNE came from two sources.[22] A standard single-page one, written by a boarding officer after a rescue tug had returned to Lee-on Solent, gave details of each completed passage. It included such data as the speed, state of tow, state of equipment, arrival and departure times and dates, what if anything was towed back, and whether the rescue tug was still serviceable. When necessary, the commanding officers wrote longer reports, on rescues, the loss of tows, and so on.

Superman, commanded by Lt Edwin 'Tubby' Turner RNR, was assigned for general duties after she had finished helping to tow parts of the MULBERRIES. One of her crew, Bertie Neilson, later wrote:

> On several occasions we were detailed to assist some rocket-firing landing craft. These shallow drafted vessels

had difficulty in taking aim if the wind was too strong and our job was to steady them while they supported our army units at Ouistreham.[23]

Superman was also employed in her proper role as a rescue tug, and on one occasion was sent to assist a Royal Navy sloop, which had been badly damaged by German batteries near JUNO beach, and was drifting inshore:

We connected up and lashed alongside and started to tow her seawards under fire from the shore battery, which straddled us until we finally got out of range but not before we had been holed at the waterline and were making water.

We managed to deliver the damaged sloop to the JUNO beach anchorage and, following a thorough inspection, it was decided to beach *Superman* on the next falling tide. This was successfully accomplished and a repair effected by Engineer Paddy Murphy and helpers by welding a section from an engine room door over the shell hole. They did a first class job which, I am told, lasted many months until her next refit.[23]

While on rescue tug duty, *Superman* spent twenty-four hours at Arromanches and twenty-four hours at one of the GOOSEBERRIES at immediate notice to steam. On 19 August she went to the assistance of the 7271-ton SS *Harpagus*,[24] which had hit a mine off Arromanches, but shortly after commencing to tow, the fore part of the ship started to sink. *Superman* cast off and began towing the ship by her stern, and managed to take her to a safe anchorage. But early in the morning of 21 August, Turner received a signal that the casualty's after part was also sinking. So *Superman* connected to *Harpagus* again, and beached her four cables west of MULBERRY B. This must have taken some doing as it was blowing a near gale (force 7) at the time.

Three days later, *Superman* went to the assistance of the new 2370-ton cargo ship SS *Empire Roseberry*, which had been mined 2 miles north-east of Ouistreham, killing ten of the crew and two gunners. *Superman* picked up survivors, but the ship sank shortly afterwards. Then on 6 September, she took the remains of *Harpagus* back across the Channel. Turner concluded his report:

> Put her to anchor at midnight 7 September four miles north of Nab Tower. At 0930/8 September reconnected and proceeded for Southampton, berthing her at Town Quay at 2030/8 September. Thence tug proceeded to Lee, going to anchor at 0925. *Superman* needs B/C (boiler cleaning) – date of last clean 1st May.[22]

THE EXPERIMENTAL MINESWEEPER AND OTHER ASSIGNMENTS

For his contribution to the success of the landings, Turner was awarded the DSC, one of four commanding officers in the Rescue Tug Service to be given this decoration for their services during NEPTUNE.[25] Another recipient was Lt CW Stanford RNR, who commanded the Assurance class *Griper*, which assisted an LCT drifting helplessly in heavy seas, an incident that was later described in *Lloyd's List and Shipping Gazette*:

> When the *Griper* arrived at the spot indicated by signals, there was no LCT to be seen, but by groping about in the gale for some time the tug found the stricken craft 11 miles away.

'Getting the tow line aboard was a problem calling for all the seamanship we knew,' said the *Griper*'s Commanding Officer. 'It was dark and the LCT was tossing about like a cork. With our second attempt we made a successful hook-up and we steamed into the gale for home. For three and a half hours we couldn't make more than two knots. Then our boiler engine fan broke down, reducing our power so that we were barely holding our own against wind and tide. For two and a half hours we managed to hold our course, and then, the tide changing, we made better progress. After eight anxious hours, with the constant threat of the tow parting in the heavy seas, we brought the LCT into sheltered water. Although such jobs are part of the routine of the Rescue Tug Service, it was nice to hear the Commanding Officer of the LCT say that the connecting-up operation was the finest exhibition of seamanship he had seen under such conditions.'

This was the second LCT that the *Griper* had rescued recently. Soon after the Allied landings in Normandy she went to the assistance of an LCT drifting helplessly into an enemy minefield, and brought her safely through heavy seas to harbour.[26]

One of *Griper*'s assignments was not so successful, but as everyone in the Rescue Tug Service knew very well, you couldn't win them all. On 24 November 1944, she and *Jaunty* were assigned the task of towing to the Far Shore a crewless 3980-ton experimental minesweeper HMS *Cyrus*. Launched the previous January, this top-secret trimaran had its three hulls held together with steel lattice trusses, so that if a pressure mine was detonated, the resulting blast would pass harmlessly right through the hull. It was steered by remote control from another vessel over suspected minefields.

As with most new experiments, the operation did not end well. It commenced in calm weather with the two rescue tugs towing in tandem across the Channel, but the weather soon deteriorated. The wind reached force 5–6 from the north-west, and as *Cyrus* was being manoeuvred on to her mooring buoy in the Seine Bay's crowded anchorage, her remote control steering gear carried away. She immediately took a broad sheer to starboard and rammed an American LST on the port bow, and became caught in the LST's port anchor cable. The two ships were eventually disentangled and the minesweeper was put on to her mooring.

The first sweep was carried out without any problems – and it would seem without any results – but the next day a westerly gale was blowing, and on returning from Le Havre, *Griper* found *Cyrus* adrift. Some of *Griper*'s crew were aboard the minesweeper to help moor her, but Stanford decided to take them off. While manoeuvring to do this, a wave swept *Griper*'s towing wire overboard and wound itself round her rudder.

With *Griper*'s crew struggling to clear the wire, *Jaunty* tried to pass a tow rope to the men on *Cyrus*, but was unable to do so. After what Stanford described as 'a very fine piece of seamanship', *Jaunty*'s commanding officer, Lt WS Lowrey RNR, held her close enough to *Cyrus* to take off the nine men aboard her, but all efforts to clear *Griper*'s screw failed, and *Jaunty* had to tow her into Le Havre where US Naval divers cleared it. But it was then found that the main engine thrust block had fractured, and *Griper* had to be towed back across the Channel.

Jaunty's report made clear the impossibility of connecting up with the drifting *Cyrus*. 'The weather was the worst I have experienced for many years,' Lowrey reported[22], '*Jaunty* being continually under water in the towing deck, with seas which at times enveloped the whole of that deck from the view of the navigating bridge.' On no less than three occasions, seas swamped the navigating bridge, strained the wheelhouse's armour-plated doors and broke the chart room door. It was not surprising that Lowrey had to conclude by reporting the stranding of the experimental minesweeper, after 'everything possible was done to get the vessel in tow'.

This loss in no way affected the high regard with which Lowrey was held by his superiors, for in August he was recommended for a decoration, and was duly awarded the DSC. The citation read:

> Lieutenant Lowrey, by his devotion to duty, promptness in carrying out his orders, and cheerful efficiency, set a fine example to his ship's company and to the other British, Dutch and American rescue tugs with which he operated. His behaviour has been in accordance with the best traditions of the Service.
>
> HMS *Jaunty* sailed for the French coast in the Assault convoy, and carried out her first rescue duties during the passage. From D-Day to the 20 July, she was employed on rescue duties off the Beaches and in the Channel, returning to UK only to tow damaged vessels. During practically the whole of this period the ship was at instant notice. The promptness with which the Commanding Officer carried out his duties was largely responsible for the saving of a number of ships and many valuable lives.
>
> In addition to her normal rescue duties, HMS *Jaunty* towed many HM ships clear of mines and mined areas, sometimes under enemy shellfire.[27]

Another rescue tug that distinguished herself was the *Mammouth*. On 23 January 1945, in a strong south-easterly wind, she was escorting a dredger, *TB Taylor*, and two hoppers from Ouistreham to the Solent, when her commanding officer, Lt H McGregor RNR, received a signal from the dredger that she was disabled and needed a tow. McGregor wrote in his report:

> This appeared impossible. The dredger was sheering
> wildly with her rudder jammed hard over and in
> addition was heeling over to port at an alarming angle.
> As I closed in on the dredger, we saw them launch
> a raft and five of her army crew jump for it. The
> wind and sea was increasing and as these men pulled
> themselves on to the raft, one was washed back into
> the sea. The dredger certainly appeared to be on the
> verge of capsizing. Her boats had been smashed, and
> she was making water in the engine room and her
> accommodation was flooding. The remaining personnel
> were clustered aft and under the conditions it would
> have been impossible to couple up. The men on board
> could not stand owing to the violence of her rolling.
> The wisest thing in my opinion was to abandon her,
> and if she remained afloat, which certainly appeared
> very unlikely, we could board her and take her in tow
> when the weather moderated. This I told the Officer in
> Charge, Captain Sessions RE [Royal Engineers]. With
> the first party leaving her, it was obvious that they
> had already decided to abandon ship. I then proceeded
> to pick up the man washed off the float and then the
> party on the raft.[22]

This accomplished, the *Mammouth* returned to the dredger. As her sea-boat would have been smashed by the heavy seas if it had been lowered, McGregor towed one of the rescue tug's Carley floats, and manoeuvred it round the dredger's stern. The next group of men jumped, clambered on to the Carley float, and were hauled back to the rescue tug. This process was repeated until the dredger's entire complement of eighteen was taken aboard. All that afternoon and through the night, the *Mammouth* stood by, waiting for the weather to improve. When it did so, the dredger's crew returned to their ship and helped couple her up with the rescue tug, which then took her to Southampton. McGregor concluded:

> I should like to report that I was very ably assisted by my two deck officers during the whole operation and that my Engineer Officer, Sub-Lt Charles Gray RNVR, at considerable risk to himself, climbed over the side on to the ship's belting and time after time was in danger of being pulled into the sea, as he pulled men on board, many of whom did not have the strength left to help themselves, and were only partly conscious after being in the water, some of them for over 30 minutes.[22]

The report was forwarded to the Director of Transportation for Twenty-first Army Group, who replied: 'Will you please arrange to pass on our thanks and congratulations to the CO of the *Mammouth* and to his crew for what was undoubtedly a very gallant and courageous rescue under most difficult conditions.'[22]

SESAME SUNK

Given the weather, the crowded Channel traffic, enemy gunfire from the shore, and attacks by enemy aircraft and E-boats, it was amazing that rescue tug casualties were so low. It was E-boats that caused the one British fatal rescue tug sinking during NEPTUNE, when in the early hours of 11 June 1944 six

of them attacked *Sesame*, which was towing a WHALE pier head.[28]
The commanding officer ordered the gun crew to open fire,
but, according to the five survivors – the commanding officer,
third officer, first radio officer and two ratings – *Sesame* was
immediately torpedoed amidships on the starboard side and sank
in fifteen seconds. The rest of the crew, who were belowdecks,
must have been killed at once. After being in the water for up
to an hour and a half, the five survivors were helped aboard the
tow and, along with its crew, were later transferred to a warship
and returned to England.

The circumstances under which the demise of *Sesame* was
discovered must have given the crew of the rescue tug *Storm
King* a terrible shock. After delivering the PHOENIX she was
towing to Arromanches, *Storm King* turned and headed for
home, but came across an abandoned PHOENIX, which she took
back to Arromanches. While returning home across the Channel
for the second time, she came upon an abandoned WHALE pier
head. 'On boarding it,' Joe Barnes, one of *Storm King*'s crew,
remembered, 'we found the tow rope to be bar tight so we
knew there was a tug on the end of it.'[29]

In his report, the NCO in charge of *Sesame*'s tow wrote
that at the time his crew were in the crew shelter.[30] A large
flash was seen, but no attention was paid to this as there had
been gun fire and flares all night. However, a minute after the
flash, the NCO, thinking the tow had stopped, looked out of
the shelter, but all he could see was a puff of smoke ahead of
the tow.

In due course, *Storm King* received a well-deserved congratulatory
signal from C-in-C Allied Naval Expeditionary Force (ANCXF),
Admiral Sir Bertram H Ramsay, for 'consistent good work
in hazardous towing and salvage operations', which was, no
doubt, also recognition of *Storm King*'s efforts, as described in
Chapter 6, to save HMS *Woodpecker* earlier in the year.

DOVER VETERANS

While the battle raged on the Far Shore, two pre-First World War vintage steam tugs, *Lady Brassey* and *Lady Duncannon*, also became involved in the fighting. Both were based at Dover and were managed by the Dover Harbour Board. The 362-ton *Lady Brassey* was 130 ft overall, had an ihp of 1200, about the same as the Assurance class. She was equipped for firefighting, and was listed in 1944 as a rescue tug in the lowest category, C (see Appendix), but was only armed with an Oerlikon and two Lewis guns.

Lady Duncannon was much smaller, half the gross tonnage of *Lady Brassey*, but both had been hired by the Admiralty in 1939, just as they had been in 1918 when *Lady Brassey*'s master, Captain CH Lambert, had been awarded the OBE 'for courage and skill displaying towing cargo and other ships out of a minefield, after they had been mined'.[31] They were commanded by RNR or RNVR officers, but the crews were civilians, and they flew the Red Ensign. There were three crews and they took it in turn to man the two tugs, making both vessels available for rescue work twenty-four hours a day.

On 24 June 1944, *Lady Brassey* was ordered to assist the 2824-ton collier *Empire Lough*, which had been hit by German coastal batteries and set on fire some half a mile south-east of Folkestone. The collier, part of convoy ETC-17, had left Southend for the Normandy beaches to deliver supplies, including ammunition and petrol, when she was hit and abandoned by her crew. By the time *Lady Brassey* found her, she was drifting south-eastwards and burning fiercely from the bridge to the stern. The rescue tug's foam firefighting appliance had little effect, and after some minutes flames began leaping to mast height, and the ammunition aboard started to explode. It soon became too dangerous to continue fighting the fire, and *Lady Brassey* was forced to withdraw to a safe distance.

The minesweeping trawler HMT *Fyldea* arrived at the scene at about the same time as *Lady Brassey*, and other firefighting ships now appeared, but they, too, were unable to approach the blazing ship for the area around *Empire Lough* was, as the trawler's commanding officer commented in his report, like a 'battlefield'.[32] Eventually there was a lull in the explosions and both *Lady Brassey* and *Fyldea* attempted to close the collier with the intention of towing her towards the shore and beaching her. *Lady Brassey*'s stern was manoeuvred under the collier's starboard bow, but was unable to connect up until Ordinary Seaman V Brockman took matters into his own hands. The rescue tug's master, VF Nichols, later wrote:

[He] at once observed the difficult position and entirely of his own initiative, without being requested to do so by me, climbed on board the burning vessel and made the tug's towing wire fast to the starboard bollard, after which he was taken back on board the tug, and we commenced towing the vessel towards the shore.[32]

Ordinary Seaman Brockman, someone wrote on the report, was just sixteen years old.

The ammunition now started to explode again, hurling burning debris high into the air, but at 5.45pm *Lady Brassey* beached the collier off Lydden Spout Battery west of Dover. By now the fire had spread to No. 2 hold on the fore side of the bridge, and the ammunition was exploding much more frequently, with pieces of shrapnel falling on the rescue tug's deck. Because of the extreme heat of the fire and exploding ordnance, *Lady Brassey*'s towing equipment could not be retrieved and she returned to Dover without it. 'As the nearest onlooker,' the trawler's commanding officer concluded his report, 'I have the highest praise for *Lady Brassey*'s seamanship and resource, and for the endeavours of her crew in a most dangerous operation.'

Four days later, on 28 June, *Lady Brassey* and *Lady Duncannon* went to the assistance of another burning cargo ship, the 825-ton SS *Dalegarth Force*, which had been hit by German shell fire while in convoy between Dover and Folkestone. Three of the crew were killed and others, including the master, were wounded. Later, he and the second engineer were awarded the OBE for their bravery under fire and refusal to leave their ship. Shells were still falling on the convoy when the *Dalegarth Force* was taken in tow by *Lady Brassey*, while the crew of *Lady Duncannon* extinguished the flames and helped save the burning ship, which was towed into Dover.

The skill and courage shown by the crews of the tugs in these two incidents was duly recognised: the two masters were awarded the MBE, and four of *Lady Brassey*'s crew, including Ordinary Seaman Brockman, received the BEM, as did two of the crew of *Lady Duncannon*. Brockman was also awarded Lloyd's War Medal for Bravery at Sea.

In recommending these awards the FOIC Dover, Admiral Henry Pridham-Wippell, pointed out the outstanding services the crews had rendered during the period, 1941–44, including their contributions to moving parts of the MULBERRY harbours:

> In my opinion these services have been quite unique, carried out as they have been in the proximity of the enemy coast and often under fire from the enemy's guns... it is difficult to speak too highly of the conduct and bearing of the crews.[33]

At the conclusion of NEPTUNE, the achievements of the tugs on both sides of the English Channel was duly recognised when the Rear Admiral commanding MULBERRY and PLUTO, Rear Admiral William Tennant, wrote in his report:

> The work of the tugs has been magnificent.
> They have worked under conditions to which
> the majority of the crews were unaccustomed.
> Nevertheless, their pride in their job as tugmen has
> been such that they have never failed to give of
> their best and to hold on to and deliver tows in
> circumstances which they could not have been blamed
> for giving up.[34]

THE SHORES OF NORMANDY

(Tune: 'The Dawning of the Day' or 'Raglan Road')

In the cold grey light of the sixth of June,
in the year of forty-four,
The Empire Larch sailed out from Poole,
to join with thousands more.
The largest fleet the world had seen,
we sailed in close array,
And we set our course for Normandy,
at the dawning of the day.

There was not one man in all our crew,
but knew what lay in store,
For we had waited for that day,
through five long years of war.
We knew that many would not return,
but all our hearts were true,
For we were bound for Normandy,
where we had a job to do.

Now the Empire Larch was a deep-sea tug,
with a crew of thirty-three,
And I was just the galley-boy, on my
first trip to sea.
I little thought when I left home,
of the dreadful sights I'd see.
But I came to manhood on the day,
that I first saw Normandy.

At Arromanches, off the beach of Gold,
'neath the rockets' deadly glare,
We towed our blockships into place,
and we built a harbour there.
Mid shot and shell we built it well,
as history does agree,
While brave men died in the swirling tide,
on the shores of Normandy.

Like the Rodney and the Nelson,
there were ships of great renown,
But Rescue Tugs all did their share,
as many a ship went down.
We ran our pontoons to the shore,
within the Mulberry's lee,
And we made safe berth for the tanks and guns,
that would set all Europe free.

For every hero's name that's known,
a thousand died as well.
On stakes and wires their bodies hung,
rocked in the ocean swell.
And many a mother wept that day,
for the sons they loved so well.
Men who cracked a joke and cadged a smoke,
as they stormed the gates of Hell.

As the years pass by I can still recall,
the men I saw that day,
Who died upon that blood-soaked sand,
where now sweet children play.
And those of you who were unborn,
who've lived in liberty,
Remember those who made it so,
on the shores of Normandy.

©Jim Radford (Shantyman, folksinger, and ex galley-boy, *Empire Larch*)

NOTES

1. ADM 199/2165, 28 March 1944.
2. *Ibid.*, 13 March 1945.
3. Roskill S. *The War at Sea, 1939–45*. Vol. III. Part 2. London: HMSO; 1954–61. p.29.
4. RAM/P Report, Encl No. 7, p.200 in ADM 199/1616.
5. Details of each tug taking part in towing the MULBERRIES can be found on www.thamestugs.co.uk
6. See www.royalnavyresearcharchive.org.uk
7. ADM 199/1616, Chapter 9, para 61.
8. Roskill S. *The War at Sea, op. cit.* p.126.
9. Con Harris, a signalman aboard *Emphatic*, wrote that one of *Emphatic*'s tasks was to tow the First World War monitor, HMS *Erebus*, into her bombardment position. *Emphatic* was also assigned the unpleasant task of landing dead bodies found in the water. From an article submitted for publication in *Towrope*, DSRTA archives.
10. *DSRTA Newsletter*, 2000; 1(3): 2–3.
11. *Towrope*, 2005 (Christmas); 5(18): 15–21.
12. ADM 199/1637.
13. *Towrope*, 2001: 3(10): 18–21. The account has been slightly abbreviated here.
14. ADM 199/1637.

15. Extracts from Dutch tugs' logs in red file B marked HMRT in DSRTA archive.

16. COTUG memorandum, dated 24 September 1944, in ADM 199/1631.

17. Report by Sir Walter Monckton in ADM 199/1617.

18. If Monckton's remarks sound partial today, *Force Mulberry* by Commander A Stanford USNR, who was Clark's deputy for force Mulberry A, describes how Clark drove his men – and himself – to exhaustion to finish the American harbour ahead of schedule.

19. ADM 199/1619.

20. See Litwiller R. *White Ensign Flying.* Toronto: Dundurn Press; 2014 for a history of HMCS *Trentonian*.

21. ADM 199/1618.

22. ADM 199/1637.

23. Letter to Len Reed from Bertie Neilson, 28 November 2001, in DSRTA archive.

24. *Harpagus* was taken to the Tyne where a new forepart was built for her, and she was renamed *Treworlas*. See www.tynebuiltships.co.uk/H-Ships/harpagus1930.html

25. After the war, Turner transferred to the Royal Navy and then served in the Marine Branch of the Royal Air Force (see supplement to *The London Gazette*, 18 August 1959, p.558). After retirement, he continued to go to sea and, as a civilian, was master of a protection vessel during the Icelandic cod wars of the 1970s.

26. *Lloyd's List and Shipping Gazette*, 6 November 1944.

27. ADM 199/1637.

28. One of the official reports in ADM 199/1637 described it as a WHALE Link, the other called it a 'WHALE Unit No. S.513'.

29. Describing the incident many years later in *Towrope*, 2001; 3(10): 17, Barnes said *Sesame* was towing a PHOENIX. Aged fourteen, he must have been the youngest member of any ship's crew at Dunkirk when his tug, *Sun King VII*, went to the aid of Allied

troops on the Dunkirk beaches. See *Towrope*, 2006 (Summer); 7(29): 21.

30. ADM 199/1637.
31. *Dover Express*, 11 November 1918.
32. ADM 1/29724.
33. *Ibid*.
34. RAM/P Report Enc. No. 7, p.199, in ADM 199/1616.

ENVOI

AFTER GERMANY SURRENDERED, the Rescue Tug Service was able to turn its undivided attention on the war against Japan. By that time quite a number of rescue tugs were already stationed in the Far East. But it was a different kind of conflict, where they were employed in more routine, but essential, matters such as towing AFDs and other heavy equipment like floating cranes. *Lariat*, for instance, with the help of *Saucy* for part of the way, towed AFD 17 from Iceland to Sydney, an eighteen-thousand-mile voyage lasting six months.

She then became the only rescue tug at that time to be officially attached to the British Pacific Fleet after it was formed from the Eastern Fleet in November 1944. She went with it to Thursday Island, New Guinea and the Philippines, and finally to Hong Kong where the Royal Navy accepted the surrender of the Japanese garrison on 30 August 1945, after Japan had surrendered on 15 August. By then, the Rescue Tug Service, for the loss of twenty tugs, 'either by mine, torpedo, bomb, or stress of weather' had saved nearly three million tons of merchant shipping and two hundred and fifty-four British and Allied warships.[1]

A fitting end to this book is the one last battle by a rescue tug, not with the enemy but with that equally dangerous, and more frequent, opponent, the weather. It comes more or less verbatim, but abbreviated, from an article published in the *South China Morning Post*, on 9 November 1945, which was written by

Lariat's second mate, Sub-Lt AHC Smith RNVR:

One of the Fleet Train tankers, *Wave King*, had
developed engine trouble and needed to be towed back
from Okinawa and *Lariat*, which was commanded by
Lt GV Reakes RNR, was sent to retrieve her. One
typhoon had already struck the area a few days earlier
and the tanker had narrowly escaped being driven
on to a reef. But by the time *Lariat* had arrived on
25 September 1945 and taken the tanker in tow the
weather was balmy and for the next three days she
covered one hundred and thirty-eight, one hundred and
twenty and one hundred and forty miles.

Another typhoon had been reported but appeared
to be travelling well to the north-west. However, by
the end of the third day a gentle swell had started to
appear and the wind had increased to twenty knots, and
a new forecast predicted that the typhoon was heading
Lariat's way. Overnight, the wind increased to forty
knots and the barometer, which had been steady until
then, started to fall. The wind continued to blow from
the north, and in the morning the sky overhead was
still clear, though clouds were gathering all around the
horizon. There was nothing unduly spectacular about
the sunset, but a few small birds sought sanctuary on
the ship, which had started to roll rather heavily, and
the gunwhales were occasionally awash.

All watertight doors, ports, etc. were now closed and
everything likely to move had been secured. Because of
the increasing strength of the wind, the tanker's bows
kept moving into the wind, increasing the strain on

the towing wire, and a further fifty fathoms was let out. From then on the wire had to be let out every fifteen minutes to prevent undue chafing, as both ships were rolling and pitching heavily. Occasionally there would be a heavy rain squall and strong gusts of wind, reducing *Lariat*'s speed through the water from six knots to a meagre two knots. By midday on 30 September the wind was north by west and had increased to fifty knots, making *Lariat* unable to keep the tanker on her course of two hundred and forty degrees.

By the Sunday afternoon the seas were mountainous, with dark clouds hanging low above them. *Lariat* occasionally rolled so heavily that the ship's bell just forward of the bridge kept ringing every few minutes. Meals were taken standing up, with our bodies jammed against a doorway. Most of the articles we had secured below were now strewn about the cabins. The barometer was now falling about one point an hour and was down to 29.0 inches (982 mb), and by the evening the wind had increased still further, to sixty knots. The waves were now higher than the rescue tug, which was rolling at forty degrees most of the time, with an occasional roll of fifty to sixty degrees, and we could only head three hundred and twenty degrees. Visibility was only a few yards and we had not been able to see *Wave King* for several hours. Another sixty fathoms of towing wire were let out, and we eased out a couple of feet every five or ten minutes.

By 7pm the wind was a steady eighty to ninety knots with gusts of hurricane force, which made the whole ship shudder and vibrate. The ship's bell was ringing

practically all the time, the wardroom furniture had
all come adrift, water was coming in everywhere, and
the awnings around the bridge ripped and banged, and
finally blew away. As *Lariat* went down in the trough
of the waves, the wind whipped the tops of the waves
off in a driving, flying sheet of spray and spume. It was
also raining hard.

In the dark everybody just hung on to anything in
order to keep balanced. We all got bruised in our
efforts to do this and it was very tiring. The ship's
head was three hundred and sixty degrees and at any
minute we were half expecting to beach on the rocks
south of Formosa. We had no idea of our speed, and
no radar. Our only communication with *Wave King* had
broken down, as water in the radio room had put out
of action every transmitter and receiver.

Some of the rolls we did were terrific and we thought
were going to turn over. There was still tension in the
wire, so we knew that *Wave King* was at the other end
but did not know what her heading was.

At 9.20pm both engines stopped and we rapidly
headed round to sixty degrees. The engine room rang
up to say that water had got into one of the control
boxes (she is diesel electric) and whole lot had gone
up in flames. Fortunately, after about ten minutes
the prompt action of the chief engineer, Sub-Lt J
McLaughlin, and his other officers managed to get the
port engine going again. Slowly we got our head back
into the wind. The water was getting into the engine
room faster than they could pump it out, despite the
fact that they were using a fire pump that was capable

of pumping one hundred tons an hour over and above normal pumps.

We were now left with one engine and one generator to supply steering, gyro, light, pumps, etc. At 11.40pm, after one terrific gust of wind, the wind suddenly dropped and, apart from a confused mountainous sea, which pitched and rolled in every direction, all was quiet. The barometer read 28.01 inches (948.5 mb).

We now managed to head back to two hundred and seventy degrees and probably made some progress, but early on the Monday morning the wind commenced again. Although it did not quite reach its previous speed it was still a steady seventy knots or so, with strong gusts. The pressure jumped up to 29.10 inches (985 mb) and remained steady until dawn. We still got occasional squalls making a lot of movement on the ship, but the sea did not look so angry. The barometer continued to rise and the wind to moderate. The temperature had also dropped to seventy-nine degrees Fahrenheit, from the eighty-four degrees it had been when the barometer had been dropping.

We were now able to assess the damage. The awnings of course had gone, so had all the gun covers, most of the signal flags; and the signals locker was flat on its face on the opposite side of the bridge. The sights of the Oerlikons had gone, so had one of the Oerlikon shoulder fittings. The platform above the bridge for taking bearings was clear of everything except the gyro repeater and the standard compass, the metal cover of which had gone. A large metal navigation desk had also disappeared; the lifeboat had come loose at its davits;

and the guards around the steering rods had all come adrift. The port steering rod was bent badly, wireless aerials were down, most of the halyards had gone, as had the ensign and its halyards.

Belowdecks was real chaos. The typewriter had been thrown across the captain's cabin and smashed a large wooden panel below his bunk; strangely enough not damaging the typewriter. As the galley chimney had blown off, and the ship was still rolling heavily, it was impossible to make hot drinks or to cook any food. Actually, from Saturday to Wednesday the ship's company lived on biscuits, bully beef and water.

Later we found out that during the forty-eight hours, Saturday to Monday, we had found from *Wave King*'s radar that we had gone astern in a semi-circle within three to nine miles of some rocks. We tried hard to get away, but we did not appear to make any real headway until Monday night, when we steered various courses between two hundred and two hundred and forty degrees according to the strength of the wind. Meanwhile, a signal had been received that help was at hand in the form of the Canadian cruiser *Ontario* and the rescue tug *Integrity*, and on Friday 5 October *Lariat* arrived back in Hong Kong.[2]

What the article didn't mention was how the *Lariat*, at the height of a typhoon, 'was troubled,' as a Rescue Tug Service document put it with typical British understatement, 'with water down her funnel'.

Admiral Sir Bruce Fraser, C-in-C of the British Pacific Fleet, acknowledged this epic when he signed a letter of commendation. It read:

> On 26 September 1945, HMRT *Lariat* left Okinawa for Hong Kong with RFA *Wave King* in tow. On 29 September 1945 the wind began to increase steadily until at 2200 on 30 September it had reached force 12. At 2230, fire broke out in the engine room, and although this was quickly got under control, the starboard engine was put completely out of action, and HMRT *Lariat* had to proceed with the tow on one engine. In spite of these unfavourable and difficult conditions, the tow was successfully completed at 0800 on 3 October 1945.
>
> For skill and determination throughout this successful towing of a 10,000-ton ship through an active typhoon area, I commend Lieutenant GV Reakes RNR, Commanding Officer of HMRT *Lariat*, and Sub Lieutenant J McLaughlin RNR, his Engineer Officer.[3]

NOTES

1. Correspondence and amendments from CCRT's secretary to Paymaster Rear Admiral Sir Eldon Manisty, 23–30 November 1945, in ADM 199/2165. After the defeat of Germany the CCRT stated, in an undated document in ADM 199/1632, that the Service had rescued 2,814,178 tons of shipping.
2. Smith AHC. 'Story of a Tug in a Typhoon', *South China Morning Post*, 9 November 1945, p.2.
3. *Towrope*, Spring 2004; 6(19), 19.

APPENDIX

FROM CAFO 796 APRIL 1942 AND
CAFO 339 FEBRUARY 1944

Fire fighting appliances are divided into the following categories:

(a) Capacity, 150 tons of water per hour at 160 lb per square in. Pyrene multiple injectors.

(b) 107 tons of water per hour at 100 lb per square in.

(c) 75 tons of water per hour at 100 lb per square in.

(d) 16 tons of water per hour.

(e) One incline inductor unit for foam equipment on wash deck service.

(f) 130 tons of water per hour at 70 lb per square in. No foam equipment.

(g) 190 tons at 120 lb per square in (no pyrene multiple injectors).

(h) No separate fire pump.

When tugs are required to work in pairs they should be of approximately the same power.

The sea-going capabilities can be classified as follows:

[A] Can proceed in any weather.

[B] Can proceed in any but the heaviest Atlantic weather.

[C] Not available for heavy Atlantic or very heavy North Sea weather.

RESCUE TUGS

(Commissioned or to be Commissioned.)

Name.		I.H.P.	Category.	Speed.	Endurance in days.	Fire-fighting Appliances.	Armament.
"Bustler" Class	"Bustler" "Growler" "Mediator" "Reward" "Samsonia" "Turmoil" "Warden"	4000	A	12–15	28–50 Food and water 30 days only	a	One 12-pdr. HA/LA. Two Oerlikons. One 2-pdr. Pom-pom. Two twin Lewis.
"Assurance" Class	"Allegiance" "Charon" "Frisky" "Griper" "Hengist" "Jaunty" "Prosperous" "Prudent"						

	"Restive" "Saucy" "Sesame" "Storm King" "Tenacity" Plus 6 completing 1944: Envoy Class	1350	A	10–12½	14–21	a	One 12-pdr. HA/ LA. Two Oerlikons. Two Lewis.
American Class (U.S.A.-built)	"Advantage" "Aimwell" "Aspirant" "Athlete" "Bold" "Cheerly" "Destiny" "Eminent" "Emphatic" "Favourite" "Flare" "Flaunt" "Integrity" "Lariat" "Masterful" "Mindful" "Oriana" "Patroclus"	1875	A	12½–14	21–30	b	One 3in HA/LA. Two Oerlikons.
	"Reserve" "Sprightly" } "Tancred"	To Royal Australian Navy					
	"Vagrant" "Weazel" "Director" (wood) "Emulous" (wood) "Freedom" (wood) "Justice" (wood)	1875	A	9–12	9–12	b	One 3in HA/LA. Two Oerlikons.
	"Marauder" "Nimble"	3000	A	10–15½	8½–15	a	One 3in HA/LA. One Oerlikon. Two Lewis.
"Empire" Class	"Empire Ace"	850	C	9–11	8–10	h	One Oerlikon. Two twin machine guns.
	"Empire Dennis"	850	C			h	One Oerlikon. Two twin machine guns.
	"Empire Dolly"	1000	C			h	One Oerlikon. Two twin machine guns.
	"Empire Edwards"	900	C			h	One Oerlikon. Two twin machine guns.
	"Empire Fred"	900	C			h	One Oerlikon. Two twin machine guns.
	"Empire Gnome"	900	C			h	One Oerlikon. Two twin machine guns.

(Continued)

(RESCUE TUGS – continued)

"Empire" Class	"Empire Griffin"	1000	C			f	One Oerlikon. Two twin machine guns.
	"Empire Harlequin"	900	C			h	One Oerlikon. Two twin machine guns.
	"Empire Minotaur"	900	C			h	One Oerlikon. Two twin machine guns.
	"Empire Minnow"	1000	C			f	One Oerlikon. Two twin machine guns.
	"Empire Samson"	1000	C			f	One Oerlikon. Two twin machine guns.
	"Empire Titania"	1000	C			f	One Oerlikon. Two twin machine guns.
"Attentif"		1000	B	10	9	g	One Oerlikon. One twin Hotchkiss.
"Barwick"		700	B				
"Busy"		1200	C	12–13	10		One 13-pdr.
"Captive"		1130	A	12	60		
"Champion"		1000	B	10	9	g	One Oerlikon. Four Hotchkiss.
"Confident"		1200	C	12–13	10		One 13-pdr.
"Crocodile"		1000	B		6		
"Danube V"		900	C	9–12	7½–18	g	One Oerlikon. Four Lewis.
"Mammouth"		1800	B	10	8½	f	Two Oerlikon. One twin Lewis.
"Mastadonte"		1800	B	10	8½	f	Two Oerlikon. Two twin Hotchkiss. Two Lewis.
"Resolve"		2700	B	10–12	8½–11½	e and g	One 12-pdr. HA/LA Two Lewis.
"Sea Giant"		2400	A	10–14	9½–15	c	One Oerlikon. Two Hotchkiss.
"Seaman"		1200	B	10	11	h	One 0.5in twin Mark IV. One Oerlikon. Three Lewis.
"St Mellons"		1250	B	9	8	c	One Oerlikon. Three Hotchkiss. Four Lewis.
"Superman"		1000	B	10	9½	h	One Oerlikon. One 0.5in twin. Mark IV. Two twin Lewis.

COMMERCIALLY MANAGED RESCUE TUGS
British Crews
Managers: Overseas Towage & Salvage Co., Ltd.
53, Leadenhall Street, E.C.3
Telephone: Royal 5678.

"Abeille IV"	1400	B	10–12½	13–14½	e	One Oerlikon. Two twin Lewis.

| "Hesperia" | 4000 | A | 12–15 | 28–50 Food and water 30 days only. | a | One 12-pdr. HA/LA. Two Oerlikons. One 2-pdr. Pom-pom. Two twin Lewis. |
| "Salvonia" | 1350 | A | 10–12½ | 14–21 | a | One 12-pdr. HA/LA. Two Oerlikons. Two Lewis. |

Managers: United Towing Co. Ltd.,
Nelson Street, Hull.
Telephone: Hull Central 15514.

| "Diversion" | 800 | C | 10–11½ | 8½–11½ | e | One Oerlikon. Two twin Lewis. |
| "Krooman" | 800 | C | 10–11½ | 9–12½ | e | One Oerlikon. Two twin Lewis. |

Managers: Messrs. Wm. Watkins Ltd.,
112, Fenchurch Street, London, E.C.3.
Telephone: Royal 5434.

| "Assiduous" | 1350 | A | 10–12½ | 14–21 | a | One 12-pdr. HA/LA. Two Oerlikons. Two Lewis. |
| "Kenia" | 760 | C | 10–12 | 6½–8 | c | Three machine guns. |

Managers: Dover Harbour Board, Dover.
Telephone: Dover 296.

| "Lady Brassey" | 1200 | C | 10 | 4 | d | One Oerlikon. Two twin Lewis. |

Managers: Alexandra Towing Co.,
6, Covent Garden,
Water Street, Liverpool.
Telephone: Liverpool Central 2015

| "Earner" | 1350 | A | 10–12½ | 14–21 | a | One 12-pdr. HA/LA. Two Oerlikons. Two Lewis. |

UNDER DUTCH FLAG
Managers: Messrs. J. D. McLaren Ltd.,
183, High Street, Dorking, Surrey.
Telephone: Dorking 3370.

"Antic" "Dexterous"	1350	A	10–12½	14–21	a	One 12-pdr. HA/LA. Two Oerlikons. Two Lewis.
"Amsterdam"	1300	C	10–12	5–7½	e	One Oerlikon. Two machine guns.
"Goliath"	1200	B	10–11	6–7	e	One Oerlikon. Two Lewis. Two Hotchkiss.
"Roode Zee"	1800	A	12–13	33–41	f	One 3in HA/LA.
"Thames"	2450	A	10–14	14–31	b	One 12-pdr. HA/LA. One 0.5in twin, Mark IV. Two Hotchkiss.
"Zwarte Zee"	4200	A	10–16	22–55	h	One 0.5in twin, Mark IV. Three twin Lewis.

BIBLIOGRAPHY

All titles published in London unless stated otherwise

Baird, D. *Under Tow*. St. Catharines, Ontario, Canada: Vanwell; 2002.

Baird, R. *Shipwrecks of the North of Scotland*. Edinburgh: Birlinn: 2003.

Behrens, C. *Merchant Shipping and the Demands of War*. HMSO; 1955.

Booth, T. *Admiralty Salvage in Peace and War. 1906–2006*. Barnsley: Pen & Sword; 2007.

Brookes, E. *Turmoil*. Jarrolds; 1956.

Buffetaut, Y. *D-Day Ships: The Allied Invasion Fleet, June 1944*. Conway Maritime; 1994.

Close, J. *Beyond the Horizon*. Hull: Riverhead; 2010.

Dear, I. *The Ropner Story*. Hutchinson Benham; 1986.

Dear, I. *The Royal Ocean Racing Club*. Adlard Coles Nautical; 2000.

Dear, I. ed. *The Oxford Companion to World War II*. Oxford: Oxford University Press; 2005.

Dimbleby, J. *The Battle of the Atlantic*. Penguin Random House, 2015.

Drummond, J. *HM U-Boat*. W.H. Allen; 1958.

Elphick, P. *Liberty: The Ships that Won the War*. Rochester: Chatham Publishing; 2001.

Fayle, C. *History of the Great War: Seaborne Trade*. John Murray, 3 vols; 1920–24.

Ferguson, D. *Shipwrecks of North East Scotland*. Edinburgh: Mercat Press; 1992.

Forczyk, R. *Fw 200 Condor vs Atlantic Convoy, 1941–43*. Oxford: Osprey Publishing; 2010.

French, D. *The Strategy of the Lloyd George Coalition, 1916–18*. Oxford: Oxford University Press; 1995.

Grove, E. ed. *The Defeat of the Enemy Attack on Shipping, 1939–45* Navy Records Society; 1997.

Hague, A. *The Allied Convoy System, 1939–45*. Maryland, USA: Naval Institute Press; 2000.

Halpern, P. *A Naval History of World War I*. Maryland, USA: Naval Institute Press; 1994.

Hannon, B. *Fifty Years of Naval Tugs*. Liskeard, Cornwall: Maritime Books; 1984.

Harvey, W & Turrell, K. *Empire Tugs*. Kendal: World Ship Society; 1988.

Hodson, J.L. *British Merchantmen at War: The Official Story of the Merchant Navy, 1939–44*. HMSO; 1944.

Houlder Bros. *Sea Hazard: A History of Houlder Bros. 1939–45*. Privately published; c.1947.

Hurd, A. *The Merchant Navy, 1914–1918*. John Murray, 3 vols; 1921–29.

Jackson, C. *Forgotten Tragedy: the Sinking of HMT Rohma*. Maryland, USA: Naval Institute Press; 1997.

Jeffrey, A. *This Time of Crisis*. Edinburgh: Mainstream Publishing; 1993.

Lane, T. *The Merchant Seaman's War*. Manchester: Manchester University Press; 1990.

Larn, R. *Shipwrecks Around the Isles of Scilly*. Newton Abbot: David & Charles; 1993.

Lenton, H. *British and Empire Warships of the Second World War*. Maryland, USA: Naval Institute Press; 1998.

Litwiller, R. *White Ensign Flying*. Toronto, Ontario, Canada: Dundurn Press; 2014.

Lloyd George, D. *War Memoirs of David Lloyd George*. John Murray, 2 vols; 1938.

Lloyds' War Losses WWI.

Lloyds' War Losses WWII.

Lund, P. & Ludlam, H. *Trawlers Go To War*. New English Library; 1974.

Lund, P. & Ludlam, H. *Night of the U-Boats* Foulsham; 1973.

Lund, P. & Ludlam, H. *Nightmare Convoy* Foulsham; 1987.

Masters, D. *In Peril on the Sea: Exploits of Allied Seamen*. Cresset Press; 1960.

Masters, D. *Epics of Salvage: Wartime Feats of the Marine Salvage Men*. Cassell; 1953.

May, E. *The World War and American Isolation, 1914–17*. Cambridge, Massachusetts, USA: Harvard University Press; 1959.

Morison, S. *The History of United States Naval Operations in World War II*. Little, Brown & Co. 15 vols; 1947–62.

Mowat, F. *The Serpent's Coil.* Michael Joseph; 1961.

Mowat, F. *Grey Seas Under.* New York: Lyons Press; 1958.

Parrish, T. *The Submarine – A History.* Viking Penguin; 2004.

Playfair, I. *War in the Mediterranean and Middle East.* HMSO, 4 vols; 1954–66.

Poolman, K. *Focke-Wulf Condor – Scourge of The Atlantic.* Macdonald & Jane's; 1978.

Rompkey, B. *St John's and the Battle of the Atlantic.* St John's, Newfoundland: Flanker Press; 2009.

Roskill, S. *The War at Sea.* HMSO, 4 vols; 1954–61.

Roskill, S. *A Merchant Fleet at War.* Collins; 1962.

Sandeman, J. *Bute's War.* Bute: Buteshire Natural History Society; 2006.

Sanders, R. *The Practice of Ocean Rescue.* Glasgow: Brown, Son & Ferguson; 1947.

Schofield, W. *Eastward the Convoys.* New York: Rand McNally; 1965.

Stanford, A. *Force Mulberry.* New York, USA: Wm. Morrow; 1951.

Slader, J. *The Red Duster at War.* Kimber; 1988.

Slader, J. *The Fourth Service.* Robert Hale; 1994.

Still, W. *Crisis at Sea: US Navy in European Waters in WWI.* Florida, USA: University of Florida Press; 2006.

Tennyson, J. *The Saga of the 'San Demetrio'.* HMSO; 1942.

Terraine, J. *Business in Great Waters.* Leo Cooper; 1989.

Thomas, D. *The Atlantic Star, 1939–45.* W.H. Allen; 1990.

Thomas, P. *British Steam Tugs.* Wolverhampton: Waine Research Publications; 1983.

Tomblin, B. *With Utmost Spirit: Allied Naval Operations in the Mediterranean, 1942–45.* Lexington KY, USA: University Press of Kentucky; 2004.

Van der Vat, D. *Stealth at Sea.* Weidenfeld & Nicolson; 1994.

Warlow, B. *Shore Establishments of the Royal Navy.* Liskeard, Cornwall: Maritime Books; 1992.

Williams, J. *Swinging the Lamp.* Hull: Riverhead; 2013.

Williams, J. & Gray, J. *HM Rescue Tugs in World War I.* Privately published.

Winn, G. *The Hour Before Dawn.* Collins; 1942.

Winser, J. *The D-Day Ships.* Kendal: World Ship Society; 1994.

Winser, J. *British Invasion Fleets.* Kendal: World Ship Society; 2002.

Woodman, R. *The Real Cruel Sea.* John Murray; 2004.

INDEX

hmcs = His Majesty's Canadian Ship
hmsas = His Majesty's South African Ship
hms = His Majesty's Ship
mt = Motor Tanker
my = Motor Yacht
rfa = Royal Fleet Auxiliary
rn = Royal Navy
rnr = Royal Navy Reserve
rnvr = Royal Naval Volunteer Reserve
ss = Steamship
sy = Steam Yacht
usa = United States Army
uscg = United States Coast Guard
usns = United States Naval Ship
uss = United States Ship

INDEX

LIST OF
ILLUSTRATIONS

First section:
1. Sketch of *Zaree*
2. *Great City* beached at St Mary's
3. *Roysterer* towing torpedoed destroyer
4. HMS *Minona*, the rescue tugs' base ship at Campbeltown
5. The remains of SS *Imperial Transport*
6. Admiralty Floating Dock under tow of *Superman*
7. Publicity photograph of 18-inch towrope
8. *Freebooter*'s towing winch
9. *Jaunty* steaming towards the sinking HMS *Eagle*
10. A stamp issued in Malta to commemorate the PEDESTAL convoy
11. *St Day* off Gibraltar where she was based during the Second World War
12. Newfoundlander Charlie Ghent who served aboard *St Day*
13. *Salvonia*
14. *Nimble*
15. *Masterful*
16. US Liberty ship, *Flora MacDonald*, under tow of Dutch rescue tug *Zwarte Zee*
17. The Commanding Officer of *Prosperous* handing out lucky heather to his crew
18. Cdr EG Martin OBE RNVR
19. Lt-Cdr O Jones RNR with his OBE
20. Lt 'Robbie' Robinson RNVR
21. *Destiny*'s football team at Gibraltar

Second section:
22. Dutch motorship *Madoera* in St John's after being torpedoed, February 1943
23. The torpedo hole in *Madoera*'s forefoot
24. The damage to the British tanker *G.S. Walden* after being torpedoed, August 1942
25. The Bustler Class *Growler*
26. *Growler*'s mascot was a dog called Pluto
27. The remains of the American tanker, *Brilliant*, being evacuated
28. *Tenacity* approaching the US Coast Guard cutter *Campbell*
29. The last hours of SS *Neptune*, March 1943
30. *Tenacity* fighting an oil fire at St John's, June 1944
31. Liberty ship *Empire Treasure* adrift in mid-Atlantic, January 1944
32. *Empire Treasure* under tow in storm force 10 winds
33. *Destiny* at St John's, November 1942
34. 'Tug' Wilson manning an Oerlikon
35. Two of *Mindful*'s officers, Sub-Lt Crawford and Sub-Lt (E) MacDonald (left)
36. Able Seaman Len Reed
37. Lt-Cdr R.E. Sanders MBE RNR
38. Sub-Lt (E) Stanley Butler RNVR
39. Conundrum used to lay fuel pipelines (PLUTO) to France
40. Rescue tugs' assembly area off Lee-on-Solent prior to the Normandy Landings, June 1944